You can return this item to any library but please
note that not all libraries are open every day.
Items must be returned on or before the due date.
Failure to do so will result in overdue charges.
Items may be renewed unless requested by
another customer, in person or by telephone, on
two occasions only. Your membership card number
will be required.
Please look after this item – you may be charged
for any damage.

Headquarters:
Information, Culture & Community Learning,
Town Hall, Bournemouth BH2 6DY

Bournemouth
Libraries

On Brick Lane

RACHEL LICHTENSTEIN

HAMISH HAMILTON
an imprint of
PENGUIN BOOKS

For Majer Bogdanski

HAMISH HAMILTON

Published by the Penguin Group
Penguin Books Ltd, 80 Strand, London WC2R ORL, England
Penguin Group (USA) Inc., 375 Hudson Street, New York, New York 10014, USA
Penguin Group (Canada), 90 Eglinton Avenue East, Suite 700, Toronto, Ontario, Canada M4P 2Y3
(a division of Pearson Penguin Canada Inc.)
Penguin Ireland, 25 St Stephen's Green, Dublin 2, Ireland
(a division of Penguin Books Ltd)
Penguin Group (Australia), 250 Camberwell Road, Camberwell, Victoria 3124, Australia
(a division of Pearson Australia Group Pty Ltd)
Penguin Books India Pvt Ltd, 11 Community Centre, Panchsheel Park, New Delhi – 110 017, India
Penguin Group (NZ), 67 Apollo Drive, Rosedale, North Shore 0632, New Zealand
(a division of Pearson New Zealand Ltd)
Penguin Books (South Africa) (Pty) Ltd, 24 Sturdee Avenue, Rosebank, Johannesburg 2196, South Africa
Penguin Books Ltd, Registered Offices: 80 Strand, London WC2R ORL, England

www.penguin.com

First published 2007
1

Copyright © Rachel Lichtenstein, 2007
The Text and Illustrations Permissions on pp. 343–5 constitute an extension of this copyright page

The moral right of the author has been asserted

Set in 12/14.75 pt Adobe Garamond
Typeset by Palimpsest Book Production Limited, Grangemouth Stirlingshire
Printed in Great Britain by Clays Ltd, St Ives plc

A CIP catalogue record for this book is available from the British Library

ISBN 978–0–241–14286–8

Contents

Illustrations

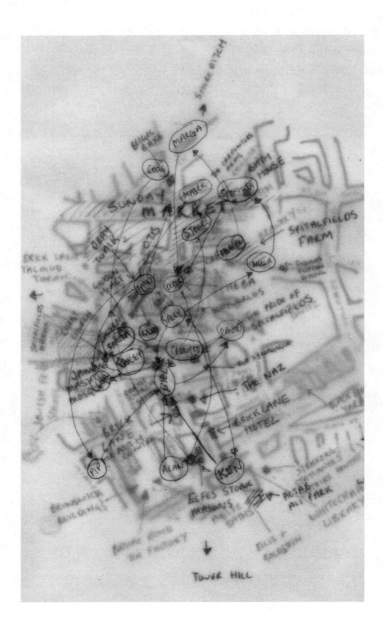

I forced myself to obey a peculiar kind of mental command:
to look around me as if I had never been in this place before.
And slowly, my travels began to bear fruit.

Alain de Botton, *The Art of Travel*

Introduction

The Past being over and done with now falls prey to our invention.

Walter Benjamin

Brick Lane had been a mythical landscape for me as a child. I heard stories about it from my grandparents, who opened their first shop, Gedaliah Lichtenstein's Watchmakers & Jewellers, at no. 67 in the 1930s. They were Polish Jewish refugees, hard-working people with a rich cultural and intellectual life. My grandmother told me about her friend, the great Yiddish poet Avram Stencl, who lived in Cheshire Street, just off the lane, in the heart of the sprawling Sunday market. Stencl called Brick Lane and the surrounding area of Whitechapel 'my *shtetl*, my holy acres, my Jerusalem in Britain'. The thriving Jewish community and the vigorous street life around him became the subject matter for most of his poetry. The first time I visited the street in the early 1990s as a young art student there were only the faintest traces left of that world.

Since then I must have walked up and down Brick Lane thousands of times, initially to search for signs of its Jewish past, checking doorposts for marks left by *mezuzahs* and rescuing books from damp cupboards in abandoned synagogues. Standing outside the site of the former Russian Vapour Baths I devoured stories from an old Hasid who owned a shop there. Over the following decade I spent countless hours interviewing members of the elderly Jewish community, collecting stories of places and people, snapshots, fragments, whispers and hidden traces until I could mentally map the area as it had once been. With the help of East London historian

I

Professor Bill Fishman I became a tour guide of the Jewish East End, relaying and gathering more information. People shared memories from childhood with me, of Yiddish-speaking homes, *cheder* lessons after school, fighting with fascists in the street. Many of these stories featured Brick Lane, the street itself, which had been at the heart of the Jewish East End from the late 1880s until the outbreak of the Second World War.

During that period Brick Lane and the surrounding area was known as the centre of the textile and clothing manufacturing industry in London. Rooms above shops and in the side streets off Brick Lane were filled with Jewish immigrants working long hours for poor pay in terrible conditions. On Saturdays, their only day off, the Orthodox men would dress in long black silk coats and wide-brimmed fur hats before making their way towards the Machzike Hadath Synagogue. The younger ones would dress up in their best clothes and wander up and down Whitechapel High Street, in 'the monkeys' parade', looking for a date. This is how my grandfather met my grandmother.

When my grandparents lived in Brick Lane every shop in the street was occupied. There were printers, hairdressers, drapers, greengrocers and tobacconists. Milliners, leather manufacturers, wine sellers and boot repairers among others. Most of the shop signs were written in Yiddish and English and the street was known as 'Little Jerusalem'. When war broke out in 1940 everything changed, the East End of London was badly bombed and many left for the safety of the countryside. My grandmother was evacuated with my father and his two brothers to a small village outside Oxford. My grandfather stayed behind in East London for two years until the building next door to his was obliterated completely during an air raid and he decided it was time to move on. The family relocated to Westcliff-on-Sea in Essex, or Whitechapel-on-Sea, as many called it. Many of the friends they had made in East London – artists and Talmudists, poets and anarchists – often visited them there. Some of my strongest childhood memories are of seeing these characters sat around the table in my grandparents house, laughing and playing cards, singing in Yiddish, arguing in Polish and Russian, the air thick with cigar smoke, the table laden with steaming glasses of lemon tea and porcelain plates filled with black bread and sweet herrings.

I returned to the streets my grandparents had willingly left to find the last of the elderly Jewish East Enders and to hear their stories. I spent my days talking with people in shops and old people's homes and walking the streets where my grandparents had walked. Over time, I began to pick up traces left by other groups of people who had lived in the area. I learned that the Latin inscription 'Umbra Sumus' above the great mosque, which was once a synagogue and before that a church, translates as 'We are Shadows'.

Following trails left by my ancestors led me to the small synagogue in Princelet Street, a narrow turning just off Brick Lane, where my grandparents married. Inside I heard about a former resident called David Rodinsky, an Orthodox Jewish scholar who had lived in the attic rooms above the synagogue and mysteriously disappeared one day in the 1960s. Fascinated by his story I secured a residency in the building, which was undergoing restoration to become a museum of immigration. The fragmented and contradictory pieces of information collected about him were eventually collated together into various forms of artwork and then a book, *Rodinsky's Room*, co-authored with Iain Sinclair and published in 1999.

At the time I was working in the old synagogue I walked past the shops along Brick Lane selling sweetmeats, boxes of mangoes, brightly coloured saris and illuminated pictures of Mecca without ever entering them. Like most other tourists, the only Bengali-owned places I used to visit then were the Indian restaurants for a cheap curry. In the early 1990s the Bhangra music spilling out of the shops, the call for prayer from the mosque and the chatter of

The folks who compose our pictures are the Children of the Ghetto. Their faults are bred of its hovering miasma of persecution, their virtues straightened and intensified by the narrowness of its horizon. And they who have won their way beyond its boundaries must still play their part in tragedies and comedies – tragedies of spiritual struggle, comedies of material ambition – which are the aftermath of its centuries of dominance, the sequel of that long cruel night in Jewry which coincides with the Christian Era.

Israel Zangwill, *Children of the Ghetto: A Study of a Peculiar People*, 1892 voices speaking foreign languages were nothing more than an exotic soundscape for my wanderings. I had no real understanding of what was taking place in the Bangladeshi community around me.

In later years I began working as an artist in local schools, spending time with the children whose parents worked in the streets in and around Brick Lane. Many of them were employed in the same trades and businesses as my grandparents' generation, as leather and textiles manufacturers and wholesalers, as shop owners and tailors. Some of the children I met had been born in Bangladesh, many of them went back there for extended holidays in the summer. They saw themselves as Bangladeshi first and British second. A decade ago nearly all of the children I worked with were struggling with English and spoke Bengali at school and at home. The next generation are far more assimilated and describe themselves as British first and Asian second. Through working with these children I began to discover more about their culture. I heard stories about life in villages in rural Sylhet, where most of the community living in and around Brick Lane have come from. I celebrated their festivals with them and got to know their parents and other local people, who slowly began to share their stories with me. I talked with teenagers struggling to come to terms with their Muslim identity, elderly people who yearned for home and successful businessmen who'd become councillors and millionaires.

In 1999 I married a Muslim man whose father used to sell spices wholesale to the restaurants in Brick Lane in the early 1970s. Through him I found out more about the Muslim religion and culture and the Asian history of Brick Lane. Gradually, like learning a new language, I was able to read the street in a different way.

I tried to make sense of this new information by reconstructing fragments of stories in sculptural forms in a studio I rented in the Old Truman Brewery at the north end of Brick Lane. When I first took on the studio in 1995, acres of space lay empty, available for cheap rent for those willing to work on a near-derelict site without heating. Brick Lane proved a fantastic location for

Zangwill's ghetto is gone. But in the side streets of Brick Lane – Fournier Street, Wilkes Street, Princelet Street and Hanbury Street – can still be heard the endless hum and whir of tailors' machines, just as it was when the great Jewish chronicler walked these same streets a century ago. The corner shop, the all-purpose store, is still there – under new management. Halal butchers, where a Muslim *kashrut* strictly prevails, signify their existence in Bengali instead of Hebrew. The Machzike Hadath is now the Great Mosque (Jamme Masjid) packed to overflowing at Ramadan as it was yesteryear on Yom Kippur.

William J. Fishman, *The Streets of East London*, 1979

a sculptor then. The largest art suppliers in London, Atlantis, had a gigantic warehouse in another part of the brewery and artists would meet there to buy materials, exchange information and ideas. A cheap lunch could be bought in one of the Indian cafés down the road, such as the Nazrul or the Aladdin, where you could buy a plate of rice and dhal for a couple of pounds. Sometimes after a long day in a cold studio I'd meet up with other painters or sculptors for a pint or two in one of the local pubs, usually the Pride of Spitalfields off Heneage Street or the Golden Heart at the top of Hanbury Street. There was a strong sense of an artists' community at that time in Brick Lane. The rich and famous were yet to move in, the streets still felt like unexplored territory and it was possible to survive financially in the area on very little. Rent was affordable and materials for making sculpture could easily be picked up off the street: fabric remnants, wicker baskets covered in pink Arabic text, scraps of leather, cardboard patterns and thousands of other abandoned things. My studio was filled with this gathered stuff as well as a special shelf that held the treasures purchased by religiously visiting the Sunday market at the top of Brick Lane.

Breakfast after a morning at the market would be a salt-beef sandwich with mustard on rye from the Beigel Bake at the top of the street. Over the years the eccentric characters I used to see in the bagel shop seemed to disappear, just like the unusual objects in the market, which became increasingly hard to find as intensive regeneration of the area changed everything. In the early 1990s parts of Cheshire Street, the densest section of the Brick Lane weekly market, were closed off as whole rows of dilapidated cottages were renovated into designer shops. Former bombsites around the Bethnal Green end of the street, which used to be filled with vans and market stalls on a Sunday, were suddenly boarded up. Then the lorries and cranes moved in and an intensive period of building works began. The market shrank, there was nowhere left for it to go. Rents for stalls went up and so did the rents for local businesses, residential property and the studios in the brewery complex. It wasn't long before price rises forced me and many other artists out. Higher-paying tenants soon moved in – web and fashion designers, production and internet companies.

Brick Lane disappeared behind a wall of scaffolding and once-empty shops re-emerged as coffee bars, estate agents and smart new galleries. Pavements were dug up and replaced with fake cobble-stones. Leather manufacturers became vintage-clothes stores, selling at hugely inflated prices the second-hand stuff you could have bought from the Sunday market for a few pence. Many Asian businessmen and some of the remaining Jewish traders couldn't resist offers to sell up and move on. Some were glad to escape to the suburbs, others reluctantly left their familiar and colourful world behind. Cafés that had served market traders and brewery workers their early-morning fry-up for decades transformed into 'lounge rooms' selling peppermint tea in small pink glasses. Peeling Yiddish shop signs were torn down and bright new neon ones hung in their place. Remnants of the past were left lying in skips dotted along the street. A lot of the characters that had originally drawn me to the area started to leave Brick Lane in droves. They couldn't recognize it any more: it had become something other, a zone in which they no longer belonged.

I found myself unable to accept this new version of the street and retreated back into the past, beyond the living memory of the Jewish experience, spending weeks in the local history library researching. I read about the Huguenot silk weavers who came to Spitalfields in the seventeenth century, escaping persecution from Catholic France. I studied etchings of them dressed in fine clothes, sitting outside their grand Georgian houses in Princelet and Fournier streets, smoking long clay pipes under the caged canaries hanging above their doorways. I learned that in order to muffle the sound of the spinning the weavers used to stuff the spaces between the attic floorboards with remnants of silk. I visited the Victoria and Albert Museum to view surviving fragments of damasks, velvets and silk brocades they had produced, and copied the intricate floral designs in my notebook. In the British Library

I pored over ancient maps from the sixteenth century, the whole of Whitechapel then a series of rural fields with a medieval priory, and before that a Roman burial ground. With a magnifying glass it was possible to read the faint scrawl across the fragile pages of diary entries from Spitalfield's residents during the time of the Great Plague. I searched through the memoirs of Daniel Defoe and read his descriptions of the area he had walked in as a child: 'Brick Lane was a deep dirty road, frequented chiefly by carts fetching bricks that way into Whitechapel from Brick kilns in those fields whence it had its name.' I called up old newspaper reports of the Ripper murders of the 1880s and sifted through vast leather-bound volumes of *London Labour and the London Poor* by Henry Mayhew, reading about the worst lodging houses in Victorian London in Flower and Dean Walk, off Brick Lane. I read stories about Irish labourers who arrived in the 1840s to escape the potato famine,

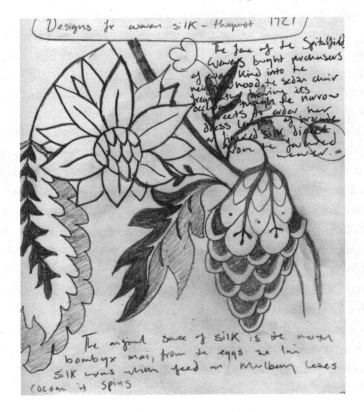

and saw harrowing engravings by Gustave Doré of life in tenement blocks.

Bidding for books about East London on ebay became a daily ritual. As they arrived wrapped in brown paper from small second-hand bookshops across Britain and America, I ripped open their packaging, searching the faded pages for stories that brought the old East End back to me. I read about the streets adjoining Brick Lane, such as Chicksand Street, where Bram Stoker's Dracula slept in a coffin of Transylvanian earth, and Hanbury Street, rumoured to be haunted by the ghost of Annie Chapman, murdered there by Jack the Ripper. Like many before me I became obsessed with the stories and mythologies of London's East End.

There was even a day, after a night of intensive reading, when I walked down Dray Walk, part of the old brewery site now filled with cafés, delis and bars, and became convinced I could hear horses' hooves echoing on the cobblestones. I had just been reading about the stables that existed there for centuries and how the horses were used to pull carts of hops up to the brewery and return with barrels of beer. Worried I had started to hallucinate I turned a corner to see two large white horses being ridden by women with spiked blue hair in tight leather outfits. 'All part of a fashion shoot for a show at Spitalfields Market,' I was told by a thuggish-looking bouncer who had received an order to eject me from the 'set' via his walkie-talkie. Another time, walking down Fournier Street, I saw a slim silhouette of a man in top hat and tails disappearing on to Brick Lane, reminding me of the description I had just read of the reformed brewer Charrington. This unusual Victorian philanthropist used to stride through the smoggy streets of Whitechapel with a leather black book in hand, ready to report on the brothel owners, pimps and madams, who shook at the sight of him. The figure I'd seen had been an actor. There were many similar sightings. The collision in my mind of past and present was accentuated by bizarre scenes, witnessed on other occasions, of people in Victorian dress waltzing down the narrow side streets off Brick Lane, which had been strewn with hay and filled with synthetic fog as filming took place for the latest BBC period drama. The area became the hottest new film and photographic location in the country. It was being recorded and rewritten by documentary makers, news crews, tourists, and photographers taking pictures to accompany Sunday supplement articles on lost Georgian London. They all came to document and consume in London's 'newly discovered' and heavily marketed 'ethnic quarter'.

My own fantasies and visual projections on to the streets and buildings around me were feeding into this constructed mythology of the place. My reaction to Brick Lane became schizophrenic; I was both fascinated by its stories and repelled by the way they were being used to re-market the area and increase property prices. In 1990, when Brick Lane was still barely on the tourist radar, my relationship with the street had been more romantic. I went there searching for the Yiddish-speaking world of my grandparents, the vibrant and chaotic Jewish East End. During the time I spent looking for it Brick Lane changed for ever. It will never again be the first stop for the next new wave of migrants in London. The dockside, where many first arrived, is now accessible only to a privileged few who can afford apartments with private walkways and river views. Dilapidated properties in Spitalfields, once split into multiple rooms for cheap rent, have been restored and refurbished and are now worth millions. The Hasidic men in long dark coats with beards and sidelocks who occupied street corners, exchanging gossip and discussing business, were replaced by groups of Asian elders doing the same, wearing long white kaftans and open-toed sandals, their beards stained orange with henna. You still see these men shuffling quickly past the bars and clubs, trying to reach the mosque further down the road without attracting unwanted attention. Scuffles sometimes break out as racist abuse is hurled across the street as partygoers drink late into the night.

The latest arrivals in Brick Lane, the 'haircuts' (as some of the locals like to call them), are the ones buying up old warehouses and turning them into vintage-clothing stores or dot.com companies. The weekends also see thousands of other incomers descending on

Lying between Middlesex Street and Brick Lane
are to be found most of the common lodging houses,
and in the immediate neighbourhood, lower still in
reputation, there are streets of furnished houses
and houses where stairways and corners are
occupied nightly by those without any other
shelter. So lurid and intense is the light which
has lately been thrown upon these quarters, that
the grey tones of the ordinary picture become
invisible.

Charles Booth, *Life and Labour of the People*, Vol. II, 1892

Brick Lane from across London to visit the many bars, clubs and restaurants. Pavements heave with tourists and visitors bar hopping and staggering woozily out of Indian restaurants clutching half-drunk bottles of wine. The noise outside the old brewery site steadily increases throughout the night as clubbers queue to get into the Vibe Bar or 93 Feet East. By midnight the street is full of revellers, although the local Bangladeshi youth for the most part stay behind closed doors as drinking is not part of their culture. Resentment is building: last year a group of Asian men petrol-bombed a pub off Brick Lane known to be the haunt of white locals. The attack has been called racially motivated. As the City moves further towards territory traditionally belonging to immigrant groups tensions are increasing. The curry houses, originally established as cheap cafés selling food for Bangladeshi men stranded here without families and home-cooked meals, have become smart new restaurants, endorsed by Ken Livingstone and Prince Charles, an essential eating experience for every tourist visiting London. While documentaries and contemporary works of fiction discuss the 'fabulous architecture', 'waves of immigration' and 'unique ethnic mix' of Brick Lane, the people they celebrate are leaving the area. Young Bangladeshis can't afford to buy there and many want to escape the drug problems and poverty that exist in the streets behind the glitz of Banglatown. A few in the community have become millionaires and housing has dramatically improved but many Bangladeshis feel confused and excluded from what is happening in their neighbourhood today.

Brick Lane continues to be rewritten and reimagined but primarily with a focus on the violent and grim aspects of its history. Magazine features and television programmes report repeatedly about heroin addiction and gang warfare. Novels revel in the poverty of the area and Ripper Tours help to keep visitors' dark preconceptions confirmed. I have attempted in this book to bring to light some of the quieter but no less remarkable stories of the people who have lived and worked in Brick Lane. So many memories of this street have already been erased or forgotten: hidden behind newly erected buildings, buried under recently paved streets like unexcavated archaeological treasures. I have tried to extract them through a series of walks, conversations, archival research, sound recordings and photographic outings. As the writer Iain Sinclair said to me recently, 'It takes a very long time to exorcise the volume of people and their dramas that took place somewhere.'

Over the last five years I have spoken with visionaries who walk the area, mapping the territory in new ways, with photographers, religious leaders, teachers, doctors, café owners, celebrities, artists and long-time residents of the street. I have met extraordinary people on the fringes of society and unsung heroes who have shared their stories with me. I have heard how the street has changed from a thriving Jewish community to an area abandoned to violence and vandalism to Banglatown and currently a tourist and heritage site. The story that follows is an exploration of a place described through the people who know it intimately. Different threads combine to create a multilayered portrait of a place, which can be read in a thousand different ways depending on your point of reference.

The East End within the East End

Brick Lane is one of those places that you come to with a sense
of recognition as if some part of your humanity has been there
before.

Iain Sinclair

The physical act of walking, tracing the steps of my grandparents,
visiting and revisiting the places where they lived, the locations of their
businesses, the synagogues where they prayed, the ground they are
buried in, is how I learned the geography of Whitechapel. Later, when
the wider history of the area became my obsession, I navigated the streets
by using the historical tours mapped out in the back of Bill Fishman's
classic book *The Streets of East London*. His carefully researched trails
led me to the sites of the first Yiddish theatre in London, the old Soup
Kitchen for the Jewish Poor, and the church hall in Hanbury Street
where anarchists met. Most documentary films shot in Spitalfields over
the past thirty years include footage of Professor Fishman standing on
the corner of a Whitechapel street, enthralling a group of students with
personal memories of the Battle of Cable Street and anecdotes about
the characters and events that make up the mythology of the area. His
walking tours are legendary and he's still pounding the streets at the
age of eighty-six, even after two recent hip operations.

I met Bill for the first time in 1991, during one of his tours, when
he stopped by the synagogue in Princelet Street where I was working
as the unpaid artist in residence. I had been downstairs invigilating an
art exhibition of mine that explored my own family history through
sculptures made from objects recovered from my grandfather's East
End watchmaking shop. As I sat in the damp basement waiting for an

audience I heard a key turn in the lock and the sound of many feet making their way into the synagogue directly above. I crept upstairs and listened as Professor Fishman gave his talk on the history of the building, including a passionate account of his memories of the Orthodox scholar David Rodinsky who lived in the attic rooms above. Bill recounted how he had seen Rodinsky bent over his books near to the window, reading by candlelight. Years later, when a consecration service for David Rodinsky was held at Waltham Abbey Jewish Cemetery, Bill read the Kaddish, the memorial prayer for the dead traditionally recited by the first-born son of the deceased.

I introduced myself to Bill when he finished his lecture in the synagogue that day and he brought his students downstairs to see my exhibition. My art needed no interpretation for him. As the son of an East End tailor he inherently understood what I was trying to express. Bill became my mentor and friend, and whenever I had the opportunity I'd join him on a walk around the area. As we wandered down Brick Lane he'd point out places he remembered from childhood, such as the site of the Russian Vapour Baths opposite the mosque: 'I can see them now,' he said, 'the devout men with their sidelocks and long beards, freshly scrubbed, with towels round their necks, and the women in heavy skirts and wigs, lined up waiting to get into the *mikvah*.'

We'd stop in Fashion Street, Bill showing me the flat where the eminent post-war playwright Arnold Wesker was born, or reading the description of the street in the opening chapter of Israel Zangwill's classic *Children of the Ghetto: A Study of a Peculiar People*. His favourite stop on his walking tours has always been the East London Mosque in Fieldgate Street, which is situated directly next door to one of the last functioning synagogues in Whitechapel. 'This is a unique phenomenon,' he said to me the last time we were there together, 'to have a Muslim settlement and a Jewish settlement cheek by jowl; the only other place in the world you might find this combination in is Jerusalem.' Bill was touched by a story he heard about the mosque: he was told that during Yom Kippur one year the imam ordered some builders at the mosque to stop work out of respect for the worshippers at the

synagogue. 'The world should learn from this example,' he said.

Bill's walks are far more than just historical tours. He is engaged with the contemporary world around him and constantly interacts with those on the street whether they are interested tourists stopping to catch the tail end of his talk or local people. He speaks fluent Urdu, learned during his seven years in the British army in India, and he never misses an opportunity to use the language. 'Salaam Aleikum!' he'll shout, while waving his walking stick about, before launching into a conversation with a bewildered Bengali elder. With a twinkle in his eye he tells me, 'When I walk these streets it's like being back in Bombay or Bangalore and I love speaking Urdu to the older people here, they are always so surprised to hear an old white man who can talk their language.' Laughing he says, 'It's the madness in my soul – I can't help it.'

Bill and his wife, Doris, have lived in Harrow for over fifty years. The distance from East London has only increased his attachment to the area of his youth. I went to visit him shortly after his second hip

A dead and gone wag called the street 'Fashion Street', and most of the people who live in it do not even see the joke. If it could exchange names with 'Rotten Row', both places would be more appropriately designated. It is a dull, squalid, narrow thoroughfare in the East End of London, connecting Spitalfields with Whitechapel and branching off in blind alleys. In the days when little Esther Ansell trudged its unclean pavements, its extremities were within earshot of the blasphemies from some of the vilest quarters and filthiest rookeries in the capital of the civilized world.

Israel Zangwill, *Children of the Ghetto: A Study of a Peculiar People*, 1892 operation to talk about Brick Lane. He was looking frailer than the last time I'd seen him, and obviously in pain, and his first words to me were, 'I'm on my last legs and don't you dare shed a tear for me when I'm gone. I've had a good long life and there is nothing to be sad about.' But I know his passing, when it does come, will hit me hard.

Taking me gently by the arm he led me through to a conservatory at the back of his house, which overlooks an immaculately kept garden. The small room was filled with sunlight and near to the French windows were two reclining chairs strewn with books and a pair of reading spectacles. Against the far wall above a table hung a copy of a painting of the former synagogue in Brick Lane. 'You see,' he said as he caught me looking at it, 'never far from my mind.' He patted a chair with vigour and we began to talk about the recent interest in the area. 'The East End is really on the map now,' he said, 'years ago no one cared.' I asked how he felt about Brick Lane today and he told me, 'The last of the Mohicans have gone, the old ones with their beards and kaftans, the anarchists and communists, the radicals and poets. It's a different place.' Without prompting, Bill launched into a lecture, putting the current story into context: 'Historically Brick Lane has always been a point of arrival for immigrants and the home of the labouring poor. When the Irish came in the 1840s no new houses were built to accommodate them. After the 1860s central areas in the city were rebuilt and there was further pressure on the East End as the poor were chucked out of their homes to build houses for the rich. This coincided with the biggest influx of newcomers the area had ever seen – eastern European Jews escaping persecution in the Pale of Settlement who were arriving in their tens of thousands. Spitalfields and Whitechapel were poverty-stricken, filled with over-congested lodging houses, unemployment and crime. The biggest catalyst for social change was in fact Jack the Ripper. The murders in the autumn of 1888 created a climate of fear and were reported all over the world, which awoke a wider population to the state of the East End. So the Ripper did more to see the old squalid rookies pulled down and decent sanitation and street lighting installed than anyone else.

'The area is being encroached upon by the City today, which is literally consuming the working-class housing and facilities. There is a new type of person living in Brick Lane now, alongside the Bengali immigrants, but I doubt the two will mix. They've taken over those Huguenot houses and changed the feel of the place for ever. They need to engage with the local community as those saints of the past like Charrington and Barnardo did. They should invest in the area, become school governors and make sure their children mix with local children.'

Like many older Jewish people Bill feels the contemporary Brick Lane has lost its uniqueness of character today. The massive redevelopment of the area and the branding of the street as 'Banglatown' have made it an entirely different place for him. Streets he knew from childhood have been obliterated completely. He remembers it as 'a mixed place where Jews, Irish and native English coexisted together'. In reality Brick Lane is probably more multicultural today than it has ever been. Back in the 1930s when Bill was roaming the streets it could be a dangerous place. The Whitechapel end of Brick Lane was relatively safe territory but if you crossed into Bethnal Green, passing the boundary of the railway bridge in the centre of the street, you risked a severe beating by the Blackshirts, gangs of fascist youths who patrolled that area. Their leader, Oswald Mosley, the founder of the British Union of Fascists, the BUF, gained much support during the depression of the 1930s in East London. A fervent anti-communist and anti-Semite, he encouraged his supporters to attack Jews, and as a young man Bill was involved in numerous skirmishes with Blackshirt gangs. He remembers seeing Mosley speak once outside the Salmon and Ball pub in Bethnal Green, 'on top of a van ranting about the alien Jewish menace threatening our jobs'. On 4 October 1936 Bill was witness to the legendary Battle of Cable Street: 'I was at Gardiner's Corner at Aldgate and I watched the Irish and the Jews pour from every corner of East London to unite to stop Mosley and his Blackshirts marching down Cable Street. Catholic dockers walked side by side with bearded Jews, shouting in unison, "They shall not pass!" before building and manning barricades that prevented Mosley's incursion and culminated in a day-long battle with the police, who tried to clear the way to let the fascists through.'

In Brick Lane itself Bill never saw these kinds of tensions. 'There was more interaction, cross-sexual relationships and a fair amount of intermarriage,' he told me. 'Today I think there is less of this, and you know what I think about that.' I did, there was nobody quite so delighted about my marriage to Adam, whose father is Pakistani Muslim, as Bill. He slaps his thigh with pleasure and grins broadly every time he hears the Muslim-Jewish surname of my children: Hasan-Lichtenstein.

Bill's childhood was spent in Philpott Street, about a mile away from Brick Lane, and he describes himself as 'a 100 per cent East End Jew and a cockney too'. His neighbours were a mix of Jewish immigrants from Russia and the Ukraine and Irish dockers. Bill lived with his grandparents, parents and four siblings in a small terraced house. His grandparents arrived in East London from Russia in 1905 after the worst of the Kishnev pogroms. 'The local police organized the raping of women,' Bill told me. 'Grandfather couldn't take it any more so he packed a few belongings and just left. He saved enough money for the trip by working as a *melamed* teaching kids their *bar mitzvah* portion, he led the family on foot through the forest in Austria to England. He was nearly seventy when he came here.'

Bill's grandfather was very religious. Every Friday night Bill accompanied him to the local synagogue: 'If noise came from the congregation while the rabbi was talking Zayde would bang his hands on the bench and shout, "Sha, sha!" and people would keep quiet – he commanded respect.' His grandfather instilled the Jewish principles of *rachmones* (compassion) and *tzedoka* (charity) into Bill: 'On many occasions I'd walk with him and his immediate response when being stopped by someone less fortunate than himself was to press a handful of coins into their hand with a solemn declaration in the Yiddish vernacular, "Thank you for asking me." Bill remembers seeing his friend, the poet Avram Stencl, doing the same thing, 'even though he was close to being a beggar himself'. These simple acts of kindness summed up for Bill the 'spirit of the Jewish East End', which he still lives by – during my many walks with him I noticed he would never walk past homeless people on the street without giving them money.

Every time I talked with Bill he brought the streets of Whitechapel alive for me, with stories from his own childhood, myths from before he was born and tales from his contemporary walks. 'As a boy I'd walk through Brick Lane, which was the centre of the sweatshop trades, producing masses of cheap clothing. Nearly all of those workshops were filled with Jewish tailors, pressers and cutters, and you could hear the hum of the machinery from early morning till late at night. In the summer the women with their headscarves on would sit outside doorways keeping out of the indoor heat. Everywhere the old Jewish ghetto-dwellers were going off to their evening services. The Huguenot houses were all sweatshops, *stiebels* and homes then and it was one big working Jewish settlement.'

A regular stop on any walk with Bill is the site of the Jamme Masjid Mosque on the corner of Brick Lane and Fournier Street, which was once the Spitalfields Great Synagogue, also known as the Machzike Hadath Synagogue. For Bill, this building exemplifies the whole immigrant experience to the area. 'Where once the Kol Nidre services intoned on Yom Kippur you now hear the sound of Muslims praying on Ramadan. The family remains sacrosanct, as do their ancient religion and culture – a bastion of defensive orthodoxy in the midst of hostile society.' Bill told me about an incident that happened outside the mosque in 1903 when it was the Machzike Hadath Synagogue. Much like the situation today within the Muslim community in the area there were tensions then between those who wanted to remain strictly Orthodox, usually the older generation, and others in the community who had discarded their religious practices. 'At the end of Yom Kippur, the most solemn day of fasting in the Jewish calendar, a fight broke out directly outside the synagogue. While the Orthodox were inside intoning for the expiation of sins, outside young anarchists were singing their own hymns, revolutionary ones. At the end of the service the doors flew open and the worshippers, many in full regalia, came out, gathering any weapon at their disposal before hurling themselves at the blasphemers across the road, standing with lit cigarettes, openly eating ham sandwiches, deliberately showing their contempt. The police were called and a few people were arrested. When the case came up the judge dismissed it saying in this country people are given both the freedom to practise their religion as well as the freedom not to practise.' This story happened outside Bill's own living memory but it has become part of local folklore.

In the 1930s and 1940s Bill would accompany his father to the Sunday market in Brick Lane, a place where many in the Jewish community went to buy cheap groceries, exchange gossip and meet friends. The market was open daily till late in the evening, apart from on Fridays and Saturdays when it would close in time for the stall-holders to get home and light their Sabbath candles before the first stars appeared in the sky. The main shopping day was Sunday, and today the East End markets still open on that day, following the tradition set a century ago by the Jewish inhabitants of Whitechapel.

Every kind of Jewish food and goods could be found in Brick Lane Market before the war: sweet herrings, candles, kosher meat, *menorahs*, lace tablecloths, religious books, *cholla*, sweet pastries and salt beef. Bill would walk up and down the stalls with his father, haggling for bargains, buying vegetables, fruit and unplucked kosher chickens. They'd always visit the bagel shop at the top of the street for warm bread and a bag of bagels before the highlight of the trip, a visit to Bloom's kosher delicatessen on the corner of Brick Lane and Old Montague Street. Every Sunday the pavement in front of Bloom's was filled with large crowds of Jewish immigrants listening to the arguments of different political speakers in Yiddish. Bill watched as 'communists, socialists and the Labour Party put up a platform and spoke passionately to those gathered there'. He was just a child and didn't understand much but it aroused his interest: 'My whole East End childhood was set against a background of radical politics, which has influenced my political orientation to this day.'

Over the years Bill has watched his community move away from East London and the visible signs of their presence slowly disappear. The last time we were there we stood outside the recently closed doors of the Whitechapel Library and he sighed, raising his hands above his head, and said to me, 'What is this place now? I just don't recognize it any more.' A few doors down from the library is a Burger King outlet, which until 1995 housed the last kosher eatery in Whitechapel, the very same Bloom's (which moved from its Brick Lane location in 1952 after the site was destroyed during the Blitz). 'It does sadden me,' said Bill, 'most of the signs of a Jewish past here have been erased except a few, like the Star of David on the drainpipe at Christ Church School on Brick Lane, probably left there by Jewish builders.'

Without expert guides like Bill Fishman it is almost impossible to get any sense of a Jewish past in Brick Lane today. His writings and memories leave a legacy for future generations. I have recorded him talking and walking countless times over the last decade and during every conversation he has never failed to mention his dear friend the Yiddish poet Avram Stencl. 'You cannot talk of Jewish Whitechapel,' he told me, 'and not talk of Stencl.'

I grew up with stories about Stencl, who was also a great friend of my grandfather. They met in Whitechapel at the Saturday-afternoon literary meetings – *literarishe Shabbas nokhmitiks* – now called the 'Friends of Yiddish', which Stencl established in 1936. My grandfather was one of the founding members of the group and when he moved

The Brick Lane I knew as a child was all Jewish places, herring people with their barrels, delicatessens, the whole street was Jewish. The hoardings above the shops weren't long enough for the names: Hertzberg, Rosenbloom, Egelnick, Waxenblatt. On the Sabbath there was no one around, it would all be closed up, every shop shut up, but of course it's different now. After the war and all that bombing the Jews moved away and now it's all Banglatown. I know why the Asians want to live there, same as us, because they've always had enemies and when you're among your own you feel safer. When I was a child Brick Lane was my refuge.

I find it so strange that they're building from the City into Brick Lane, into what they call a very prestige area. If the old-timers got up and saw there was flats going there for half a million pounds they wouldn't believe it. If my father came back from his grave and saw this he'd say they'd all gone *meshugge*.

Leslie Kay, 2002

out of Whitechapel after the war he continued to attend, travelling up from Essex every week until his death in 1986. When he first joined the meetings were filled with prominent Jewish intellectuals and guest speakers from New York and Germany who performed Yiddish classics, sang songs and discussed politics. The meetings were packed-out noisy affairs with hundreds of people, standing room only. They still take place weekly at Toynbee Hall and have become one of the last surviving remnants of the once-flourishing Yiddish community of Whitechapel.

Stencl was a regular visitor to my grandparents' house in Westcliff-on-Sea. My father remembers seeing him sitting in their front room with my grandfather, laughing, playing cards, talking of politics and friends. 'He was like a warm and affectionate uncle,' said my father, 'who'd pinch my cheeks vigorously and speak to me at great speed in Yiddish. As soon as he arrived my mother put a plate piled high with steaming hot food in front of him while lamenting at the holes in his jumper and his fingerless gloves. To her it was a *mitzvah* to feed him and an honour to have such a great man in her house.' I must have seen him as a child but have no clear recollections, only half-remembered details, which have further fuelled my fantasies of the Jewish East End. When I moved to Whitechapel as a teenager I began to learn more about Stencl and discovered that much like David Rodinsky the reality of his life had been far from romantic. He was desperately poor and his financial circumstances became worse as the remaining Jewish community moved out of the area, cutting him off from his primary source of income. He had earned his living since the 1930s by personally distributing and selling the Yiddish magazine he edited and contributed to, *Loshn un Lebn* (*Language and Life*), outside Jewish meeting places and even on the street. As his audience died out or moved away he sold very few copies and often appeared like a beggar, poorly dressed and underfed. He never married and lived in small cheap rented rooms around Whitechapel. The few possessions he owned were destroyed a number of times, as he was bombed out repeatedly during the Blitz. His poems survived because he always carried them around with him, stuffed into the pockets of his old coat.

After the war he was given a council flat in Greatorex Street, at the end of Old Montague Street, off the Whitechapel end of Brick Lane, which remained his home until he died. He became a familiar face in Brick Lane, tipping his trilby hat to everyone he met, walking the streets in his shabby old coat, speaking in Yiddish to anyone left who would listen. He liked to write surrounded by the people of Whitechapel, the inspiration for much of his work, and he could often be seen scribbling away on an old notebook in the Lyons teashop on the Commercial Road or in the warmth and comfort of the Whitechapel Library, located on Whitechapel High Street near the south end of Brick Lane. Stencl was one of many immigrant Jews using the library then. From its opening to the outbreak of the Second World War the reading rooms were filled with the sound of Jewish schoolchildren discussing their homework, their parents and grandparents arguing in Yiddish, groups of intellectuals planning meetings and events, all of them escaping the confined spaces of their tenement homes to read, learn and meet friends at the free public library.

Bill Fishman started using the library when he was about ten years old. 'The staff there were fantastic,' he said, 'you'd get all the help you needed. The building was known as the "University of the Ghetto". We all went. My father would read Yiddish newspapers, for us literature and history. The Whitechapel Arts group used to meet there in the reference library. Joseph Leftwich told me this, he was a survivor and met Jacob Epstein the sculptor there and Rosenberg the poet. The group started about 1905, a period of a lot of flourishing literary circles in the East End. The library was a marvellous training ground for these young immigrants, they got a higher education there that most couldn't afford. The intellectual elite among the Jewish immigrants met in the library not in the synagogues: Rosenberg, Mark Gertler, Bomberg, the poet Rodker and Jack Bronowski the mathematician, scientist and writer, and of course Stencl, who'd write his poetry there and sometimes give readings.'

Whitechapel Britain

Pumbedita, Cordova, Cracow, Amsterdam,
Vilna, Lublin, Berditchev and Volozhin,
Your names will always be sacred,
Places where Jews have been.

And sacred is Whitechapel,
It is numbered with our Jewish towns.
Holy, holy, holy
Are your bombed stones.

If we ever have to leave Whitechapel,
As other Jewish towns were left,
Its soul will remain a part of us,
Woven into us, woof and weft.

Avram Stencl

2

The University of the Ghetto

When I came back to the library after the war I arranged to buy books in Urdu, Gujarati and Hindi and it took me back to when the Yiddish borrowers stood chatting away in their own languages, in exactly the same way fifty years before, and I was there for both those happenings.

Bernard Levine

The Whitechapel Library provided shelter, a site for learning and a well-used meeting place for local people from 1892 until its closure in August 2005. During this long history the library adapted to the needs of its users more than any other public library in the country. The first ethnic librarian in Britain, Mr Bogdin, a specialist Yiddishist, was employed at the Whitechapel Library in the 1930s. In 2000 the library was the first in the country to stock books in Somalian.

Like so many historical buildings in the area the library has been sold off. It will soon be converted into part of the Whitechapel Gallery next door. Aware of the need to remember the long history of the library the Whitechapel Gallery commissioned oral historian Alan Dein and myself to create an audio archive of memories of the library in 1999. Alan and I spent many months interviewing users and staff, one of whom was Denise Bangs, the head librarian, who had worked in the building for over twenty-five years. When Denise first started her job at the Whitechapel Library she found the place eccentric. It took her a while to get used to the extraordinary mix of characters who visited the place: City workers, old Jewish ladies, beefeaters from the Tower of London, and people with no fixed address, such as 'Atlas Annie', nicknamed because she came

34

every day to read the huge reference atlas. One of Denise's longest-standing and most regular visitors was Deborah Cohen, who had come every Thursday since her sixteenth birthday in 1934. 'We had a frustrated librarian who planted their own books in the Russian literature section,' said Denise of another visitor, 'just in the right place. Never found out who they were or why they did it.' Denise felt her time working at the library had taught her to be more tolerant: 'Lots of people came here with problems and just needed someone to talk to. Some people arrived at nine and stayed all day. We were their only port of call and were available to listen to them.'

The library has been at the heart of the community in and around Brick Lane for over a century. Jewish artists and intellectuals like Stencl and Gertler used to share their desks with Irish dockers, sometimes the worse for drink, who'd come in to look at the *Lloyd's List* to see when the ships were coming in. Later the Bengali community mixed with City workers and other locals, all using the building as a refuge of some sort.

The last time I visited the building when it was still being used as a library was on a wet day in late July 2005. Denise was at the front desk, head bent low, helping an elderly man put some books into a plastic bag. She told me the library would close to the public within a matter of days. Although her own working future was uncertain she was more concerned about what would happen to the library regulars. 'Go and look for yourself,' she said to me, pointing in the direction of the reading room. 'Where will they go?'

Leaving Denise at the mahogany information desk I passed the local history section and entered the ethnic reading room on the ground floor. Four wooden school desks were arranged in a line in the centre of the room, next to a long Victorian reading table. The walls of the narrow room were painted in a sickly lime-yellow colour with bits of grey concrete peering through in diseased patches. Around the room were rows of utility shelves half filled with tatty books in Arabic, Bengali and Urdu. Fluorescent lights hung on chains dimly illuminating the desks below and casting long shadows on the ceiling, helping to hide the watermarks and peeling paint. I sat down and started flicking through a copy of the local paper. Sitting opposite me was an older Bengali man of indeterminate age, wearing a thick black woollen hat and a stained grey suit. He'd shuffled in out of the rain carrying a heavy bag that seemed to bend him over almost double with its weight. He'd raised a few curious looks when he first came in but nothing more. Now, with repeated moans and groans, he pulled a square cardboard box covered in many layers of brown parcel tape out of his bag, which he proceeded to write on with a black marker pen and then tie up with blue string. Behind him a young Asian man in a white *shalwar kameez*, skullcap and grey jerkin scanned the Arabic section of books before picking one and returning to his desk, where he started to read, swaying back and forth, his lips moving silently while he traced the text with his finger. Directly in front of me sat a middle-aged white man staring at the wall, his folded arms resting on the desk, his face fixed in a permanent grimace. Two female students sat next to him, heads bent over their books, chewing worn pencils in their mouths. A young black man sat on the other side of them, fast asleep, snoring quietly. After about ten minutes the fire alarm rang and everyone was thrown into a clumsy huddle on the noisy

It was a treat to go with my mother to the
Whitechapel Library. I stepped into the
building with anticipatory pleasure. I came from
a poor working-class home and the library was
both awe-inspiring and daunting. The grand
staircase, with an iron balustrade, it was like a
mansion I'd only seen in films. There was
decorum, self-imposed respect, a bit like going to
shul. I always remember when I saw an old man
drop a prayer book there and he kissed it when
he picked it up. That Jewish love for books has
stayed with me. The place smelled of books and
polish. The oak tables must have been polished
every day, I can imagine an old lady shining and
rubbing the tables in the night after we'd gone
home.

Harold Rosen, 1999

Whitechapel High Street outside. The pavement here is the widest in London, built especially for pedestrians, and the large group of people spilling out of the library still left enough room for the constant stream of people passing by. The rain stopped and the sun came out, the young student who'd been sitting near me was blinking violently in the bright light. An excited group of Bengali girls in tight jeans, wedge-heeled open sandals and brightly coloured scarves stood together whispering secretively. A tall Somalian man flicked his newspaper impatiently behind them. The Bengali man in the woollen hat appeared, standing near to the entrance, with frightened eyes, holding his heavy parcel close to his chest. Two shaven-headed scruffy-looking students came downstairs from the music library and lit cigarettes, sheltering in the doorway. A couple of American tourists – wide hips, flowery skirts and bum bags – sauntered past and joined the crowd on the pavement, waiting for someone to start a tour, confusion slowly spreading across their faces. Next to the railing beside the road a teacher tried to control a chattering class of schoolchildren, pointing and jumping around, most of them with brown skin and silky black hair. I saw Denise waiting by the large wooden doors of the library entrance; when she got a nod from inside she stood on tiptoe and tried to shout over the deafening noise of sirens, dieselly traffic and the cacophony of different languages being spoken. 'It's OK,' she said, blushing slightly, 'you can go back in now.' I turned and watched this truly diverse group of people wander back into the library and felt sad that the next time I came the doors would be permanently closed.

I always felt welcome at the Whitechapel Library.
I used to go from when I was a child, and later, as
a teenager, with my friends when we had
nothing to do. It was one of the only places apart
from the mosque we were allowed to go to
unaccompanied. Boys and girls used it as a
meeting place. We are not supposed to mix but
we could there. We had to take the books to show
our parents we had been. It was a shelter, a safe
place where we couldn't be chucked out.
Otherwise we had to go into the parks, which are
too visible and dangerous in terms of racial
attacks.

Zoinul, 1999

3

Two Brick Lanes

The battle against racism and fascism cannot be won by outsiders
who march into an area, chant slogans, and then march out
again; it can only be won by the most dedicated, rooted and
persistent commitment to undermine and destroy the injustice
and neglect on which such movements thrive.

Revd Kenneth Leech,
Brick Lane, 1978: The Events and Their Significance

If you stand outside the Whitechapel Library and look directly across
the busy road and slightly to your left you can see Altab Ali Park,
a small patch of green named after a young Bengali tailor stabbed
to death there in a racist attack on 4 May 1978. The park has
become a contemporary meeting place for the Bengali community
and a starting point for political marches against racism and the
war in Iraq. Mapped out in limestone in the grass of the park is
the skeleton outline of the church the area was named after, White
Chapel. According to Iain Sinclair, 'it was the original pilgrims'
church to make your devotions to before you went into the City
of London'. White Chapel Church had a doomed history, burning
to the ground and being rebuilt at least four times. 'The last time
it was destroyed,' says Sinclair, 'they found little coffins in the roof
filled with the remains of children, which have never been explained.
The lead from them was melting and running into shimmering
streams into the street.' Iain is fascinated by this space and feels
it has mystical qualities: 'Groups of homeless alcoholics who hang
out in that field never cross inside the old church boundary,' he
said. 'There is nothing to stop them but they cluster instead around

one anonymous old tomb. If you go to the drinking fountain at the entrance there is a hole which acts like a telescope, pointing directly at that tomb as if there is a secret geography underneath Whitechapel all the time that people subconsciously respond to.'

Living high above ground, in a flat overlooking this park, is a long-time resident of Whitechapel and good friend of Bill Fishman, the Reverend Kenneth Leech. Bill encouraged me to speak with him about Brick Lane, telling me, 'He's a socialist Anglican priest who has lived and worked in the area since the 1950s. In my eyes he's a modern-day saint. You may have seen him marching through the streets of Whitechapel in his cassock and dog collar.' Reverend Leech agreed to meet me after receiving a phone call from Bill. 'Fishman's been knocking on my door for nearly half a century,' he said. 'He always puts a smile on my face when I hear his cheery voice calling up on the intercom as he passes by on one of his many walks around the area – "It's Fishmania here!" he'll boom, and then up he'll come and we'll sit and chat for hours.'

The reverend asked me to be quick if I wanted to talk with him as he'd decided to retire to his home town of Manchester after forty years of serving the ministry in the East End. After being buzzed into his flat I climbed a few floors up a winding staircase, leading into a bright and spacious room strewn with books and papers. A short, softly spoken, bald-headed man appeared from behind a closed door, wearing trainers, casual trousers and a bright red T-shirt with a tortoise on it, and introduced himself as Ken. Not the cassocked priest I had been expecting. He led me across the room, dodging piles of papers on the way to a battered old sofa under a window with a perfect bird's-eye view of Brick Lane.

Ken Leech is legendary within certain political circles and is known as the anarchist preacher who fought the fascists in Brick Lane in the 1970s. 'Back then Brick Lane was famous for all the wrong reasons,' said Ken, 'but it still had almost mythical status. In the early 1970s, at the height of the National Front activity, I was taking part in a demonstration and wearing my cassock, so I was fairly recognizable, and this group of young people wearing badges saying "Brick Lane against the Nazis" came up to me and one of them said, "Excuse me, sir, where is Brick Lane?" They were standing right in it and had no idea. I often had to explain to people that Brick Lane is one street and not a town.'

Looking out of his window down on to Brick Lane Ken pointed out to me all the new building projects currently taking place, including a hotel at the Whitechapel end of the street. Ken told me he has seen far too much of the grim and violent past of the street to be entirely negative about the current changes but he remains concerned about ordinary Bengalis who live in the area and don't feel part of it any more. 'They can't afford to eat in the restaurants,' he said, 'which are geared to tourists and City workers. I think a build-up of resentment about these problems has caused consider-able damage and I expect the attack on the Pride of Spitalfields pub was something to do with these feelings from local people about the influx of wealthy incomers into the area.'

These kinds of tensions are not new for Ken. Since arriving in East London in 1958 he has been trying to build bridges between different community groups. His first East London residence was in Cable Street, to the south of Brick Lane; 'the site of political battles in the 1930s but in the 1950s one of the most multicultural streets in the city', said Ken. 'It was the heart of the so-called coloured quarter then; a red-light district and the most notorious slum area of London. My neighbours were very mixed, I had Somalis to the left of me, Nigerians next door and Maltese people opposite.'

Ken lived in Cable Street until he finished his studies. In 1964 he moved north of the lane to his first parish in Hoxton, the heartland of the National Front, which 'was a complete culture shock. I'd just assumed the whole of the East End was multiracial – but not Hoxton. Shortly after I arrived the general election took place and Mosley, a candidate for the borough, got a lot of votes from members of my congregation. They didn't see any moral dilemma between voting fascist and being Christian. This was a real turning point for me.'

Ken worked tirelessly to change the attitude of his congregation for the next ten years before moving to St Matthew's Church in Bethnal Green, just off Brick Lane, where the funerals of the Kray twins took place. I witnessed both of their funeral processions, Ronnie's in 1995 and Reggie's in 2000, as they passed along Bethnal Green Road, which was lined on both occasions with thousands of mourners waiting to pay their last respects. Many older people looked genuinely distraught. At Ronnie's funeral I saw an elderly lady faint and another throw herself in front of the hearse. Many, like me, just came to see the spectacle, street theatre at its most extreme, as black horses with feathered plumage pulled the ornate glass-and-wood Victorian carriages containing their coffins for miles, led by a solemn entourage of local villains dressed in leather trench coats and top hats. I asked Ken if he had officiated at either of their funerals and he told me firmly he had not.

In the 1970s, when Ken was the priest at St Matthew's, the National Front was at its height, the Bengali community were expanding, and racial attacks were commonplace. The atmosphere was tense, as gangs of skinheads repeatedly charged down Brick Lane, smashing windows, throwing concrete blocks and bottles. The police did little to stop it. Schoolchildren were let out early

On Sunday 11 June 1978 a one-hundred-and-fifty-strong fascist window-smashing squadron, bussed in from as far as Dagenham, Putney and South Ockenden, attempted a Kristallnacht on the Lane. An eyewitness wrote, 'They thought that the Asians were cowed and it would only be a few minutes before they could wave their Union Jacks down Brick Lane. They were wrong. Asian youths know well how to defend themselves. Faced with this strength and courage the racists had no option but to run back from where they had come.'

David Widgery, 'Ripe Bananas and Stolen Bicycles', *Marketa Luskacova: Photographs of Spitalfields*, 1991 and rushed straight home. Stories of young men having their ears slashed off and being beaten beyond recognition started to circulate. The community lived in fear: 'paki-bashing' was commonplace and any Asians out alone at night were risking their lives. 'Most Bengalis wouldn't move north of the railway bridge unless they moved in gangs of twelve,' Ken told me. 'I knew a woman who ran classes in the borough for English as a second language at the Bethnal Green Institute but she could not get students to cross over into what they considered to be fascist territory. Jerry White's book on the Rothschild buildings says elderly Jewish people would always tell him don't walk through Bethnal Green at night because it's not safe, and it was exactly the same in the 1970s, you hardly ever saw Bengalis north of the bridge. It was almost as if there were two Brick Lanes.'

For the Bengali community around Brick Lane it was a nasty time. By 1974 the National Front had a strong physical presence in the area, most visibly at the top of Brick Lane on the Bethnal Green Road. Every Sunday morning gangs of skinheads wearing braces and Doctor Marten boots would stand there, waving Union Jacks and selling fascist papers, spitting and hurling racist abuse at any Asians that walked by. Disgusted by what was happening on his own doorstep Ken made it his personal mission to reclaim the site where they stood. He gleefully told me how he engineered a peaceful way to oust them from their position: 'There was a meeting at the Montefiore Centre about the presence of the National Front at the corner of Brick Lane and Bethnal Green Road and the intimidation and the violence. About four hundred people came. It was a very angry meeting. There was a police officer there called Inspector John Wallace, the community relations officer, who said in an unguarded moment, "We can't do anything about the National Front because they're not breaking any laws, but if anti-racists don't like them there I suggest you turn up first."' Between fits of laughter Ken continued: 'So I wrote a letter to the *East London Advertiser* saying that Inspector Wallace at a public meeting in front of hundreds of people said this and we thank the police for their support and

I was the only one in my family who wasn't a member of the NF. I have a cousin who was in prison for attacking an Asian family. I'm ashamed to say my family were part of the lynch mob at the top of Brick Lane every Sunday with their placards and chants. When the market closed they'd run amok down Brick Lane smashing up shops and beating people up. My cousins used to sing a chant as they went up Brick Lane, 'Ding dong the lights are flashing, we're going paki-bashing.' They all wore the skinhead gear.

As a white teenager I was constantly approached by people trying to give me stickers with slogans like 'Ain't no black in the Union Jack'. If you rebuffed them you ran the risk of violence. It was serious for me because many of those people were in my immediate family. I had a secret friendship with an Asian girl and if my family had found I was mixing with a 'paki' I'd have been in real danger. I felt like an outsider from the community I grew up with. When I started to go out to pubs and clubs on the gay scene it was such a relief to find a community where I fit in.

Eddie, 2005

propose that we occupy the site from ten in the morning. I knew the NF would turn up at eight and the police would be there from seven but of course we'd secretly arranged to be there at five and take over the site. At the beginning there were only about thirty of us but it grew to four thousand at one point.' He shakes his head remembering. 'It was ironic because the police told us it was impossible to take action against the NF as they weren't breaking any laws, but within five weeks of our occupation they got an injuction from the commissioner saying that anybody on the site would be arrested. It was only when anti-racists non-violently occupied the site that anything was done. But it did change things, particularly when the Bengalis joined in – that's when the atmosphere really changed.'

Things got worse though before they got better. Altab Ali's death in 1978 marked a turning point in the political awakening of the Bangladeshi community and many more local Bangladeshis joined Ken in his occupation at the top of Brick Lane. Eventually the racists were driven out but the action took years to take root and was not without its risks. Ken, one of those always on the front line, had repeated death threats posted through his letter box, some written in human blood. If he was ever physically attacked he didn't mention it but when things became 'too hot' he would retreat to the safety of a Quaker commune, housed above a leather manu-facturers, which overlooks the old National Front site.

4

Brick Lane is a River

If I set out from my house in Hackney, it's like getting into a canoe, I don't even have to walk, I just flow South straight down into Brick Lane.

Iain Sinclair

I have spent a lot of time in the Quaker commune at the Bethnal Green end of Brick Lane with one of its founding members, a remarkable eighty-five-year-old German lady called Marga. She has lived in this rambling alternative community since its foundation in the early 1970s. The walk from Ken's home to Marga's takes you from one end of Brick Lane nearly to the other, starting at the busy intersection with Whitechapel High Street and ending at the junction with Bethnal Green Road.

The Whitechapel end of Brick Lane (officially called Osborn Street, but most still refer to it as Brick Lane) has always had a down-at-heel feel about it until recently, when a new hotel was built there. Tourists now frequent this part of the street, wandering in and out of the glass-fronted building with maps and guide books, or sitting in the bar on the ground floor on large cubed seats, looking out at a *halal* chicken fast-food outlet, fashion wholesalers and a travel agency offering cheap flights to Mecca, Jordan and Bangladesh.

A little further up is A. Elfes Ltd Monumental Stone Masons, the only remaining overtly Jewish presence in the street. The large showroom is filled with marble tombs and headstones engraved with Hebrew inscriptions in gold leaf. The business has been there since 1945 but the stone masonry takes place somewhere else now. The Brick Lane site is used for display only and is often, to the annoyance of the owners, mistaken for a tourist attraction or some kind of museum. Next to Elfes is one of the few empty yards on the street, probably already bought by property developers waiting to convert it into high-spec flats. An alleyway near by acts as a frame to the City skyline less than a mile away, the giant Swiss Re Tower, the 'Gherkin', appears to loom over Brick Lane. On the pavement women wrapped from head to toe in black *burkas* try to push babies in buggies laden with shopping up the street while hordes of tourists and City workers go against the flow of local traffic to reach the restaurants and bars at the other end. The sounds of horns, car radios and sirens mask the music coming out of the Asian wedding services shop a bit further up the street.

This section of Brick Lane is noisy, bustling and raw, and apart from the hotel it belongs mainly to the Bangladeshi community that live there. There's an eye clinic, a chemists, and the Sonali Bank, the first Bangladeshi bank in Britain from which people can send money directly back home to their families. On the corner of Hopetown Street and Brick Lane is a lone pub called the Archers, frequented by the last of the white cockneys in the area and visiting building contractors who sit outside on metal chairs in hard hats and dirty jeans drinking pints and pointing at the Ripper Tour guides in their deerstalker hats and cloaks, leading grisly tours through the backstreets.

Crossing over Wentworth Street you arrive at the Brick Lane Health Centre and the decorative metal arch that announces you are now entering Banglatown. In between the health centre and the Shiraz Hotel and Restaurant is a narrow alleyway leading into Flower and Dean Walk, one of the first purpose-built housing estates for Bangladeshi families, once the most notorious Victorian rookery in London. Zaman Brothers grocers takes over much of the next row of shops. Outside, giant jackfruits are piled up on the pavement next to boxes of ripe mangoes. Inside, sacks of basmati rice sit next to coffin-shaped freezers filled with large fish, whole and stiff, imported from the rivers of Bangladesh. You don't see any tourists in here, unlike Taj Stores further up the street.

Just past Zaman Brothers is the Brick Lane Police Station, and surrounding it an electrical shop, a money-transfer agency and newsagents selling Bengali papers and Bangla tapes, their windows covered in posters advertising Bollywood films. On the other side of the street is one of the largest businesses operating in Brick Lane, the Modern Saree Centre, which has been trading since the late 1950s. Big-busted Asian mannequins draped in hand-embroidered saris stand in a row in the window. Walking up towards the mosque on the corner of Fournier Street and Brick Lane, you pass the last of the textile wholesalers and manufacturers. As you reach Fournier Street you enter a different zone. From here over fifty restaurants line Brick Lane on both sides of the street, all the way up to the Old Truman Brewery site, selling an English version of curry to a lunchtime City crowd and an evening clientele mainly made up of visiting tourists. A new development is the touts outside, aggressively hustling passers-by with promises of the 'best curry in the street'. It's considered a sign of true belonging if they don't bother you as you walk past. Many of the restaurants appear empty in the week, particularly the recently refurbished ones decked out in chrome and glass. The white middle classes come to Brick Lane for the burgundy wallpaper, kitschy decor and garish murals.

Set back from the street behind iron railings, between Fashion and Fournier streets, is the Victorian building of Christ Church School, where 90 per cent of the pupils are currently Bangladeshi. When the school opened over a hundred years ago it was filled with Jewish students from Russia, Poland and the Ukraine. Past the school is the now derelict Seven Stars pub, a few Asian sweet shops and the Al Barakah store for the devout, selling prayer mats, religious books and clothing. Directly opposite, behind large gates, on the site of the former Russian Vapour Baths, is a vast wholesale Bangladeshi cash-and-carry warehouse. The London Jamme Masjid Mosque sits on the corner of Brick Lane and Fournier Street. When afternoon and evening prayers have finished the pavement outside the mosque is packed with men in ankle-length white kaftans coming out of the building.

The only obviously Jewish shop sign left in the street is C. H. N. Katz, the string and paper bag wholesalers at no. 86. I became a regular visitor to this shop after showing some of my artwork in Mr Katz's window as part of the 'Whitechapel Open' in 1994. When first approached about the exhibition the elderly bearded Hasid had shooed me away until I unwrapped the small metal sculptures I had made, preserving in resin objects from my grandfather's East End shop – broken clock pieces, a pickle fork from Jerusalem, ivory tags for watch repairs. We struck up a friendship of sorts and I'd often pop by to see him until rent rises forced him, like so many others, to pack up and move on. The shop sign above the doorway remains, but the old bell has been removed and replaced by a set of three chrome buttons with signs that read 'Vamp', 'Gallery' and 'Loft'. The window, which apart from my temporary exhibition had contained only a few faded balls of twine and piles of paper bags for over fifty-seven years, has now become a permanent venue for art installations.

Mr Katz had been a regular fixture on Brick Lane for decades and used to pray in the Machzike Hadath Synagogue opposite his

shop twice daily until it became a mosque in 1976. Walking past that building recently I saw two white girls with blonde ponytails sitting irreverently on the steps eating chips from one of the *halal* fried-chicken places on the street. Three Bengali teenage boys stood on the pavement opposite. 'You can't sit there. It's sacrilegious!' one of them shouted flirtatiously. 'Yes we can,' they hollered back, 'free country, innit!' 'Slags!' one of the boys shouted, before stomping upstairs to a minicab office, from which he spat in disgust on to the pavement below.

From here to the site of the old brewery, among the numerous curry houses, are a few off licences selling bottles of overpriced Chardonnay for tourists to drink in the unlicensed restaurants. There's an Asian barbers, Azeem's Hair Stylists, at no. 69, which is always busy. It's an entirely Bengali crowd in there, men only, most of them young, wanting hairstyles that imitate their gangster rapper heroes. The Shampan on the corner of Hanbury Street is the end of 'curry row' and the beginning of the Old Truman Brewery site, now famous as a venue for performance art, fashion events and video shoots. By far the most interesting artwork I have seen in the area was located on this junction in 2001 as part of a temporary exhibition of interactive art entitled 'Curio'. The curator of this show, Alana Jelenick, described it as 'a four-week intervention into the tourist zone of Banglatown'. Alana invited seven artists whose work she sees as exploring fantasies about the 'other' to respond to the street, which she feels is so often misrepresented by the media. 'The East End has been used to connect up different stories of violence and crime,' she told me, 'of revolutionary politics, of authenticity, of poverty and exoticism, of foreign cultures, both long gone and vibrant. People come for Jack the Ripper or the "cockney paradise", for Victorian slums and deprivation, for deconsecrated synagogues and Eastern European shop names, for curry and Asian cool.'

Like me, Alana came to the area as an artist with a Jewish background, seeking cheap studio space and a connection to the streets her family had once inhabited. When she first arrived, herself a new migrant from Australia, she said, 'I was like every other white middle-class person who moves here. I went to the local library and got out books on the Ripper or Dan Leno's Limehouse.' The longer she spent living in East London the more she realized this easily consumed history was in fact a myth. She didn't trust the tour guides with their repeated stories of the arrival of the Huguenots, the Jews and then the Bengalis, feeling that these histories were used to promote the idea of London as a multicultural city rather than being a representative truth about the people who live in the East End. Alana believes most visitors and journalists come with stereotypes of Brick Lane in mind and leave with them confirmed. After twelve years living and working in the area she feels she can now legitimately call herself an East Ender, but the longer she stays the uneasier she feels about how the area she calls home is being represented. 'Most reportage about Brick Lane services the idea that London is a refuge or a sanctuary,' said Alana, 'or that people have lived harmoniously together here for centuries. The real, complex stories of the people who live here have not been revealed by this simplistic version of the area. But I live here and daily experience the disparity between myth and reality. The history of the area, as with anywhere, is more complex and diverse than is usually believed. We hear and tell stories that suit us and diminish the evidence of others. This is what I wanted to bring out in "Curio".'

I think Alana most successfully achieved her aims in Curio with the inclusion of a site-specific soundscape by the artist Mohini Chandra entitled *Flow*. Installed directly at the busy junction of Hanbury Street and Brick Lane were three public-address speakers attached to a large metal pole that threw out the sound of free-flowing water. Designed to interact with the street, the range of watery sounds increased or decreased in volume and intensity relating to the level of noise and traffic on the roads and pavements. Some saw the work as an echo of the different waves of immigration that had passed through Brick Lane. Others in the Bangladeshi community told Mohini it made them long for home, the sounds a constant reminder of the rivers they had left behind in Sylhet. Mohini made the piece as an alternative way to map the city and its cultural and physical flows. Alana felt it inverted the associations about migrant communities and focused instead on the largest new wave of incomers, tourists. 'The microphone picked up the noises on the street, which are predominantly tourist noises,' she said, 'as everyone who actually lives there became background noise. As the night wore on and more tourists came the sound increased. When there were hardly any people around the sound was of quiet dripping. When many people passed by the sound was of a torrent of water flooding through. This metaphor, the idea of "being flooded" and "waves of immigration" are usually used in a negative way for migrants. Here it was transferred to the hordes of tourists and art seekers who unknowingly interacted with the piece to make its point.'

Hanbury Street marks the end of one zone in Brick Lane and the beginning of another. This central part of the street, from Hanbury Street to Quaker Street, is dominated by the Old Truman Brewery site. Just beyond Dray Walk and my old studio is the central brewery building, concealed behind a mirrored wall, which reflects back into the street those walking past. The Georgian brick exterior is hidden from view like so much in the street. Just past Woodseer Street is the first of the Brick Lane bridges, a covered walkway with arched windows connecting the two halves of the brewery site. Iain Sinclair is fascinated by this crossing, which he sees as a strange imitation of a Venetian bridge over a river, like an energy gateway. 'Part of its power lies in the fact that nobody really notices it,' he said. 'Brick Lane with its bridges becomes like Venice, a city of the dead, a city of dreams, which you navigate by following watery paths.'

Past Shoreditch Station is the second bridge in Brick Lane, which originally carried railway traffic to and from Bishopsgate Station. This is the bridge, mentioned earlier, that cuts Brick Lane effectively in two; those living in the Whitechapel end have traditionally been afraid to cross this boundary and enter the sometimes hostile territory of Bethnal Green. Apart from on Sundays, when a market is held here, this part of Brick Lane is desolate. The metal walls of the railway bridge are covered in torn posters for local gigs at 93 Feet East and the Vibe Bar, as well as flyers for demonstrations against the war in Iraq. The only other decoration is a large mosaic cemented on to the wall, which I helped to create over ten years ago with children from two local schools.

Further north, the leather wholesalers near Sclater and Cheshire streets have been replaced recently with estate agents, designer furniture shops, a hairdressers and an alternative therapy centre. The street is particularly congested around the two bagel bakeries near the Bethnal Green end as cars and taxis fight for parking space. The oldest bakery is at no. 155 Brick Lane, having been established there in 1855; the Beigel Bake, at no. 159, has been at that site since 1970. Marga, my friend who lives at the Quaker commune near by – which Ken Leech used in the 1970s as his hideout – says the Beigel Bake is the only one to go to. 'It is what makes Brick Lane special,' she told me. 'It's open twenty-four hours a day. If I get hungry in the middle of the night and want to buy some bread, all warm and smelling beautifully, or some *cholla* freshly cut, I can pop down the road and there it is. It's never closed.' There can't be many eighty-five-year-old women who would venture into a bakery in the East End at three in the morning, but Marga is quite unlike anybody I have ever met.

I got to know her while working on an exhibition called 'Keeping Pace for the Women's Library', about the lives of older women in the East End. Our first meeting took place at the Nazrul curry house on Brick Lane on a freezing January day in 2002. As I sat waiting for her I began to worry about her slipping on the icy pavements outside. At exactly one o'clock a tiny slim lady with long white hair pulled into a loose bun breezed into the restaurant wearing trainers, a brown cord jump suit and a bright orange scarf. She scanned the room quickly and marched straight over and introduced herself, shaking my hand firmly and fixing me with her piercing blue eyes. I mentioned the ice and asked if she'd had a good journey here. She raised an eyebrow and said, 'Having just returned from solo trips to South Africa and Australia I think I can manage to walk down my own street quite safely.'

Her accent is hard to trace, and when I mentioned this she laughed. 'When people ask me where I am coming from I say, like you, on this planet, we're all swimming through the cosmos together, we're just human beings, you know.' She feels at home living in the cosmopolitan, noisy, energetic atmosphere of Brick

Lane. 'I like the interaction, and every time I walk down the street there is something new to see.'

Marga came to Brick Lane originally because the Quaker community she was involved in wanted to carry out social work in a needy part of London. They felt Brick Lane was the right place and established the commune, which has had up to thirty people living in it at any one time. Marga moved there in 1973 with her husband (who died in 1988) and since then she has watched an ever-changing group of people come and go from the building and the streets around her.

As we sat enjoying our curry she told me a story about the restaurant we were sitting in. She has been going there since the early 1970s when she first moved to the area. Back then the whole Quaker community had been regulars at the Nazrul. They'd had an account, and used to go in a large group every week to eat there. The Nazrul had been more of a café when it first opened, with Formica tables and large jugs of water on the tables. The majority of the customers had been Bangladeshi men, for whom the eclectic group from the commune had been quite a novelty. Marga struck up a friendship with the owner, Ali, and received an invitation to his daughter's wedding. 'It was quite an experience,' she told me. 'I'd never seen anything like it before. There were over five hundred people attending and I was the only white woman. It took place in the Brady Centre around the corner.' Ali had good reason to ask Marga. She'd been instrumental in helping the family in their battle to receive citizenship for their daughter, who was going to be deported back to Bangladesh. As we talked a surly young waiter came over and snatched our plates away the second we'd put our forks down. Marga smiled wearily. 'It's different now, you see, no time to stop and talk. New people run the place and they need the seats for the next lot.'

We finished our meal and walked back up Brick Lane together, Marga striding ahead with me struggling to keep up with her. 'How does the street compare to when you moved here in 1973?' I asked, panting behind her. 'It leaves me a bit cold today, to be honest with you,' she said with a nod in the direction of the new estate agents

in front of her. 'I tend to walk quickly through nowadays, heading only for the few places I like to visit, like the Spitalfields City Farm and the beigel shop. Sometimes I'll meet my granddaughter in the Mohib for a chicken korma but most of the time I tend to avoid it.' 'And on Sundays?' I asked. 'Do you visit the market? It's right on your doorstep, you must have seen a lot of changes over the years.' Ignoring the cue to delve into stories of the good old days Marga told me about her weekly visit to the Sunday market to buy walnuts from two old ladies in their nineties who've been there for over fifty years. 'Every Sunday on my way to Spitalfields Market I buy a bag of walnuts from them and we stop and chat. I take the walnuts to feed squirrels in St James's Park and amuse the tourists, who take pictures of me on their videos because the squirrels walk up my coat because I have what they really like, real walnuts.'

We walked quickly in silence to the top of the street and when we reached her building she asked if I'd like to come and see her computer paintings. I followed her up a steep flight of stairs above a leather shop and arrived in one of the communal kitchens in the building that overlooks Bethnal Green Road and the top of Brick Lane. From the large sash windows running along the length of the room I could clearly see the site where the NF once lurked. I imagined Ken hiding out here in the early days of his campaign, out of breath, heart pumping, watching the vicious gangs of skin-heads below scouring the streets to find him. In the centre of the industrial-sized room sat a long wooden table covered in empty mugs, a jug of water and half a loaf of seeded black bread. Catering-sized jars of pulses, honey, rice and herbal teas were stacked along shelves and next to the fireplace. In the far-left corner next to the window was the community's shared computer. After making us both an elderberry tea Marga sat down, logged on and quickly found the file containing her vibrant computer-generated paintings. Hundreds of studies of her daily life flickered on to the screen. Geometric patterns mixed with figurative line drawings and text, describing meetings with friends in Brick Lane, swimming in Hampstead pond, circle dancing, parties and celebrations. As we viewed her online gallery a number of young people who lived in the community drifted in and out of the kitchen, including a professional clown just back from a trip to Japan, a Danish student and an eco-warrior from France.

Marga told me, 'Sixteen young people live here with me from across the globe. There's a young woman who's just returned from doing a research project in the Amazon with shamans, an acrobat from Sweden, a teacher from Greece, all sorts of people with such stories.' Unsurprisingly Marga finds the commune a really stimulating place to live. She's never alone or bored and thinks living with young people keeps her attitude fresh.

She took me on a tour of the building. The first stop was the meditation room. The only furniture inside was a futon covered in a cotton throw. A few fern plants stood in pots in one corner and an ethnic rug lay on the sanded wooden floorboards. Marga invited me to sit cross-legged and barefoot with her on the rug. As we sat relaxing I commented on the calmness of the space. She told me there was a battle raging within the commune about the room. Some people wanted to rent it out as office space to create more revenue. 'The landlord has nearly doubled our rent in the last year. After thirty years here the future of the commune looks uncertain. Many people have already left due to rent rises. There used to be an organization beneath us called Avenues Unlimited but they had to move.'

I wanted to talk with Marga about her early memories of the street but unlike many older people she hates to reminisce. She preferred to discuss the present and talked at length about her favourite places in the area, in particular Spitalfields City Farm, which is situated behind Allen Gardens, off Brick Lane, on a former railway goods depot. 'I love it there,' she said. 'You can touch the animals running freely and happily, buy free-range eggs and silver beet. I know the farm almost from the beginning and have Polaroid film of people and activities there, spinning, weaving and making pottery.'

Marga's mental picture of the area, like her perspective on life in general, allows her to edit out undesirable elements and focus on the positive. She believes she achieves this enviable outlook through a unique system of daily therapies she has personally constructed.

While sitting with her on the floor of the meditation room I was witness to one of her 'five daily therapies' as a faint beam of winter sun fell on to the floor when the grey clouds momentarily parted. 'Quick,' said Marga urgently, 'we must bathe. I haven't done my solar therapy yet today. When the sun is shining I'll drop everything and go flat out, quarter of an hour on my back, quarter of an hour on my front, totally relaxing.' Giggling like a schoolgirl I lay on the floor with Marga and joined in.

As the last of the sun disappeared we put our shoes back on and Marga completed the tour of the rest of the commune. She led me round scruffy narrow corridors and into a number of communal lounges including the one where she had nursed her husband till his death on the sofa there nearly twenty years ago. We climbed another flight of stairs and she led me through a tiny door out on to a roof garden covered in flowering plants lovingly tended in terracotta pots. We sat on a makeshift bench, a plank raised off the ground by two bricks, listening to the calming sound of children playing in St Matthias's schoolyard below. Marga pointed out the spire of the church where Ken worked for so many years. 'I took pictures of all this being built,' she said, pointing to a new block of flats behind the school. 'I've been walking the area for years with my Polaroid camera,' she told me before inviting me up to her private room at the top of the building to see them.

After two more flights of stairs we reached Marga's tiny space in the attic. A life of collecting was evident everywhere. Her bed was covered in a deep-red throw from Morocco, a gift from a friend. Beside it was an installation made from orange peel and plant cuttings. The walls of her room were decorated with drawings and postcards received from friends all over the world. I sat down in the only available floor space while Marga searched under piles of belongings for the boxes containing her Polaroid archive. Eventually she found one and we spent the next couple of hours sifting through the faded images. The photographs included recordings of building works that have taken place in the street since the early 1970s, but most of the images were of people: Marga with her husband,

Marga in the kitchen of the commune teaching friends German; and parties and celebrations, all carefully documented. We couldn't find the pictures of the Asian wedding she had attended but she promised to look for them the following week when I was to return as she had kindly agreed to introduce me to Derek Cox, a youth worker from Avenues Unlimited, the organization that had moved from the floor below hers and into new premises on Brick Lane.

I could see Marga was tiring. I had taken up a lot of her time. We kissed goodbye and arranged a time for the following week. 'See you on Tuesday,' I called as I reached the bottom of the stairway. 'Will do,' she called back. 'Jolly good show. Jolly good show.'

5

Avenues Unlimited

It is here that Sikh, Muslim and Jew, gypsy, cockney and skinhead walk on common ground. The language of this wide humanity is evident in the names of the traders, the stonemasons, the tailors, the torn posters of Asian cinema and in the slogans of the graffiti.

Mark Holborn, 'Marketa Luskacova', *Marketa Luskacova: Photographs of Spitalfields*

Marga took me to meet Derek the following week. We walked together back down Brick Lane, past Shoreditch Station and a row of shops before turning into a narrow alleyway next to a café, which ended in an iron stairwell. I followed Marga up the rickety staircase into an unlit corridor. She pushed open an unmarked door to her right and we entered a brightly painted hallway covered in posters. An old racing bike leaned against the wall. 'He's here,' Marga said, turning to me with a grin. I followed her towards the sound of female voices and laughter coming from the far end of the hall and we entered a tiny office. A middle-aged white man, sitting at a desk, was speaking on the phone, wearing jeans and a pale blue shirt. Marga waved to him and whispered to me, 'That's him, that's Derek.'

Sitting next to Derek was an older Bengali lady dressed in a black sari with gold trim, talking animatedly with two young Asian women. The older woman stood up to greet us and offer tea. The muffled sound of pop music and the click clack of balls being hit by pool cues could be heard coming from the adjoining room.

Derek hung up the phone and walked over to give Marga a hug, his huge frame towering over her. Thankfully Marga gave me a great

introduction; Derek made it clear he had little time for media types or interlopers into the area. Marga left shortly afterwards and in a quiet moment Derek shut the door and began to tell me the story of his long time in residence in East London.

He'd grown up in a working-class home in Guildford and had left school aged fifteen with no academic qualifications. After three years in the army based in Hong Kong he decided to become a youth worker; his first job was at St Hilda's Youth Club just off Brick Lane. It was 1963, the era of the Kray brothers, and Derek described the whole area as 'dark and gloomy, especially Brick Lane, which was depressed and seedy'. There were certain establishments on the street he was scared to enter, such as a restaurant near the railway bridge called Chucklers, a notorious Maltese-owned place that was well known for its connection with drugs and gang activity. There was a big Greek Cypriot and Maltese community in Brick Lane in the early 1960s as well as many Jews still living in the area: 'I remember this fish and chip shop run by a Jewish guy who'd always charge me double because I wasn't Jewish.' Another place Derek remembered was Harry Fishman's grocers by the brewery: 'He was an ex-policeman who was always getting robbed. His shop was filthy, dark and hardly had anything in it and you wouldn't really go in there unless you had to, which is exactly how most people felt about Brick Lane at that time.'

In the 1960s the busiest part of Brick Lane was around the Truman Brewery site: 'They employed thousands of local people and the brewery was what Brick Lane was known for then. Because Truman's stored a lot of maize there were rats everywhere, they ruled the street. Grey Eagle Street and Old Montague Street were filled with terrible tenement slums and drug dealers. The whole area was dismal. Christ Church was derelict and unused, with loads of homeless and drunks in the gardens. You've got to remember there were no tourists, no restaurants, you have to completely put out of your mind what it looks like today. There were still a lot of sweatshops and tailoring workshops around, it was a working place and the furniture industry was very prevalent then, particularly cabinet making. The building we're sitting in now used to be a factory that made furniture.'

Fashion Street, Flower and Dean Walk, Thrawl Street, Wentworth Street. Through which shall we go to Brick Lane? Black and noisome, the road sticky with slime, and palsied houses, rotten from chimney to cellar, leaning together, apparently by the mere coherence of their ingrained corruption. Dark, silent, uneasy shadows passing and crossing – human vermin in this reeking sink, like goblin exhalations from all that is noxious around. Women with sunken, black-rimmed eyes, whose pallid faces appear and vanish by the light of an occasional gas-lamp, and look so like ill-covered skulls that we start at their stare.

Arthur G. Morrison, *Palace Journal*, 24 April 1889

Derek's first home in the area was a bedsit at St Hilda's: 'The local residents called our digs the brothel as there were unmarried men and women living together. The white working-class community were very traditional about this sort of thing.' When he took over the youth club there was nothing there, just a filing cabinet with two letters in it. One banned them from the local swimming pool and the other banned them from a campsite in Buckinghamshire. Derek transformed the club into a coffee bar and ran late nights at which two distinctive groups of young local people came to hang out: 'One was the Rockers in their leather, they were real motorbike guys and mainly white and in the minority. The other was the Mods, they were a multiracial group with a lot of Nigerian boys, one or two from the Caribbean, a lot of Maltese, Greek Cypriots, Turkish Cypriots, white guys and many Irish. There was still a big Irish community in the area, fifth-generation dockers and all the sons of the brewery workers. There were no Asian people then, we had a couple of Jewish guys, a few mixed-race with Bengali dads and white mums who were called the "Bengali wives" because they married Bengali seamen. So you had all these different kids, from a real variety of backgrounds, sticking together because they were Mods and they lived in the East End. They all had short haircuts and a few who could afford it had scooters. There were many territorial fights, vicious, with broken bottles, if anyone tried to come into their patch. There was friction between the two groups so another youth worker, Richard Howser, took the Rockers to a different youth club in Barnet Grove and I had the Mods. It was less tense that way. They used to leave me on a Friday night and go up West clubbing, taking drugs the whole weekend. The only one I'm in touch with from that time is called Peter. Many of them died young. I had a good time with them most of the time but one night someone allegedly put pep pills in my tea and I went off sick for a few weeks. When I came back nearly all the kids were in prison or borstal. They were tough kids.'

Drug problems have dominated Derek's job for the last forty years. In the 1970s it was almost exclusively young white men who were addicts. Now Derek works with Bangladeshi and Somalian youths in the area, many of whom have drug problems and are consequently also involved in turf wars. 'There's always been gang activity around here,' said Derek, 'like the Krays, who I got to know in the 1960s when they tried to open a gym in St Hilda's. The pattern has repeated itself over the decades because there isn't enough in the area for young people to do so they get caught up in the wrong things, hanging out on the streets. In the 1960s there was really nothing so a big part of my job was to try to set things up. In the 1970s we did a lot for young Bangladeshi men – there were few women here then. At that time the Jewish community was moving out, but there was a residue of older Jewish people around.'

Derek left St Hilda's in 1965 and started working at Avenues Unlimited, a youth project. 'At the beginning there were only two workers,' he said. 'In 1970 we expanded and moved to the Bethnal Green end of Brick Lane. There was a factory below us and above us it was derelict until the Quaker community moved there in 1973, and that's when I met Marga.' In 1980 Avenues Unlimited moved to its current location on Brick Lane.

Derek offered to show me around the building. We went first into a room adjoining his office, which had a large pool table in the centre. Around the walls were photomontages of the work he has been involved in over the years. One of the frames was filled with a collage of pictures of Asian women in saris, picking vegetables from large vines growing above them. 'I'm particularly proud of that project,' said Derek. 'In 1966 I set up a committee that established Christ Church Gardens; it took five years of hard work to get it open in 1971. That's what I keep telling everyone, it's almost a waste of time to try to come here and get something going in a year or two; you can't just rush in and out, if you stay for a long time there's a two-way respect, then you can start to achieve something solid. I'm very proud of the garden, it's the only place (apart from maybe a few rare back gardens) where you can grow *dodi* and other vegetables from Bangladesh. It's now run by Peter, one of the ex-Mods from the youth club days.'

Another collection of images showed Derek in a playground,

surrounded by cheering children. 'I am most proud of my estate-based work,' he told me, 'where I've been visiting the same places for years. I have got to know whole generations of families this way.' Derek walked me over to another board that showed a group of Somalian and Bengali boys out together on a day trip to the countryside. 'This youth club is currently working very hard to try to bring these two communities together. They are both Sunni Muslim but from very different cultures, one African and one Asian, and both competing to adapt to a Western culture, and they don't mix well. The Somalian community today are like the Bangladeshi community twenty years ago, and they need extra support.' Derek feels the Bangladeshi community is now well established in Brick Lane and will be part of the area for a long time, although he is aware many Bengali people are being forced to leave the area as it becomes more and more expensive to live in. I asked him if he felt the spirit of the old East End had gone during the time he'd been working there. 'Absolutely not,' he replied. 'Now the extended families are in the Asian and Somalian communities. A lot of people bring grandparents over from Bangladesh or Somalia so they can be cared for, and families live together, sometimes three or four generations under one roof. They look out for each other and their elders in the same way Jewish and cockney families used to here.'

As we were talking the door burst open and a young Bangladeshi man dressed in a loose-fitting track suit and trainers, swaggered into the room, winked at me and gave Derek a friendly slap on the back before walking over to the pool table and chalking up a cue. After Derek introduced us, the young man, Atiqul, said to me, 'You should speak with my grandmother. She's one of the first people to come to Brick Lane from Bangladesh. I'll ask her, no problem.'

Before I left Derek handed me a business card and I noted he had modestly failed to tell me he had an OBE. It was apparent from his interview that he underplayed much of the work he had achieved and I hoped to find out more about him. I went back to the office a few weeks later to talk with Derek again but he was out. Atiqul was in the back room playing pool with some friends. He told me his grandmother had gone to Bangladesh and couldn't get back because of the floods, but he'd be happy to speak with me as long as his friends could come too. We waited for Derek to return, and with his consent I went into a back room with Atiqul and two of his friends. One of them lit up a cigarette as I began setting up the recording equipment and they jostled and poked each other while whispering energetically in Sylheti. For the first few minutes after the microphone was switched on the boys were very quiet, speaking only to introduce themselves as Saleck, aged twenty-one, and Atiqul and Bodrul, aged nineteen. Then, after some muffled giggling, the boys began to talk to me.

The three friends had grown up together on the same estate round the back of Brick Lane. Bodrul came from Bangladesh as a young baby and the others were born in London. When I asked about their earliest memories Derek was the first person they mentioned. 'He made our childhood fantastic,' said Atiqul. 'He took us camping abroad and on many activities in the area, we done so many things, day trips every week from the age of six or seven. He took us to the cinema, swimming, everything we wouldn't do with our families at home.'

I asked the boys to tell me about their homes. Bodrul said, 'Six of us live together in a tiny one-bedroom flat,' before falling on the floor in hysterics, followed by the other two. It took quite a while for them to compose themselves.

'He's still young, he doesn't mean it,' one of his friends tried to apologize through his tears.

'Sorry,' said Bodrul, 'I'm just joking, it's a three-bedroom flat, very nice.'

'We can't help it,' said Atiqul, 'that's what we do together, we laugh a lot.'

After a few more minutes of hysteria the boys told me their families all come from the same part of Bangladesh, from small villages in Sylhet, where their grandparents know one another. They have all been back to Bangladesh at least three or four times in their lives

and would like to go more but, as Bodrul said, 'It depends on the financial way, you can't just go tomorrow.'

When I asked if they liked visiting they all responded positively. 'Yeah, man, it's wicked,' said Bodrul, 'magnificent, but of course now we can't go, it's flooded and we're worried 'cause the phone lines are dead and we can't get hold of our relatives.'

'His uncle, yeah,' butted in Atiqul, 'had a shop, right, and it completely blew away but that's normal, right, the shops are made of bamboo and that and right near the water and in the rainy season they just get carried away with the water. It's terrible for them, they can't barely go out the house or nothing because of the floods.'

'There are so many people there who'd like to be here,' said Bodrul quietly, 'because of all the problems and chaos there, yeah, we're the lucky ones.'

'Would you describe yourselves culturally?' I asked them.

'We see ourselves as British first and then Bangladeshi,' said Atiqul.

'British Asians,' said Bodrul while the others nodded vigorously, 'that is how we define ourselves.'

'Did you mix with many white people when you were growing up?' I asked. They all shook their heads.

'On our estate, when we were kids, it was 100 per cent Asian community, there was no mixed-race kids on the estate or at the school we went to, which was Thomas Buxton,' said Bodrul, 'just off Brick Lane.'

As they said this I realized they were about the right age to have been involved in an arts-based project I conducted with that school exactly ten years before, which resulted in the mosaic now installed next to the railway bridge on Brick Lane. I asked if they remembered it and Bodrul said, 'Of course. I loved that project. I did the mosaic of the orange hand. I remember it really well, it was really nice, it's up in Brick Lane now, innit, and when I go past I tell these guys, that's my hand I made there.'

The *Spital Square Mosaic* was funded by Bethnal Green City Challenge. I was the artist who ran the project back in 1995 while working as the education officer for Chisenhale Gallery in Bow. Thomas Buxton School, as Bodrul said, which had an almost exclusively Bengali intake at the time, worked on the project with St Anne's Catholic School. The two schools are situated opposite each other on Buxton Street, and prior to this project had never worked together before. The creation of the mosaic took over six months and involved one hundred and twenty pupils from both schools. The children filled giant twelve-foot-long sections of concrete with colourful designs that reflected different aspects of the local area. They made mosaics of *menorahs* and *mehndis*, mosques, churches and synagogues, Huguenot spinning wheels and sewing machines.

The completed artwork was placed in landscaped gardens on the site of the old Spitalfields Hospital directly behind Spitalfields Market. At the time we thought the mosaic would be a permanent fixture in the area as there was a known archaeological site underneath the gardens and we were told the land could never be built on. The project attracted a lot of positive media attention and was filmed by *Blue Peter*, whose team came to the launch party and handed out *Blue Peter* badges and balloons. Bodrul told me he'd been excluded from the party after being caught bunking off school, but he remembered the importance of the event for the children in his school.

A few years after the launch party I was travelling past the site on the top deck of a no. 8 bus when I saw large sections of the mosaic being pulled out of the ground by a forklift truck and dumped into a skip. Outraged, I got on the phone to the council and was

put through to various people, none of whom could tell me why the mosaic was being removed. Eventually I spoke to a sympathetic person who promised to do everything in their power to save it. I heard nothing about it for months and watched as the site was transformed into an archaeological site – the remains of a medieval priory and stone pulpit were excavated along with a basement full of bones and the burial site of a wealthy Roman woman. Shortly after these discoveries the site was filled in and now a vast office block stands there, bringing the city forward, right up to the edge of the adjoining Spitalfields Market.

I was never informed of the fate of the mosaic and encountered it again only by chance in 1999 in the old railway arches in Brick Lane, where the launch party for the book I co-authored with Iain Sinclair, *Rodinsky's Room*, was held. Looking around the derelict site I happened to lift a large tarpaulin and there, stacked underneath, were the twelve large sections of the mosaic. About a year later, with no consultation with either myself or the schools, the mosaic suddenly appeared on Brick Lane arranged on opposite sides of the street near the railway bridge, with a concrete border of red, white and green topped by a yin-yang symbol, which had no relationship to the original concept of the work, which was about celebrating cultural diversity in the area. Unsurprisingly, the out-of-context mosaic is now covered in graffiti and has become meaningless to those who walk past it, apart from the few teenagers who still live in the area, such as Bodrul, who remember making it.

I asked Bodrul how he felt about Brick Lane today compared to ten years ago when he was involved in making the mosaic.

'I don't like it so much,' he told me, 'because of the bars and things like that.'

'It is bad for the old people,' said Atiqul. 'When they walk to the mosque every day they have to walk past all these drunks who abuse them. Every time they go to the mosque they have to be clean and if they walk on alcohol and stuff like that then they're not clean. One time I've seen those drunkens, right, and there was an old man walking past the Vibe Bar and this guy took the old man's hat off and just run off with it, taking the piss and that and I remember that 'cause I saw it but I felt I couldn't do nothing about it because there were too many people there and if I did say anything they would've come on to me.'

'They would have thrashed you, man,' said Saleck. All three of them said they felt more threatened now than they did ten years ago.

'Back then,' said Atiqul, 'we used to walk around the streets and feel safer and there used to be more prostitutes around and we used to beat them up.'

I was witness to just such a horrible incident, about ten years ago, when I came out of the Pride of Spitalfields in Heneage Street after a night with some friends and saw a gang of young Bengali men whipping a young woman, in high heels and a short skirt, in the face. My friends and I chased them away but the image of this violence has never left me. 'Please tell me you didn't actually beat them up,' I said to the boys.

'No, he's exaggerating,' said Bodrul, 'we used to tell them to go away from here because we didn't want our young brothers or nephews to see this stuff.'

Wanting to change the subject Saleck interjected: 'The area hasn't improved for the average Bangladeshi person here. Of course it is good for the few people who actually own those bars and restaurants but for us kids it's just pushed us out. We had a good youth ten years ago but now, the kids locally, they ain't got no place to go apart from this youth club that Derek runs. Before we had more clubs in our area but now the rents are too high, we've been pushed out.'

'A lot of people are leaving because of this and to get away from the drug problems,' said Bodrul. 'There are a lot of drug problems in our community and all over East London. It's hard to avoid it, you have to mix with the right people and follow the right path.'

'There's more gangs in the area than before,' said Saleck, 'and Derek has really helped us stay away from this. We come to this youth club, it's a safe place, we play snooker, just have a laugh and catch up, yeah. We like to be in Brick Lane.'

'Everyone all around the East London respects Brick Lane,' said Atiqul. 'It's the place where we get together for the Mela, with friends, family, and we enjoy the food, music and funfair and, even though lots of people from outside come to it, it feels like our day. I love Eid, as well: our friends hire cars and cruise around together up and down Brick Lane. We have fun and enjoy ourselves and if we have any trouble with outside people we always run back to Brick Lane because once we're here they can't do nothing to us. We're safe here. It's our home ground.'

'The problems are more turf-war kind of stuff,' said Bodrul. 'I don't see a lot of racism here these days. I've got one neighbour who's black and one who's white and I'm in the middle as an Asian. Who's going to be racist about who? We've had it easier than our parents, but when we were younger, back in school, that's when we suffered with it a bit because we were troublemakers then. Like when I was at Thomas Buxton. When I bunked off school, that's when I'd experience the racism. When I was alone out on the street, not in a group.'

When I asked if they wanted to bring up their own families here they all said no. 'I don't want my kid to go through what I've been through and what I've seen,' said Saleck. 'The muggings, the drugs, gang fights and prostitution, these things were all part of my childhood, getting stopped and arrested all the time, getting chased by the dogs and the police. Every time we are in a group together the police will always stop us even if we're just walking along just talking. Now it happens even more because of the terrorist worries. We get followed, people we know are spied on.'

'We have already moved a bit further out from Brick Lane,' said Bodrul, 'but this is the hood, where we come and meet up every day.'

I asked them why they came here and I was moved to discover they are all studying under Derek's guidance to become youth work-ers themselves. Atiqul told me, 'Derek inspired us to do this, he's one of the best persons I ever knew, he's 100 per cent behind us, encouraging us all the way. Because of him we are here, if not we'd probably be on the streets selling grass or something. We know lots of people our age who are addicts and some who have died. We're talking about heroin, that's the main problem around us. We had a friend our age who got into this trouble and he went back home to try and sort it out and had an overdose and died. It's them people who've got too much stress who get into drugs, they've got nothing to do, no job, just sitting around on the estate, girlfriend dumped them, stuff like that. Our parents are aware of it, they try and guide us to the right way but at the end of the day it's our choice.'

'We do feel our parents are old fashioned,' said Bodrul. 'They're very traditional and we want to mix the traditional with our new British culture. They want to do things a different way to us so we clash. For example, with my mum and dad I'm always having a debate about the way I want to present myself, what clothes I wear and stuff like that. If we lived in Bangladesh our parents would try and arrange a marriage for us when we're about fourteen, and his parents tried to do this,' said Bodrul, pointing at Saleck. 'His parents would say to him go and have an arranged marriage and mine would say it's up to you, son. It all depends on the family, but nowadays in general the parents are a bit more laid back. Hey, it's the twenty-first century! Us Wheeler House kids, we're really lucky because we had Derek around and our parents trusted Derek and let us go off with him. And we looked up to him and he was one of our people. He's like an uncle to us, and to some of us he's more like a father or a brother even. We've known him since we were born. The great thing about Derek is he's become Muslim: he's converted because of all the years he spent in our community and this makes us really happy.'

I asked if they went to the mosque regularly and Bodrul told me, 'On Fridays I go. Our religion is a way of life for us. Our parents are really religious but we just live our lives. We try to pray five times a day but things get in the way. Like I might meet a girl today or go to the mosque, which one would I choose? It's going to be the girl, innit. It's the temptation but we still have it there in the back of our minds pulling us back. It's like the drinking:

we're not supposed to drink but sometimes we do but we keep it in moderation. If I have kids I'd teach them just the same as I've been taught, and I do respect the religion.'

A few days later I popped in again to see Derek and asked if he'd mind talking with me about his conversion. He smiled broadly and told me he'd be delighted to. Derek became a Muslim after thinking about it for a long time. He grew up as a Christian but had become increasingly uneasy with the idea of Jesus as the Son of God. In February 2002 he went to Bangladesh on one of many visits and began to ask questions of a Muslim colleague of his, and started to pray with him. Over the next few years he learned more and adopted other practices, such as fasting and reading the Koran. He converted officially in 2005. 'I feel much more patient and calm now, much more at peace in myself,' he said. 'I'm told I'm lucky because all my previous sins have been forgiven. I know I'm at an unusual age to embrace the Muslim faith. The actual process involved many people in the community speaking for me. I had an interview with the Imam and I went to a few friendship circles in the mosque. I believe there is only one God and that Allah is the servant and messenger and that all the other prophets are important. There's still much to learn. Knowledge is as important as prayer and you should never stop seeking the truth. I pray now five times a day. With the older generation it has changed things for me within the community. Some of the younger ones find it hard, they feel guilty seeing me praying five times a day while they don't want to any more. They tell me they were born Muslim and they have chosen to reject it, but I hope they realize I am making no judgements on them. I feel very positive about it. I never look back any more, I just look forward to the future. It was a personal journey for me. I pray every day for the blessings I have in life and try to go to the Brick Lane mosque down the road whenever I can.' I asked Derek if I could go inside the mosque but he told me it was for men only. 'They are planning to refurbish it,' he told me, 'and add a women's section, but if you want to I'll speak with the Imam there, I'm sure he'd talk to you.'

6

We are Shadows

The light of Judaism, flickering in many a house of worship,
quite extinguished in others burns brightest in Brick Lane, at
the Machzike Hadath, the Spitalfields Great Synagogue.
                                    A. B. Levy, *East End Story*

The Imam of the Brick Lane mosque, the Jamme Masjid, agreed
to meet with me – as long as Derek came too. On the day of the
meeting I walked up to Avenues Unlimited and found Derek at his
desk on the telephone. He was trying to get through to a mobile
phone company for someone in the Bengali community who spoke
little English. While Derek made his calls I went into the bathroom
to change into the appropriate dress in which to visit the mosque:
long skirt, high-necked top and a wide scarf wrapped around my
head, covering my hair.

As we walked up the stone steps to the large wooden doors of the
mosque's main entrance at no. 59 Brick Lane I felt a real sense of
anticipation. I have walked past the mosque a thousand times before
and have always wanted to go inside and see for myself this place
that is embedded in the memory of so many elderly Jewish people
who once lived in Brick Lane. Over the years I have heard stories
about: Jewish anarchists clashing with Orthodox leaders there; of
the funeral of a famous rabbi that took place there in 1912, which
was attended by thousands of mourners; and various tales of the
grandeur of the building and the excitement of the High Holy
Days. The building has become part of British Jewish history, one
of the first purpose-built synagogues in this country for the ultra
Orthodox and a major seat of Jewish learning that upheld the strict

moral, ethical and kosher codes of the old world of Hasidic Eastern Europe. I was also curious to find out what the building currently represented to the Muslim community of Brick Lane.

Derek led the way through the doors into a sparsely decorated entrance hall with a high ceiling and a tiled floor covered in places by a few mismatching rugs. On the wall was a chalkboard with the times for the daily prayers written on it. An elderly man wearing a long white kaftan and loose trousers was standing beside it in his socks, mixing a tin of *paan*. He looked up at us briefly and smiled, showing teeth stained red from years of chewing the tobacco mixture, and nodding in recognition to Derek. We walked past him into a narrow corridor off to the right and stopped next to some square wooden shelves, where we took off our shoes. A young man appeared from a doorway in front of us and Derek went over to speak with him. A couple of bearded men wandered past, giving me a few sideways looks, before Derek called me over and ushered me inside a small office overlooking Brick Lane.

I sat down on one of three chairs placed around a large desk covered in a plastic lace tablecloth and piled high with books and papers. Sitting opposite me was a kindly looking man, possibly in his late fifties, with a chest-length black beard peppered with grey streaks, wearing a cream *shalwar kameez*, a white waistcoat and a crocheted *kufi* on his head. He introduced himself as Mr Choudury, the Imam of the mosque. I asked him if he would mind if I recorded the conversation and he very politely said he would. In a thick Bengali accent he asked if I was affiliated to any newspaper at all and I feared the interview would be over before it started. I assured him I was not and that I wanted to speak with him only for the purposes of this book. 'I have no interest in getting my name in the papers,' he told me. 'I'm constantly getting approached by journalists but it is not what I am about. They only want to come here to try and get a sensationalist story. I have no desire to be a celebrity of any kind, although many have visited here – Ken Livingstone, Jeffrey Archer, Michael Portillo and the Archbishop of Canterbury. We have many foreign visitors too and they are all welcome but I don't want my picture in the papers.' The young man I had seen earlier came into the room and offered us some refreshment, reappearing shortly afterwards from the basement with 1 tray filled with sugary biscuits and china cups of strong tea.

Mr Choudury has been based at Brick Lane since 1991. Like most of the people who worship at the mosque Mr Choudury is a family man who comes from Sylhet. The majority of those worshipping in the mosque are, like him, older men from the same part of Bangladesh: 'But Muslims from other countries and sects are also welcome, which is why the Brick Lane mosque is more popular than others locally. We are not politically affiliated to any sect or group. We have no Middle Eastern connections so we have less trouble than other places. People come to this mosque from African and Pakistani backgrounds. We are proud that this mosque is a gathering of different Muslim communities.'

He talked for some time about the plans to remodernize the building, which include a new room being built upstairs for women to pray in and the installation of a minaret outside – a tall slender tower that will be attached to the mosque on the corner of Brick Lane and Fournier Street, allowing the *muezzin* to call the faithful to prayer. 'We need this very much,' he said, 'there is a lot of noise in this area and it will be very good for people locally who want to pray to know when to come to the mosque.' There has been some local opposition to the plans, from conservationists who want to protect the Georgian nature of the exterior, but it seems as if the plans will be going ahead. 'All the communities here need to learn to live with one another,' he said.

Mr Choudury explained that the mosque was open all day but most worshippers came during the five set prayer times, which change with the seasons, adapting to the sunrise and sunset. As we talked a constant stream of young people walked past and went down the stairs near by into the basement. 'There is a large *madrasah* here,' said Mr Choudury, 'a religious school that is open from five till seven every day. Children attend from the age of seven to learn about Islam. Their parents have a responsibility to teach them something of the Koran but they learn Arabic here and how to be a good Muslim.'

'There is a very good system in the Islamic faith for teaching the children,' added Derek, 'and you will find the young people here are very knowledgeable about their religion, and extremely literate, with many of them speaking Bengali, English and Arabic fluently.'

I asked Mr Choudury how the mosque was funded and, with his hands clasped together, he told me, 'This is not a rich mosque and it operates entirely on voluntary donations from the local community – and for the most part the community in and around Brick Lane who attend the mosque are poor. There is no government or council funding, just voluntary donations like in a church.' We talked about the difficulty of attracting young people to the mosque and Mr Choudury regretted they did not have the money for a gym or PlayStations like other mosques locally, 'but we do have two football teams,' he said beaming. He was excited that women would soon have their own space to pray in the building and was proud of how the building was used by all different generations of people in the community: 'During the last ten days of Ramadan religious people live and sleep in the mosque, praying all day, devoting their time to worshipping and reading the Koran. It is seen as a spiritual retreat. They have a pre-dawn meal, the *fajr*, before the first of the five daily prayers, and then they will break the day of fasting with the communal meal, called *iftar*, the women come with the food. The mosque is often filled to capacity every Friday and during Ramadan, with up to three thousand people worshipping at once. People who have grown up in the area and then moved away will travel for miles to come here on a Friday and throughout the month of Ramadan.'

At certain times during Ramadan it is impossible to move in Brick Lane when the mosque empties out – thousands of men dressed in white robes pour out of the building, filling the pavement and spilling on to the road. When I first witnessed this I was instantly reminded of the time I spent in the Orthodox Jewish community of Tzfat in northern Israel, the birthplace of Kabbalism.

During Yom Kippur, the most holy day in the Jewish calendar, when religious Jews fast all day and spend their time in the synagogue repenting their sins, the religious men of Tzfat wander the streets of this ancient city, moving from synagogue to synagogue dressed in long white robes, called *kittels*, which symbolize purity – reminiscent of Muslim men during Ramadan. The streets of Tzfat are old, narrow and impassable by car but Brick Lane is a major thoroughfare in East London with constant heavy pedestrian and auto traffic travelling up and down. I asked the Imam how they coped for space during Ramadan with so many extra people entering and exiting the mosque. 'Sometimes the pavement does get blocked up – particularly if the worshippers mix with tourists going past – but we seem to manage quite well; there are no major problems,' he said.

Mr Choudury felt that relations between the mosque and the rest of the population on Brick Lane were good most of the time although the amount of alcohol being consumed around the building bothered him very much. 'It's a shame that even these restaurants right opposite the mosque are serving wine and beer now,' said Derek. 'It makes it very problematic for people coming in and out of the building. Sundays are especially difficult, with extra people coming to the area, and other times at the weekend, when there are many drunk people around, shouting and making a disturbance. Some of the people here find it a bit threatening.' Physical violence between tourists and the Asian community occasionally breaks out. 'In the early 1990s it was worse,' said Derek, 'particularly up by the Vibe Bar where it was very unlit, and there were a lot of gang problems in that area. There are still gangs but they tend to fight among themselves and leave the rest of us alone.'

'Have the changes in the street made it difficult for parents to bring up their children as good Muslims?' I asked the Imam.

'Yes,' said Mr Choudury, 'of course many essential things are near by, like access to the mosque, the *madrasah* and *halal* foods, but there are few places for young people to go around here and they are surrounded by the temptations of alcohol everywhere in

Brick Lane. In the last few years we have seen more parents than before bringing their children to the mosque, trying to give them a good Islamic education as they are becoming aware of the other dangers around them.'

'Are the parents ever worried that if their children come to the mosque they might get targeted by extremists?' I asked.

'This is a very traditional mosque,' said Mr Choudury firmly, 'old-fashioned and much less political than other places, and people locally know that. We will not tolerate religious fanatics here. There is no chance for them to have a base in this mosque. A few have come before to try and recruit our young people but we have wheedled them out straight away, even informing the police about them.' We discussed how things had been for the local community and the mosque since the London bombings on 7 July. Unlike some Bengali teenagers and restaurant owners I had spoken with, who told me they had suffered more racial abuse on the street after that date, the Imam said there had been no problems at the mosque, although he was aware other places had experienced difficulties. 'I know a brick was thrown through the window of a mosque in Whitechapel,' he said, 'and the place was cordoned off for a few hours when a suspected bomb was found, but it turned out to be a hoax.'

The young man who served us tea came back into the room and whispered into the Imam's ear. The corridor outside the office had filled up since we started talking. More women were arriving to drop off their children and a steady stream of men were coming into the building and taking off their shoes to go into the mosque. I knew it was nearly time for the Imam to get ready for early-evening prayers. I asked if he would be willing to be photographed for the book. He politely declined but offered to show me around the downstairs of the building and gave me permission to take a photograph inside the mosque. Derek left to go to another meeting and I noticed the warmth and friendship between the two men as they parted. 'I have known Derek for fifteen years,' said the Imam. 'He is a wonderful person and a respected member of our community. Without him I never would have spoken to you.'

I followed Mr Choudury through the wooden doors off to the left of the central hallway and into the main mosque building. We entered a vast room devoid of furniture and covered in a carpet made up of individual prayer mats pointing towards Mecca. On the far wall hung two clocks. A single microphone stood in one corner and the building felt cold. The Imam saw me shiver slightly and smiled. 'It's a bit chilly in here,' he said, 'but you soon warm up when you start praying. It is good exercise, all that bending.' There were a few older men seated cross-legged in one corner talking among themselves, and a few others dotted about the room sat on their knees, bent over in prayer. I could just make out the remains of the women's balcony, which had been blocked off when the building ceased functioning as an Orthodox synagogue. The only other feature I recognized from the old photographs I had seen of the synagogue were the large marble pillars that split up the huge space and had once supported the women's balcony, and the ornately carved wooden Georgian doors leading out to Fournier Street. I asked Mr Choudury if the large brass chandeliers hanging from the centre of the room could have been inherited from the former synagogue – he wasn't sure.

Mr Choudury led me through to the room next door where the ablutions take place. The room was long and narrow and covered in blue tiles. There were two rows of small square wooden stools facing the walls, which have taps placed along them at regular intervals. Underneath the taps was a long trench with drainage for the water to escape. He explained to me that Muslim men use this room for the ritual cleaning of hands and feet before they enter the mosque and that there was a much larger room for washing upstairs where a thousand people can go together at once.

When we left this room I noticed that a queue of people had formed in the hallway wanting Mr Choudury's attention. I thanked him for his time and left the building, walking back into the bright lights and chaos of a night on Brick Lane.

The contrast of the street with the interior of the mosque was

The Synagogue is only dimly lighted. Here and there a few worshippers are sitting in the pews repeating their prayers or reading a tattered volume. In one pew sits an old man writing by the aid of a tallow candle, which he has stuck on the little shelf in front of him. He is writing out one of the tiny scrolls which, encased in a capsule of tin or glass, forms the *mezuzah*, the amulet which every Orthodox Jew places on his doors; or perhaps the miniature manuscript is intended to be placed inside the *tephillin* – that is, the phylacteries which are bound round the head and the left arm for the morning prayers. Remembering that the *mezuzah* and the *tephillin* are direct Sinaitic ordinances, we look at the old man writing by the gleam of the candle in the gloomy synagogue with feelings of awe and reverence.

George R. Sims, *Off the Track in London*, 1911

startling – the atmosphere inside was quiet, religious, holy. Although I had never been inside a mosque before, I felt comfortable there. The down-at-heel feel of the building reminded me of Orthodox synagogues I had visited in Eastern Europe, New York and Israel, where the energy focus was on prayer and community. The old men in traditional clothes talking together in small groups, the women modestly dressed collecting children from a religious school, the washing before prayer, the rhythm of the calendar year – all this was very reminiscent to me of the culture and practices in Jewish Orthodox circles.

I wanted to find out more about the building when it had still been functioning as a synagogue, so I set myself the task of finding someone who had worshipped in the former Machzike Hadath. The Jewish community had sold the building in 1976 so I presumed there would be plenty of people still alive who had once used the synagogue, but if there were, they proved to be hard to find. The synagogue had been famous for its strict observance of Jewish law, including the preparation of kosher food. When the kosher butchers and restaurants moved out of the area so did the last of the ultra-Orthodox community. After failing to find someone locally I tried writing to the rabbi at the new Machzike Hadath Synagogue in Golders Green (the congregation moved to premises there when the building was sold) but had no response. Then one day, quite by chance, I came across someone working practically opposite the mosque who used to be a regular visitor to the great synagogue.

I walked into Epra Fabrics on Brick Lane after noticing an elderly man serving behind the counter, wearing a *yarmulke*, the skullcap traditionally worn by Orthodox Jews. He introduced himself as Mr Epstein and told me he had been in business in the street for over fifty years. When I asked if he had ever worshipped at the Machzike Hadath he replied, 'Of course. It was my local synagogue, I used to *daven* there all the time. It was large and grand with proper seating and looked very impressive. Many who lived here didn't join as a member because they liked their little *stiebels* where they

My earliest recollections of the Machzike Ha-dath Synagogue go back to my boyhood. What a magnificent appearance it presented during the High Festivals! What a splendid array of Talmudic scholars along the honoured Eastern Wall! The *shool* overcrowded with extra chairs all round the *bemah* and in front of these, personal prayer stands suitably covered, with everybody keyed up to the importance of the occasion. One just felt the holiness of the place. And with what fervour were the prayers uttered! When the moment came for the Congregation to recite a prayer they could hardly wait for the *chazan* to finish his part before they would burst out in one loud accord impatient to show their devotion. And when the *sepharim* were carried to the *bemah*, how all thronged to kiss them! And the occasional banging by the *shammas* on a heavy *machzor* often accompanied by a loud 'Shah' to silence the more audible women-folk in the galleries hidden from view behind lace curtains.

Bernard Homa, *A Fortress in Anglo-Jewry*, 1953

could speak Yiddish and meet people from their home town. It was more the gentry that prayed there and it was considered expensive to be a member, it was the posh *shul* round here. People used to dress quite formally and the services were all in Hebrew. It was the synagogue of the ultra Orthodox. As the community moved away they struggled to get a *minyan* and the place became run down. It was too big a premises for the small community left so they moved to a new site in Golders Green and sold the building off to the emerging Muslim community in the 1970s.'

Shortly after my meeting with Mr Epstein I took a trip to the Jewish Museum in Finchley (formerly known as the Museum of the Jewish East End) to try to find out more about the building when it had been a synagogue. The curator there found two large boxes of material in their archives relating to the Machzike Hadath. One was filled with the personal effects of the Kamenitzer Maggid, who was a kind of rent-a-rabbi who gave sermons at the synagogue in the early 1890s. Inside was a dusty collection of handwritten notebooks in Yiddish and Hebrew, and a tiny red leather-bound notebook filled with reminiscences of his early childhood in Russia as well as a beautiful wood-and-copper plate negative, showing a man wearing a top hat and prayer shawl, the traditional dress for High Holy Days. In the back of one of the notebooks I found a prayer in English, which honoured Queen Victoria: 'She is our beloved mother. The most distinguished person of our age and she is the person through whom the lord was sanctified. Victoria is her name and during her reign truth reigns. Let us pray to prolong the life of our queen.'

In the second box I discovered papers and notes relating to the founding of the synagogue, many of which were in English. I read that the Machzike Hadath congregation had been founded in 1891 by Orthodox Jewish immigrants from Eastern Europe who felt the practices of the established Anglo-Jewish community, particularly those relating to *kashrut*, were not strict enough for them. In 1897 the Machzike Hadath Society bought the building on the corner of Brick Lane and Fournier Street, which had been erected by

These pious Jews are distinguished by their scrupulous observance of the Sabbath. They will not even carry their handkerchief on the Sabbath day because it constitutes carrying a burden. That is forbidden, so they tie it round their waist as a girdle, where it becomes part of their clothing and so allowable.

George R. Sims, *Off the Track in London*, 1911

French Huguenots in 1743 and originally functioned as a Protestant church called La Neuve Eglise. It was used briefly from 1809 as a mission for converting Jews to Christianity before becoming a Methodist chapel in 1819 and was then sold towards the end of the century to the Machzike Hadath Society. Its English name was the Spitalfields Great Synagogue and the congregation at its peak numbered over two thousand. The synagogue, just like the mosque today, was open all day long with a continuous succession of services held throughout the day as well as study circles and special daily classes in the Talmud. Attached to the synagogue was a large purpose-built *cheder* called the Brick Lane Talmud Torah, which had similar aims to those the current *madrasah* has for the Muslim community on the same site. The Brick Lane Talmud Torah was the most Orthodox Jewish educational institution in the area at the time. I found some notes from a general meeting dated 1895 stating that ten teachers taught over five hundred children Hebrew there daily. They were all 'poor foreigners' and the most needy among them were provided with boots and clothing by the synagogue.

Much of the material I came across about the Machzike Hadath related to the synagogue's first rabbi, Abraham Werner. Born in 1837 in Tels, Kovno, he held posts as Rabbi in Weger, Russia, and in Tels before moving to Helsingfors as Chief Rabbi of Finland. In 1891 he was persuaded to move to London and run the Machzike Hadath, where he stayed until his death in 1912. In his obituary in *The Times* (21 December 1912) he was called 'the most learned man in London in Talmudic and Rabbinic literature'. His funeral was the largest in England at the time with twenty thousand people lining the streets of East London to see his coffin come out of the synagogue on Brick Lane and make its way to Edmonton Cemetery where he is buried. He was a peace-loving rabbi who was dearly loved by members of his community and widely respected throughout the East End.

Inside the archive box was a book documenting the story of the Machzike Hadath called *A Fortress in Anglo-Jewry*, written

From 7 a.m. onwards morning services follow one another with hardly a pause, and in the afternoon *minyan* succeeds *minyan* for *mincah* and *maariv*. Mourners who work in the East End know that here they can find a quorum for Kaddish. If, in the morning, they come without *tefillin*, then *tefillin* are provided; if they have forgotten how to bind the phylacteries to their forehead and arms they are shown.

A. B. Levy, description of the Machzike Hadath, *Jewish Chronicle*, 1948 by Rabbi Werner's great-grandson Bernard Homa. It reproduces a photograph of the interior of the synagogue. The book includes affectionate stories about the great rabbi: 'He was once approached in the synagogue by a very deserving case and was so impressed by the circumstances that he gave the man in question the three golden coins he had just received as his weekly salary; and when he reached home he had nothing left to give his wife who had been relying on the money to meet her domestic obligations. "The man's need is greater than ours," was his simple explanation.'

Homa described his great-grandfather's house as: 'a hive of activity, all day long there was a succession of callers. People came with personal and religious problems. Some came to discuss Talmudic lore or to ask the rabbi to check whether their chicken was kosher or not.' I had heard similar stories about Rabbi Werner from one of his great-great-granddaughters, Rachel Hoffbrand, a good friend of mine. I had known her for some time before I found out her relationship to Rabbi Werner. In 1992 she came to visit me while I was working at the old synagogue in Princelet Street. Leaning against the wall of the office downstairs she noticed a faded photograph in an old frame with cracked glass. She bent down to inspect the picture further and told me with surprise that it was a photograph of her famous relative. I like to think Rabbi Werner would be happy to know that Rachel met her husband, the oral historian Alan Dein, at the consecration service held for David Rodinsky at Waltham Abbey Jewish Cemetery after I invited them both. They now have three children, the eldest of whom is called Abraham, after the rabbi.

As I was leaving the Jewish Museum I bumped into David Jacobs, who works in the offices near by. We had met by chance years before, during the Rodinsky project, in the basement library of the Jewish Historical Institute in Warsaw. David helped me to locate the burial site of Rodinsky and since then I have often called on him for advice. He is exceedingly knowledgeable on all Jewish subjects with a particular area of expertise on the Jewish East End and British Jewish cemeteries.

I asked David if he knew anything about the Machzike Hadath and he told me he had taken pictures of the building in the 1970s and had numerous bits of ephemera in his archive from there. David told me he was one of the first people into the building after it

The funeral of Rabbi A. Werner was marked yesterday by unparalleled scenes. Early in the morning the coffin was removed from his house to the Spitalfields Great Synagogue and great crowds assembled around the building, which was guarded by a strong force of police . . . At one o'clock the coffin, which was covered with a plain cloth, was carried out of the Synagogue where a crowd variously estimated between 20,000 to 30,000 waited. As a mark of honour the coffin was to be borne a considerable distance followed by pupils of the Brick Lane Talmud Torah. The procession and over 220 carriages waited along the Whitechapel Road and the coffin was carried through Brick Lane. The police, who numbered over 100, had great difficulty in restraining the people who, in their anxiety to touch the coffin, pushed and jostled each other to such an extent the bearers could barely make any progress.

Manchester Guardian, 23 December 1912

closed. 'There was all sorts of stuff lying around on the floor so I gathered it up to save it,' he said.

He described walking into the building on that occasion: 'It was the first of many synagogues I explored and it had a magical effect on me and was the beginning of a long-term passion. The full name of the synagogue was the Machzike Hadath, Shomrei Shabbat, which translates roughly as "Guardians of the Faith and Observers of the Sabbath" or "Upholders of the Law". The people in the kosher wine shop opposite the building, Mendel Chaikin & Co., told me about the synagogue. Mendel was one of the founding members of the synagogue and used its vaults to store and brew his kosher wines. I entered the synagogue via a side door in Fournier Street. It was open so I just gave it a little shove and pushed my way into a small vestibule before going into the synagogue itself. It was in very poor condition; there were windows broken and leaves and debris covered the floor. All the ritual objects had obviously been removed but there were things left around like various papers and a clock face with Hebrew numbers on it. It was dark, dusty and quite spooky walking in there for the first time. I felt like an intruder and I

was quite nervous – it was the first time I had done something like this, but it must have made a big impression on me as I went on to document in a much more formal way many abandoned synagogues in the East End. It was 1972, shortly after it had closed, and it felt as if the Jewish community had only just vacated it. From there I took the clock face, which had fallen on to the floor, and I gave it to Bill Williams in Manchester for his museum there. Of course thirty years later I regret that I didn't do more. It took a long time after it had closed before it reopened in Golders Green.'

```
To: Rachel.Lichtenstein@hotmail.com
From: D.Jacobs@sternberg.syn.co.uk

Look Rachel, when I got home after our
meeting I found this photograph of the key
to the Machzikei (!) Hadath Syn. Taken more
than 10 years ago in the owner's offices in
Kingsbury London NW9
July 26th after 1100 or sometime on
July 27th but not lunchtime

David Jacobs
```

7
Holy Wanderers

Brick Lane has become an artificial construct, a pseudo China Town, disguising the fact that behind the façade are people living in horrendous poverty.

Alan Dein

I met Alan Dein in the early 1990s through our mutual passion for the Jewish East End. Like me, he moved to the area to explore the lost world of his grandparents and became a tour guide under the tutorship of Professor Fishman. As the Jewish landmarks on our tours began to disappear, Alan campaigned to preserve what was left for future generations. He managed to secure Grade II listing for the façade of the old Soup Kitchen for the Jewish Poor in Brune Street and the Jewish water fountain in Whitechapel. He spent over a decade walking the streets and photographing every remaining Jewish shopfront in East London, and has conducted hundreds of oral-history recordings, capturing the stories of those who remember Jewish Whitechapel.

When the Kosher Luncheon Club in Greatorex Street closed in 1995 Alan was devastated. 'Its passing is a tragedy,' he said. 'The menu, the Yiddishe atmosphere, there is nowhere else like it, where are all those old-timers going to go now?' There was only one place left – Bloom's on Whitechapel High Street, the very last kosher restaurant in the area. Alan told me about his Great-Uncle Lou who had worked there as a waiter: 'He was a wonderful character, a bit of a *schloch*, a little unkempt, with ruffled hair and hunched shoulders, and when he served you, the soup would be slopping over the bowl and his thumb would be stuck in whatever was left. There was nothing unusual about this service, people went to Bloom's for the rudeness of the waiters. The place was famous for it – the food there was kind of chucked at you. By the 1970s Uncle Lou was one of the only Jewish waiters left, the rest were Greek Cypriots.'

In the 1960s, when Alan was a child growing up in Hendon, a family visit to Bloom's in Whitechapel was a big social event as the place was packed full of neighbours and friends from the suburbs of North London. They travelled miles to eat there because Bloom's offered a sense of the old world. 'It had a *hamishe* atmosphere,' said Alan, 'it was always particularly busy if a showbiz person was there – Barbara Windsor, Cliff Richard, those types.' Alan was fascinated by the shadier characters who hung out there – the local gangsters and wheeler-dealers. Bloom's had originally opened in Brick Lane in 1912, then moved further along to the corner of Old Montague Street in the 1930s and to its Whitechapel location in the 1950s. In 1996 the Whitechapel High Street branch closed, but the other Bloom's in Golders Green, which opened in 1965, is still doing great business and the walls of the restaurant are covered in murals depicting nostalgic scenes of Jewish East London. In its last few years of trading, the Whitechapel branch of Bloom's still had a small group of regulars coming from Ilford, Redbridge and North London, but the majority of the customers were non-Jewish City workers, who liked its white tablecloths and celebrity reputation, but still thought of Brick Lane as a bit too rough to venture into.

Alan grew up in north-west London but his family on both sides had settled originally in East London after arriving as Yiddish-speaking immigrants from Eastern Europe. His mother's family all lived in Cable Street and ran 'a legendary fleapit cinema, which was bombed to shreds during the Blitz'. The whole family helped out in the business, the grandmother worked in the box office, the daughters sold snacks, his grandfather and his brothers were the projectionists, and if the film was a Western they would dress up as cowboys to introduce it. Alan's other grandmother's story was less romantic; orphaned as a young teenager she had brought up

her younger brother alone in horrendous poverty in Whitechapel. So Alan's childhood was a mixture of East End stories, one of nostalgia and the other of a place too painful to remember, both of which were a bit more edgy than the comfortable suburban world of Jewish north-west London where he grew up.

Most of his older neighbours in Hendon originally moved there from Whitechapel. 'They spoke with that accent, moved with those mannerisms and threw in a bit of Yiddish when they talked,' said Alan, 'so although I was removed from East London physically, it was part of my growing up, it was all around me.' His first independent trip there at the age of thirteen was to buy comics from Brick Lane Market. He instantly fell in love with the other-worldness of the market culture, the Jewish and non-Jewish cockneys mixing with the burgeoning Pakistani and Bengali communities. 'It was only one hour away from Golders Green,' said Alan, 'but like entering a different world.'

Despite his family's close connections to the area his parents were horrified when in 1979, as a young man of nineteen, Alan chose to move back there. They couldn't relate to his desire to be closer to the streets his grandparents had so willingly escaped from, nor could they understand what Alan found so attractive in the run-down fabric of the area. He tried to explain the 'poetry of the place' to them, 'the sense that time had ebbed away and the rawness of what is left had been exposed, all that peeled paint, scuffed and rubbed brickwork, the graffiti, the rubbish, the faces of the people'. They shook their heads in disbelief. In the twenty years he lived there they never visited his small flat in Stepney Green. The poverty and the grime held no romance for them.

Alan studied at the City of London Polytechnic in Old Castle Street, in the heart of the post-war Jewish East End. He regularly bunked off lectures to wander around the streets, which were still littered with bombsites then and full of derelict buildings. He described Brick Lane in the late 1970s as 'a working place with a mixture of Jewish, Asian and white working-class people. The Truman Brewery was still operating and, come clocking-off time, you would see sixty or seventy white men walking down the street in their overalls towards the pubs, betting shops, cafés and tube station.' The other visible presence were the skinheads and the NF. 'We were quite anarchic socialist students,' he told me, 'and they were the enemy outside our door. Around the corner to the college was a fascist shop in Goulston Street called the Last Resort where a lot of skinheads hung out. There seemed to be gangs of white thugs everywhere and it was tense.' On numerous occasions Alan saw attacks in the streets, mainly in Brick Lane – Asian shopfronts being smashed up or Bengali people being spat on or kicked as they walked by. 'The atmosphere was threatening, it was a period of great pessimism, a depressed time economically, and Brick Lane felt like an area on a downward slide.'

The Jewish presence in the street was fading fast. Alan began to document what was left. This is when he began photographing every remaining Jewish shop sign in the area. At the same time David Jacobs was running around rescuing abandoned Jewish artefacts, like the enamel sign that used to hang above the Russian Vapour Baths in Brick Lane, which he found in a skip in the mid 1970s.

In Brick Lane itself Alan remembers a few Jewish shops, a religious bookshop, a wine merchants, a sweet shop and in particular Izzy

I lived near Brick Lane since 1932. I remember
going to Mother Cohen's Soup Kitchen in
Wentworth Street after school, she made fish
soup, all kosher. In Old Montague Street was a
salt-beef shop and on the right-hand side was
Black Lion Yard, which was all jewellery, it's
called Hopetown Street now. It used to be a
court way into Whitechapel, filled with jewellers,
a delicatessen and a dairy. There were no
toilets inside the buildings and those that had
'em were like millionaires. In the lane were a lot
of Dutch Jews that we called Hutz, and a lot of
the Polish and Russian, they lived around
Commercial Road and Whitechapel, we were two
different communities.

As you got to Brick Lane near Old Montague
Street there was the Mayfair Cinema and next
to it the fish and chip shop. I saw *Gone with the
Wind* at the Mayfair, Laurel and Hardy films
and George Formby. The boys used to climb in
through the back without paying, and a lot of
kissing went on in the back row. We used to take
food into the cinema, potato latkes, chopped-
liver sandwiches, things like that, it used to
smell like a Jewish restaurant, I'm talking about
the 1930s, and then war came and we all got
evacuated, it started to change.

Marion, 2002

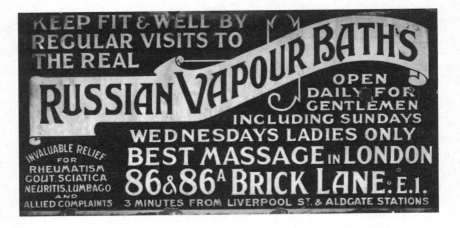

Weinberg's printing shop. 'He used to print loads of Bundist and trade-union leaflets,' said Alan, 'but mostly made a living printing bar mitzvah and wedding stationery. When he retired the Museum of the Jewish East End took the entire contents of his shop.' Alan's presiding memory of Brick Lane in the late 1970s is of 'people going about their work, which was mainly in the rag trade. There were bits of cloth everywhere, people carrying fabric to be made up, cardboard patterns on street corners, with piles of material fragments and lots of tailoring shops on the street.'

From 1979 to 2001 Alan lived among the tattered and torn remnants of old Jewish London. He felt Brick Lane used to be a place that wrote its own laws and was run by the people who lived and worked there. He finally moved away because 'there is no mystery left in the area any more'.

Alan became one of the first oral historians to capture on sound the Jewish community of East London. He started recording these life stories in 1987 while working at the Jewish Museum with David Jacobs, collecting material for the first major Jewish East End Festival, which took place that year. 'It was amazing,' he said. 'There were exhibitions and concerts all over the East End; you couldn't do it today because most of those people are dead.' Alan interviewed hundreds of Jewish ex-East Enders for the festival including the great Yiddish composer Majer Bogdanski.

The window display in Mr Weinberg's Brick Lane printing shop used to tell a typographical history of migration, adaptation and assimilation in the notepaper printed for Minsky (Furs), Whitechapel, Manchester and Bradford; Elegante Fashions, Berwick Street; the London Chess Conference (Chairman S. Reuben); the business cards of Labovitch the Glazier who becomes David Glassman; and the change of address cards sent out for the move from Hackney to Woodford.

David Widgery, 'Ripe Bananas and Stolen Bicycles', *Marketa Luskacova: Photographs of Spitalfields*, 1991

I met Majer in September 2000, thanks to an invitation from Bill Fishman to attend a formal dinner at one of the Oxford colleges attended by many great Yiddish academics. The first time I saw Majer he was sitting on a bench in the walled gardens of the university, wearing a worn jacket, trousers that were slightly too short and a flat cap. His eyes were closed and he was rocking back and forth as if in prayer while singing a haunting Yiddish melody. He sat near to me in the banqueting hall and continued to sing at the top of his voice throughout the meal, banging his fist on the table as he did so, seemingly unaware this might cause offence to the various professors and historians who got up to speak about the importance of Yiddish. Bill told me Majer had taken over as the chairman of the Friends of Yiddish group after Stencl died. 'He's the real thing,' said Bill. I spent most of that evening talking with Majer, and at the end of the night I asked if he wanted a lift back from Oxford to Whitechapel with me. He was eighty-eight years old at the time and more than capable of travelling by train but the offer was graciously accepted. As we talked I discovered Majer was from the same area of Poland as my grandfather.

About six months after that first meeting I went with Alan Dein to interview Majer for the audio archive we were compiling about the history of the Whitechapel Library. 'I have been a regular visitor there since 1947,' Majer said as he opened the door to his small council flat near Tower Hill. 'There were masses and masses of shelves of Yiddish secular books at the Whitechapel,' he said, 'and upstairs was a beautiful Judaica section, Gemaras, Talmuds; a half of the library was Yiddish books then. It seems natural now to have all the Eastern languages there, what is a library for if it is not to satisfy its readers?' Majer led us into a tiny front room and we searched for somewhere to sit as every surface was covered in books. They were piled up outside the bathroom, on top of the table, in every cupboard and across the green leather settee. He quickly cleared some space for us and sat and spoke for nearly two hours, telling us his remarkable life story, laughing nervously throughout.

He had been born in 1912 in a small town in southern Poland, the eldest of five children, and brought up in a strictly Orthodox household. He married young and moved with his new wife to the city of Lodz. When war broke out he joined the Polish army and within a few weeks he'd been captured by the Russians as a prisoner of war. 'They deported us to the Gulags,' said Majer smiling. 'I stayed there for about eighteen months in sub-zero temperatures, not many survived.' After being freed he left for London, and joined ranks with the British army. Soon after he was sent to fight in Italy, at Ancona and Monte Cassino, where he won an award for bravery, 'It was a very bloody, costly battle,' he told us. 'I belonged to the few lucky ones who did come back.'

After the war he was unable to return to Poland because of the possibility he'd be assassinated, either by the Russians because they were worried Gulag survivors would tell the West about their experiences, or by the Poles because he was a leader of the Bund, an illegal association of Jewish Socialists. He had no desire to return to Poland anyway. All his family and friends had been murdered, there was no one to go back to and 'the Jews who did return', said Majer, 'found their houses possessed and were sometimes beaten or even killed'. Majer wanted to stay in England and leave the army but to do so he had to convince the commander that he had somewhere to live and a job. Majer had only one friend in the whole country, a fellow Bundist from Poland who was living in Cheshire Street. On his first afternoon off he went to Brick Lane and was devastated to find his friend had moved on. He got talking to the landlady of the flat, a war widow called Mrs Levy. 'I know you have no room for me,' he pleaded, 'but if you say I could live with you I promise that once I'm out I won't bother you.' She agreed to help him and also recommended that Majer went to meet someone she knew in the tailoring business, and suddenly he had the two things he needed to get out of the army.

In September 1947 he went to Cheshire Street to thank Mrs Levy for her help in getting him discharged. She told him a couple had just moved out of the room above hers that day and Majer was welcome to it. Majer remained in Cheshire Street with Mrs Levy for thirty-six years and the two of them developed a special friendship. She had lost her husband and Majer had lost his beloved wife, Esther, in Auschwitz, and although neither of them ever remarried Mrs Levy became Majer's family in London and he hers. 'First of all, living with this widow,' said Majer, 'she looked after me in every sense of the word. She fed me and cleaned for me and washed my clothes, but in the end our roles reversed. She became a bit unsteady in her mind and then I looked after her.'

I went back to speak further with Majer a number of times and he talked in more detail about his time in Brick Lane after the war: 'The whole of East London and the City was one gigantic ruin. People came back from the countryside and the army to find their homes destroyed. Even the houses still standing were completely unstable. So many left and went somewhere else and it took years to rebuild. I had no choice so I got used to it. Brick Lane was a hard place to live then. In our flat it was cold all the time. There was no bathroom, the toilet was in the yard and you had to walk down steps, which would be treacherous in the winter.'

The only compensation for Majer about living in such dreadful conditions was that Brick Lane, Cheshire Street and all the side streets down to Whitechapel were all Jewish then. People spoke Yiddish to one another and all the shops were Jewish shops with Yiddish signs. 'On Friday night you walked around and in every window you could see the Sabbath candles,' he said. 'People would greet you, "Good Shabbas," all the time. There was the Machzike Hadath Synagogue, and quite often I was approached by the *shamas* there, who spoke with me in Yiddish in a rough way, "Bad boy, you haven't done *mincah*, come in." He needed a tenth for a *minyan* as someone needed to say Kaddish. You can't say no to this, what does it take, half an hour. So occasionally I went there to be the tenth man or for Kol Nidre. And then there was the *yeshiva* next door, where they studied the Talmud in Yiddish, everywhere Yiddish. Even in the synagogues now you can't hear a Yiddish word. There were a number of Yiddish theatres in the area then and they played six days a week, eight performances, Saturdays and Sundays. People came from all over, every night it was packed out to audiences speaking and listening to plays and musicals in Yiddish.'

His eyes glistened as he remembered, and speaking quietly with a trembling voice he told me, 'Before my eyes Yiddish Whitechapel has disappeared. But Brick Lane was once the heart of it all, there was those ladies who sold the bagels who could curse so nicely people came to hear the curses. On the corner of Old Montague Street and Brick Lane was a wonderful fish and chip shop, you got very good portions for the price. The steam baths was bombed so I never saw it but many people spoke of it. After the war under the railway bridge there was an electrical shop full of gadgets and next to it a café, a place where the underworld congregated. In Cheshire Street prostitutes gathered in the street and made a lot of noise at night. There were street fights with knifes, it was a rough place, everything had been bombed to pieces, it wasn't somewhere most people wanted to come back to. Brick Lane looked like a ghost town, I was afraid to go near the buildings in case they tumbled down, roofs were caved in but people still came to the theatres from all over town.'

In 1953 Majer became a home tailor with his own small workshop at no. 10 Wilkes Street, on the second floor, making high-quality ladies' clothes, jackets and skirts. 'When you have to make a living from this kind of physical work you have to work very hard,' he told me. 'Sometimes, coming home from the theatre, I would walk past the workshop, which was just off Brick Lane, and come up for another hour and a half to work after already having done a ten-hour day.' Back then his workshop had been one of many in a large dilapidated Georgian weavers' house. The first, second and third floors housed different sorts of clothing manufacturers and a printer was in the basement. Majer worked there for about fifteen years. The roof leaked, it was freezing cold and overrun with rats and the building was in a bad state of repair. A few years ago he had been walking past the building when he saw a tour guide standing in front of it pointing to his old workshop and 'talking about those

French immigrants, the Huguenots who built it, and how it was listed. I couldn't see why, I thought it was hilarious.'

Shortly after my last meeting with Majer I received a telephone call from the poet Stephen Watts telling me the sad news of Majer's death on 4 September 2005.

8

A Whitechapel Poet

My Whitechapel, my *shtetl*, my holy acres, my Jerusalem in Britain.

Avram Stencl

Stephen Watts is a familiar figure to many living in and around Brick Lane. He has been resident in the area for over thirty years, working as a poet, helping on voluntary projects in hospitals, libraries and community centres, taking part in local demonstrations, watching, listening and recording the life around him. I often see him at local events or chatting to someone on a street corner or walking at great speed around the streets, easily distinguishable by his shoulder-length white hair.

I met him for the first time in 1991 when he visited my exhibition in Princelet Street. Since then we have become friends and sometimes, if we run into one another, I'll manage to persuade him to join me for some food at Sweet and Spicy on Brick Lane. Financial worries often dominate our conversations. Like Stencl before him, Stephen exists on the poverty line. 'Why don't you sell off some of your books?' I tried suggesting once. His face visibly darkened, he would rather starve than part with a single volume – words are holy to the Whitechapel poet.

We met recently outside Spitalfields Market and went and had coffee in the nearby Arts Café in Toynbee Hall, where Stephen has his office. He looked even thinner than usual and seemed exhausted. As we sat down he took off his glasses, which I noticed had been fixed together with a plaster and a broken paper clip, and rubbed his hands up and down his face and through his long hair. We talked of Stencl and Stephen's great friend who had recently died, the writer W. G. Sebald, and about Bill Fishman. Stephen first met Bill about thirty years ago when he saw him giving a talk at Mulberry School. 'He began his talk with the words "If you walk down Brick Lane from one end to the other,"' said Stephen, 'and this became the first line to one of my poems. He had a power of presence when he talked, which almost mapped itself into my own way of thinking about the past and present history of the area. The fact that there was such a person as Bill Fishman, talking in such a passionate and scholarly way in the seventies, was very inspiring.'

About an hour later I watched Stephen leave the café and walk wearily up the stairs to his office above, determined to tidy it up. His office currently resembles an eclectic art installation. The walls are covered in bookshelves that reach to the ceiling and heave with thousands of volumes, including hundreds of poetry books in different languages. The floor is alive with orange peel, tea bags, towers of polystyrene cups and stained coffee filters, which Stephen sees as resembling sunflowers. An ever-growing collection of stones, bone and pieces of worn wood retrieved during his many walks is scattered among the debris. This material has grown to such an extent, spreading over every surface, that it has become almost impossible to move in the tiny room. Somewhere, buried in the centre of all this, is the ancient computer where Stephen sits and writes. The chaos and financial hardship have brought Stephen to his knees, and he teeters on the edge of clinical depression, nevertheless he still manages to remain engaged with the world around him, writing the most extraordinary poems about Whitechapel since Avram Stencl.

Stephen arrived in East London in 1974 at the age of twenty-two because his wife, who taught English as a second language, passionately wanted to work in the East End. Before this he had spent three years living alone in a shepherd's hut in a remote part of the Outer Hebrides after dropping out of an English degree at Oxford University. It was there that he began writing poetry. 'It was wonderful, and physically very hard,' he told me, 'there were

Whitechapel to me was the portal for any form of imaginative life about London. It has always been a place of immigration, criminality and people arriving who could disappear and reinvent themselves, and the two zones, the City and Whitechapel, were side by side, connected by these little labyrinth passageways that you could go through and emerge into this other place. It had everything, the market, the church (which you could never get into at that time as it was always locked) and the hospital, which to me defined a secret city, and the interactions between it in terms of street trade and people who had come from all over the world who survived a new life here.

Iain Sinclair, 2004

no roads, running water or electricity. I led a solitary life, cooked off a stove fuelled by driftwood collected on the beach and spent my days contemplating and wandering around the countryside, which inspired me immensely. The rock there is among the oldest in the world and the landscape is horizontal, you see bird flight and your sense of the weather is really sharpened – I learned how to tell when it was going to snow twenty-four hours before it started.' The contrast between this barren ancient land and Whitechapel seems extreme but Stephen finds many comparisons between the two places.

'In both, the English language is not predominant,' he said. 'The Outer Hebrides is a Gaelic culture and when I arrived in East London there were still strong traces of Yiddish language and a presence of Bengali. Also back then both places had 25 per cent unemployment rate, a lot of poverty and many people who drank heavily because of social pressures. So you could say I felt at home in Whitechapel instantly, particularly when I saw the docks, which compare with the expanses of flat water in Scotland. There were even cormorants at the Isle of Dogs, and I had a strong feeling I was meant to be there.'

When Stephen first came to London he went to the top of thirty tower blocks, 'to get a different sense of the city, mapping it mentally from a bird's-eye perspective, trying to achieve that sense of being closer to the clouds experienced in the Outer Hebrides'. He'd walk huge distances using Whitechapel as the starting point and travelling as far out as Edgware and Barking. 'I'm sure my love for walking is connected to my grandfather's life in the Italian Alps,' he told me. 'He worked as a shepherd and travelled great distances on foot. As a teenager he drove sheep from the high Alps down to Cremona to winter pastures, an eight-day walk, sleeping in the hills at night.' Stephen plans to repeat this epic trek on foot and would have little trouble physically achieving it: 'Walking was just built into my body before I can remember.' He has already completed part of the journey and has undertaken thousands of long walks in other countries and other cities, but Whitechapel keeps drawing

him back. 'The place has its own poetry,' he told me. 'A sense of communities past and present, the evidence of the role of migration for three, four hundred years, and the traces of different languages that have passed through, particularly in Brick Lane, where words hang in the air, fragments of speech and noise. There is a tidal wave of sound and memory rushing down that street.' Stephen often describes Brick Lane as a stream of water.

When I asked Stephen specifically about his first memories of Brick Lane he said, 'I've walked up and down that street so many times it's impossible to remember exactly, memory is buried away and is hard to recover.' He did recall walking down Wentworth Street in 1974, arriving at the Rothschild buildings, which were derelict and made an astonishing impression on him, the residues of past lives still present. Another early memory is of walking across Brick Lane and into the ABC Café near the station, which is the first place he consciously remembers hearing Yiddish spoken. 'So many, so many memories,' he said, struggling and stuttering for the right words, 'I never took a camera with me on my walks, which in some senses is a shame but in others not as it fixes the fluidity of thought too much; walking and thought and language have to be fluid.' He talked about the many demonstrations he has taken part in over the years, particularly in the 1970s, supporting his Bengali neighbours in their fight against racism: 'I marched with thousands of others to Downing Street after the murder of Altab Ali. It was one of the first significant events in a long-term struggle to successfully change the atmosphere of Brick Lane.' He sat in silence for a while remembering before saying, 'Last summer I did a poetry workshop with some homeless people and some very different memories of Brick Lane came up, memories of Irish people in the area and memories of pubs like the Seven Stars, and the sense of violence between individuals, which was probably more prominent if you lived on the streets.' Later that day he emailed me the latest version of his extraordinary poem about Brick Lane.

Brick Lane Mela Poem

Ghosts come pouring out the houses
words have clogged
my throat: this mild winter I'll put
on my mountain scarf and go out in
the dark:

I'll slowly walk down the slight curve
and incline of the Lane,
my hand in the hands of my friends in
a tight drizzle towards the fizz of far
light

Toward the tunnel of dark air that
is neither light nor real,
but either must be Bethnal Green or
else is Beani Bazaar or the relic of a
curling dream

And as I walk I am talking to ghosts
and they are
my friends and they answer with mild
herbs of speech to calm me, as surely
as I shamble

Past the oast-houses and mud fields of
Shuttle Street
and even as I curve back on Woodseer
a tinsmith is hammering cups next
to Banglatown C&C

And a man is pushing a trolley through
        Sylhet Town
and I'm become as old and young as I am
and I float in curved space in the black
        light of this lane

Here is Kafka's Dora who opened a café
        with her brother
at 53 Brick Lane after the war. Here's
the string shop intact with its window
        nailed to the moon

And my friend Nazrul Islam, the one
        who wrote 'Vidrohi'
on the back of his hand. I am talking
to ghosts as I talk to my friends and
        here in her car

Comes Shamim Azad, just in time as I
        treat myself to a bowl of dhall:
join me dear friend, help coax lemon in
the lentil or fold the curd and unbone
        the ilish-fish

And here is Nazrul Naz buying papers
        at the last Sangeeta
translating Obaidullah while the whole
vortex of Brick Lane rears up and curls
        round on its circle

Bill Fishman walks due south talking
        to his dead dad,
Majer Bogdanski plays his violin stood
in the middle of the Lane and no-one
        wants to complain

I walk out in the dark light of the road
              & hear the rotting of a sufi music
and I fall apart – or how else would I find
the mad-rapt sound I need and nowhere
              else can find

Let me hear music or I will not go mad
              and I want to lose
this sense and arthritis and spinning tin
of rationed time that ends and begins
              just where the Lane

Disappears: let me lose all sense or I'll
              not see what's looming
at the edge or hear the singers in the Mela
or taste the clay-baked fish and lassis of
              this swimming street

Raw musics burst in my head and make
              stilt paths for my feet
as I shamble histories on this rooted coil
and seek the ever-precious venoms of
              the curly snake

David Rodinsky walks by hand in hand
              with Rachel
Lichtenstein: and Miriam Nelken rides
her drunken bike on toward the flower
              meadows of her mind

Jeff Perks painted Brick Lane seamless
              as a garment,
Avrom Stencl's sat beneath a thorn tree
talking to the birds and the drunk men
              pelted with night's rind

Look at how they shine in the resident
    air, yet no-one
sees them – because they are not there:
but I know they are & think of them
     ghostly, ghostly

I see Dan Jones & Polly & Pola Uddin
    outside Café Naz:
It was the cinema where anti-Nazis met.
Look: Tassaduq Ahmed has stopped
     in the road to talk.

North of all time and of sound a lion cub
    is nose-sniffed
by a hair-singed hound: and just around
the edge a singer staggers in amongst
     hob-nailed boots

In the Knave Of Hearts market women
    and men drink away
the cold, while outside street kids talk to
donkeys and invisible singing birds
     perch on nothing's

Branch and in the Bar, men and women
    lift glasses that are half-full
and Marketa Luskacova frames their lives
with pilgrims and holy wanderers from
     the nomad world

Or by sleet-fires the aged young take
    their tinnies and their tea,
burning cardboard on palettes of wood
because nobody else knows what it's
     like to have stood

In the exact phases of their lives. Peace
                    to their blood, as
to their eyes: they are ghosts of whom
I speak, songbirds sit in their duffelled
                    hoods

And the Chicken Man of Leyden Street
                    car-washes
bloodied feathers from off his dungarees,
then ups and buys warmed beigels that
                    ooze cream-cheese

Up Sclater Street men as old as me gob
                    on bacon butties
and from enamel cups off table tops –
like all of us have always done – drink
                    pints of tea

Back in the mela-storm of the day I'll
                    nip into the Meraj or
my Sweet & Spicy and write this poem
on dough-fresh chapatti in milli-script
                    until it's done

And up above, the round filled moon is
                    clay-baked bread,
as if Kulkuta Sukanto had not died young
or beautiful Jibanananda was living still
                    in Barisal

Then he'll take this world and place it in
                    its turning clay or
microwave it til the darkening of the day
until it glints and pecks like songbirds
                    in wet trees

Or when the city gets up off its knees
        to weep
and tower blocks shed their pastel skins
and walk beyond the herded city limits
        in sheets of sleet

I'll think back to this clay & sand and
        brick-limned lane
back through ha'penny candle-lighters
and silk attics and weaver birds and
        straw floors

And mulberry fruit and horse manure
        and way-paths
winding through suburb fields, and mud
and more and the housing of the mad
        & all of human betrayal

And wattle & pleasance & jugular woad
        until I pull myself from
such streams to strudel from the all-night
baker's or burfi and jelabi from Ambala
        & Alauddin

This street's become the river of our spate
        and all of us are flowing:
all the living and the dead who congregate
eeling a way through life & maelstromed
        outside doubt

As we walk along the middle of the lane,
        all cars banished,
all traffic body, blood and unboned cloth
gone in the trick of music, or the magic
        of the mela

Such fish we are here: slabbed carp with
          blinded eyes, raw dog-fish,
stilt-walking fish and neon ray fish, deep
mud fish and perch and pike, and then
          a dream of hilsa

And here somewhere between midnight
          and the dawn – in
the heat of it and nearly at its heart, all of
pain and succour and the bone mounted
          beneath our skin

All the cream of it, all the ice-cold of it,
          here where we stand and
raw history gushing us past on the river
of our street, not holding back coiling
          waters of our spate

9

The Basement Writers

The aims of the people
from far distant shores,
walk in the footsteps
that used to be Yours.

Sally Flood, 'Brick Lane'

During the many years Stephen Watts has lived in East London he has been actively involved in two local literary groups, the Friends of Yiddish and the Basement Writers. Chris Searle, an inspirational English teacher who once taught at Sir John Cass School in Stepney, established the Basement Writers in 1973. Two years before, he made national headlines after being sacked from Sir John Cass for publishing a book of poetry written by his pupils called *Stepney Words*. The school governors felt the poems were 'too gloomy' and gave a negative view of the East End. They forbade Searle from publishing the book but he went ahead anyway after Mr Weinberg, the legendary printer in Brick Lane, agreed to produce it at trade price. The day after Searle's dismissal the children at Sir John Cass went on strike. They went to school in their uniforms and stood outside the gates, demanding his reinstatement. The strike was highly publicized, with a full-page spread in the *Sun* and a march to Trafalgar Square, which was shown on the news.

After two years of legal battles Searle got his job back. 'The action of the children left a powerful impression on me,' he told Alan Dein when being interviewed in 1997 for a BBC Radio 4 programme about *Stepney Words* entitled *The Fire in Our Hearts*. 'There was a collective commitment and strength, the headmaster came out with his loud hailer demanding the kids return to their classrooms but they would not budge, there were thousands of them standing outside not moving, it was incredible.' Alan had decided to research this story after coming across the book of poetry at a jumble sale. Decades after the event he managed to track down Searle, some of the governors of Sir John Cass and some of its former pupils. One of those pupils was Alan Gilbey, now a Bafta-award-winning cartoonist and screenwriter who lives on Brick Lane. He was also one of the founding members of the Basement Writers when he was still a schoolchild.

Alan Gilbey currently runs an alternative East End history walk in partnership with the actor Steve Wells. 'The walk is called "The Back Passages of Spitalfields" and is billed as "the antidote to history walks".' Early one Sunday evening in August 2005 I waited with a crowd of about twenty people at the top of the escalators outside Liverpool Street Station for the walking tour to begin. The promotional leaflet for the walk, a pastiche of one of Gilbert & George's paintings, is covered in quotes from celebrities and journalists who have gone on the tour. 'Social history meets street theatre in a funny and informative stroll that is unlike any other guided tour in London,' I read on the back. Eventually two men in suits and ties marched on to the concourse with a loud hailer and started collecting money for the walk. The tour began with Steve Wells announcing in his booming voice, 'As Doctor Johnson said, "When a man is tired of London he should be glad he doesn't live in Croydon,"' followed by Alan introducing himself as 'a genuine cockney born within the sound of a car radio being stolen'. The tone was set. For the next hour and a half we followed them around the streets, stopping at most of the familiar tourist spots and some stranger venues as well, such as a dark passageway near Bishopsgate smelling of urine where we were told to scream 'Aahh shutup!' if any Jack the Ripper Tours walked by. Later Alan Gilbey told me they had established Back Passage Walks in frustration at the Ripper Tours that dominate

the area. 'So many amazing things have happened around here,' he said, 'yet all they ever go on about is bloody Jack the Ripper.' When we reached the car park in Bell Lane where one of the Ripper victims was found, Alan put on a spooky voice and said, 'Behind you is the scene of murder most foul, Jack the Ripper's multistorey car park. In about an hour you'll see hundreds of tourists staring at this in abject disappointment because of the complete lack of fog or dismembered prostitutes.' In Hanbury Street, where the remains of Annie Chapman, the first victim, were found, Alan pointed out that 'tour guides have been dropping by to describe it ever since. This is great fun if you are a tourist with a taste for blood, but bloody annoying if you live here and have children with bedrooms overlooking these nightly narrations of horror ("Mummy, what's a severed uterus?").' Irritation with the Ripper Tours runs high among many local residents, and Alan is desperate for them to stop 'this pathetic industry. Jack the Ripper doesn't deserve all this attention,' he said, 'if people want to celebrate meaningless slaughter, why not give credit where real credit is due? The Ripper killed five people while 55 per cent of children died in East London in the 1880s due to poverty and disease before they reached the age of five. Compared with the Premier League performance put in by pestilence and neglect, Jack the Ripper was an old bloke with a beer-gut booting a ball around Hackney Marshes.'

I roared with laughter as Alan and Steve used street theatre, silly props and stand-up comedy to tell the history of the area. The quirky tour finished with a firework display on top of a post box and an invitation to come and have a pint in the Golden Heart pub. I followed them inside along with about ten other people from the tour. We ordered some drinks and sat down in the small wood-panelled back bar.

'Do people ever react badly to you?' I asked Alan after he'd pulled out a sign from his bag which read 'cool person' and held it above the head of a media type standing near the bar. 'I haven't been beaten up yet,' he replied, 'but we do get heckled a lot. Last week there was a guy coming down Brick Lane in trendy clothes saying, "Oh here come the tourists," and I said, "You must be the

On the left is THE MOST SYMBOLIC
BUILDING IN THE EAST END. This simple
Grade-II listed structure with its large windows
really has been all things to all people; a place
where each successive Spitalfields community
has worshipped their version of God. Just look at
the dates.
1743 – Huguenot Chapel.
1809 – Methodist Church.
1897 – Jewish Synagogue.
1975 – Muslim Mosque.
2010 – Conran Restaurant.

Alan Gilbey and Steve Wells, 'The Back Passages of
Spitalfields', 2005

cockneys." He huffed off, people just don't expect to be answered back.' Above the bar Alan pointed out a photograph of two of the area's most famous residents, Gilbert & George, doing the cancan with the landlady, Sandra. 'I always wondered what would happen if we met,' he said, 'and one day we did. We were walking down Fournier Street dressed exactly like them and they were walking on the other side of the pavement in the opposite direction. They didn't acknowledge us and we didn't acknowledge them, we just marched past swinging our arms in unison just like they did. It was hard to keep a straight face.'

I used to see Gilbert & George in the Market Café opposite Christ Church in Fournier Street, a place that looked like it had been transported directly out of the 1950s with its Formica tables, counter filled with bakewell tarts and large urns of tea. It was run by a brother and sister who invited you into the kitchen to choose what you wanted to eat. The food was fantastic, huge portions, very cheap and quintessentially British – sausage and mash, roast dinners with over-boiled cabbage, crumble and custard. The café had originally catered for the market traders and used to open at about five in the morning. Gilbert & George used to go there every day to have their lunch. 'People started to call up and try and book tables when they found out,' said Alan. 'Twats, it's a café.'

Alan feels he has the credentials to sneer at such behaviour, being a born-and-bred East Ender. He grew up on Cable Street, his mum still lives there, and his grandmother lived in nearby Juniper Street. 'I've got a real poverty photograph of her,' he said, 'standing in her best apron on a bit of old carpet. Her street was known as Incubator Street because of the amount of babies they had there.' He describes his childhood as odd. He rarely went to school and spent most of his time watching television. 'I was an expert on *Thunderbirds*,' he said. The only teacher to get through to him was Chris Searle. 'One day he turned up at my front door with a poem I had written in this published book, *Stepney Words*,' said Alan. 'I couldn't believe it.'

When Chris was reinstated as English teacher at Sir John Cass in 1973 Alan started to go to school more, and that was when the Basement Writers began. The original members were all young kids like Alan from the school. Later, other writers, such as Sally Flood and Gladys McGee, joined and the dynamics of the group changed. 'We'd put on quite alternative plays and read poetry at places like the Half Moon Theatre on Mile End Road. Looking back it was very ambitious for a bunch of East End kids with no training or money.'

As well as putting on these kinds of entertainments the Basement Writers also ran a bookshop from the Whitechapel Gallery, which led to the formation of the Eastside Bookshop, which has recently moved from near the London Hospital to new premises on Brick Lane. When Alan left school he started working at the bookshop and running drama groups. 'We did a play about the Battle of Cable Street in the synagogue in Princelet Street,' he said. At that time he also started to do history walks with Bill Fishman and began working on weird historical-collage comedy plays, which eventually developed into the Back Passages Walks.

Alan moved to Brick Lane about fifteen years ago when Cable Street became a bit too threatening. 'The man living above me was a white guy dealing drugs to Bangladeshi teenagers,' he said. 'I came home one weekend and the kids in his flat had rioted and thrown all his furniture out the windows.' The only place he could afford to buy a property at that time was in the new Ballymore development at the top of Brick Lane because 'it was cheap and no one wanted to live there', he said. Alan still has the brochure from 1991 and he told me, 'On the map on the back they've excluded the name Brick Lane, probably because the reputation was so bad they thought they'd put people off buying there. There is no mention of the street in the local attractions. It does say you are a short walk from the Barbican but fails to point out there is a street market outside your door every Sunday, and this was a shock for some people who moved in and started up a petition to stop the market,' he said laughing. 'Most of the flats were bought by investors who

Watney Street

Chattering, talking holding up the traffic.
Women shopping buying fruit, food
On the lookout for a bargain.
Man on the corner selling stolen purses
One eye on the cash box
One eye on the look out
Fruit seller shouting 'buncha bananas',
Someone buys some don't know they're half rotten
One selling toys made in Hong Kong
Old men under the arch selling broken plates.

Alan Gilbey (aged eleven), from *Stepney Words*, 1971

rented them out to City workers as a weekday bolt hole and at the weekends they were empty,' said Alan.

Unlike the close-knit East End community he had grown up in Alan now found himself living among a transient population, where he didn't even know his neighbours. 'The day I moved in,' he told me, 'I dropped a tin of paint accidentally on the hall carpet and all the people who lived in the block walked past while I was trying to clear it up. I tried to make a joke, "Just doing some decorating," and they just sniffed, no one even said hello, and it's been like that ever since.' Alan feels ambiguous about the area today and gets annoyed when people accuse him of living there because it is fashionable. 'When I say I moved there because it was the cheapest area to live in no one ever believes me. Now I feel it's got too commercial for many of the arty types I know, and they've moved on.' Alan has no plans to leave Brick Lane. The flat serves his needs and he quite likes living there: 'At least you can get a decent cup of coffee here now,' he said.

Another long-term member of the Basement Writers Group who still lives in the area is Sally Flood. Her memories of Brick Lane stretch back further than anyone I have spoken to. She was born there in 1925, went to Thomas Buxton School as a child in the 1930s, lived through the Blitz there and worked at a dress-making factory on Brick Lane in the 1960s and 1970s. She still visits Brick Lane weekly, to attend computer classes in the Old Truman Brewery.

'Brick Lane, the width and breadth of my childhood,' is how one of her poems starts. Sally has been writing poetry since she was a child, but she never showed it to anyone until she joined the Basement Writers at the age of fifty. 'Poetry just wasn't what working-class people did,' she said. Chris Searle was the first to publish her work, and her poems are now included in numerous books and anthologies. She has given readings on radio and television, in theatres and festivals. From 1985, with her friend Gladys McGee, she set up creative writing courses. When she retired, she started giving poetry workshops in local schools, including Thomas Buxton School, where she helped young Bangladeshi pupils write about their own experiences of living in East London.

Today she lives in the house where she raised her seven children, just behind the London Hospital in Whitechapel. It was there that I went to talk with her about her memories of Brick Lane. Finding time to schedule a meeting with Sally, in between her acupuncture appointments, computer classes and poetry readings, was always a struggle, and my visits were often cut short by a phone call from a friend or a relative dropping by. 'You've got to keep busy,' she'd say smiling, 'life is a gift, isn't it, and you can't waste it.'

Sally grew up in an Orthodox Jewish household in Brick Lane, one of seven children herself. Her father was a cabinetmaker whose workshop was in Gibraltar Walk at the Bethnal Green end of Brick Lane. 'He was out at six in the morning till ten at night,' she said. His parents had arrived in London from Russia in the 1880s and settled in Brick Lane. They lived near the railway arch opposite a gramophone shop and rented two rooms on the first floor. Sally remembers their small apartment as being 'very dark and filled with big pieces of wooden furniture. On the mantelpiece were two candlesticks and on the wall was a faded photograph they brought with them from Russia. There wasn't any other decoration in there and it was noisy – the train used to rumble right through their flat.'

Her grandfather, Hillel Grodinski, an imposing figure, with a long beard and ringlets, was an important member of the Orthodox community in Brick Lane. 'He often came to our house to teach my brothers Hebrew,' she said. 'He wouldn't teach me because I was a girl but I used to sit outside the door and I learned my "Baruch Atah Adonai" just through listening.' He also taught Hebrew at the Brick Lane Talmud Torah School in the 1920s and 1930s, and spent many years working as the *shamas* at the Machzike Hadath. Sally visited the Machzike Hadath only once and remembers 'the *davening* and the wooden pews and watching the men through the partition'. A couple of years ago she revisited the building to pay

her respects to someone in the Muslim community who'd died. 'It was a strange experience to return to the old synagogue of my childhood,' she said. 'The building itself didn't really look that different to me.'

Her grandmother dressed in long heavy skirts and wore a *sheytl* with a bun. 'The night before she married at the age of fifteen,' said Sally, 'she had to shave her beautiful long hair off, which I thought was dreadful. She came from a well-to-do family. Zayde was poor but he was a Hebrew scholar and that's what used to happen in Russia in them days, scholars were matched up with wealthy families – it was a great honour to have a scholar in the family. She never spoke English, had no interest in it whatsoever. She spoke to me in Yiddish and I understood her perfectly but now I can't speak it.'

On Friday nights Sally's grandparents joined them for Shabbas. Sally's mother found it stressful because the grandmother would thoroughly inspect the house on every visit to ensure they were keeping a proper kosher home. 'It was her main mission in life,' said Sally. 'She was extremely orthodox, but kind also. We didn't have a bath at home and once a week she took us to the public baths in Cheshire Street. I was quite young when my sister came running into the house one day after visiting Buba and said she couldn't wake her up – she was dead in her chair.'

Her childhood memories of Brick Lane itself are reminiscent of Bill Fishman's: 'I remember the man with the organ-grinder coming down the lane and we'd go out and listen and dance and the mothers used to throw money out to them. The rag-and-bone man would come by most weeks as well and the milkman with the urns on the back of his cart. On Saturdays, after a traditional lunch of *chol-lant,* everyone dressed in their best clothes, and walked around the neighbourhood. Everyone knew each other. The atmosphere was fantastic. Sunday was for shopping, a trip to Brick Lane Market for groceries, *schmaltz* herrings from Marks & Sons delicatessens, a live chicken from a yard in Old Montague Street, which was slaugh-tered out the back and then taken home and feathered and we'd finish up at Bloom's for a salt-beef sandwich.' Like Bill, Sally was fascinated by the speakers outside Bloom's – she remembers seeing Phil Piratin, the Jewish Communist MP, talking there, and Max Baer, the American heavyweight boxer, who visited the area before the war and spoke about the persecution of the Jews in Russia. 'I just didn't know of these things before hearing them there,' said Sally. 'I remember Baer in particular because he kissed my mother on the cheek. She thought he was marvellous and talked about it for weeks.'

Thomas Buxton School, which Sally attended in the 1930s, was an imposing red-brick Victorian building. 'Most of the children were Jewish,' said Sally, 'but I always remember this one child called Anna who wasn't. She was very blonde, with beautiful long flaxen hair, but I never spoke to her because we didn't mix, the Jewish and the non-Jewish children. The boys were in another part of the building.' When Sally was quite young the family moved from Brick Lane to nearby Chicksand Street, where the community was more mixed. 'Next door to us was an Irish family,' said Sally. 'Every Friday night the father would get drunk and bang on our door and shout, "Come out and fight, you filthy Jews!" but the rest of the week we were friends. On the other side of us were the Fullers, who had a fruit stall on Brick Lane. They used to sell the Irish sweepstake and my mum always bought a ticket from her. One year they won the top prize and moved out to Essex and got a big house with a field and their daughter Ivy learned to ride a horse.'

On the corner of Chicksand Street and Brick Lane was the Mayfair Cinema. If Sally's grandparents weren't around, her mother would give her sixpence on a Saturday morning and she'd go and spend hours there. 'I'd buy peanuts outside from an old ice-cream-type of van,' she said, 'and take my lunch with me. There'd be two pictures, variety and then the news. Once I had a bad experience there, a man sat next to me and suddenly I felt his hand on my leg, so I shouted at him and the usher threw me out. My mother wouldn't let me go again.'

In 1937 the family moved to Bethnal Green, 'to a flat with a brand-new bath, even if it was in the kitchen'. Away from Brick Lane, the area was predominantly white working class and Sally experienced a lot of anti-Semitism there. As war broke out she was evacuated briefly to Norfolk for seven months, which she hated. When bombs fell in a nearby field one night she wrote to her mother and begged to come home. 'She was on the next train to come and get me,' said Sally. Their nearest shelter was at Bethnal Green tube station: 'Everyone used to just throw their blankets down and God help you if it touched somebody else.' She narrowly missed being involved in the Bethnal Green tube disaster on 3 March 1943, when one hundred and seventy-three people were crushed to death in a stampede to get inside. It was the worst civilian tragedy of the war and Sally still finds it hard to talk about it. When Bethnal Green Station closed she sheltered in a warehouse in Backchurch Lane, near the Bethnal Green end of Brick Lane. As the bombing intensified she was evacuated again, this time to Torquay, where she was employed making uniforms. While she was there her family home was completely bombed out. 'We lost everything we owned,' she said, 'it had been turned to rubble. Brick Lane, particularly around Sclater Street, was completely decimated.' Luckily her family were all in the shelter in Backchurch Lane at the time.

She returned from Torquay to the worst of the bombing and began working in Aldgate as a dressmaker. 'Doodlebugs were flying everywhere,' she said. 'It should've been terrifying but because of my age I did not find it frightening at all, it was just a bit of an adventure, it was exciting.' Sally earned well at the time, doing cabbage work, making things to sell in Brick Lane Market. 'You could buy dresses without coupons there during the war,' she said, 'there was a black market going on. We'd make up big bundles, about sixteen a bundle, roll them up and send them off. I made really good money because I was fast at this piece-work.'

In 1947 she married a non-Jewish man called Joseph. Her father didn't speak to her for seventeen years: 'He tore his waistcoat. He cut me off. He wanted to make a traditional *shidduch* for me but

I didn't want it. If my grandparents had still been alive I couldn't have married Joseph, it would have killed them.' It was too painful for Sally to remain living in the same area as her family, so she moved with her new husband to Whitechapel, where she had her seven children. For the next twenty years she was a busy mother, working part time taking on dressmaking jobs.

Once her children were all at school, Sally returned to Brick Lane in 1967 to work as an embroiderer at Axington's in Princelet Street, staying there for fifteen years. Her sewing machine was next to the window on the third floor, overlooking Brick Lane. 'On the factory floor there were machines along one wall, and the Hoffmann presses on the other side, and we were arranged so that we couldn't talk to each other. I sat there every day looking out on to the street, dreaming and doing my work,' she said. 'I wrote a lot of poems then but I always hid them. You had to keep your head down in that place. It was an intense working atmosphere. If anyone approached me, anything I was writing would go straight under my sewing. I lost a lot of poems that way. Conditions in the factory were bad. I wrote a poem about it called "Man's Hell", which begins, "The steam of labour pollutes the air, God help the coming generation, if this is living where does Hell begin."'

Axington's was a big company that employed hundreds of dressmakers, pressers and embroiderers. 'There was a mechanic in the basement so if anything went wrong with the machines he'd come straight up and fix them,' said Sally. The company was also known as Paris Vogue because they worked with Ossie Clark, who'd come to the factory floor, and Sally used to work with him creating new samples. 'I did meet some great people while there,' she told me. Such as Joe Philips, a Jewish man, a tracer, 'who worked by himself, behind a separate curtain, to stop the chalk from coming into the rest of the factory'. He died three weeks after he retired, 'probably from swallowing the chalk for all those years', said Sally. He worked at Axington's all his life and lived on Brick Lane. 'The love of his life was music. Whenever somebody went away he would ask them

Living above us was a Jew and a gentile, a
mixed marriage, and I never saw any relations
going there probably because of this. They had
one son, he was very clever, Geoffrey Goldsmith,
he didn't fit in and was a bit bullied, there
weren't many Jewish people in our flats and he
was a bit fat and couldn't run and climb and do
all the stuff we could do but he was really clever.
He took me to Hebrew classes with him in Brick
Lane and I'd wait outside. My mum took this
picture of me and him at our Coronation party,
we were good friends.

John Gardiner, 2004

to bring him back some records, Greek, Italian, he loved that kind of music. He'd done this room up in his flat, with special amplifiers and all his music collection, and his dream was to retire and sit in that room all day and enjoy his music.'

By the 1960s Brick Lane had changed entirely from the place Sally knew as a child. It seemed rougher to her, more run down. 'There was a trimming shop directly opposite the factory,' she said, 'and a few doors along was this little café, and you used to see all this dodgy business going on, the cabs would pull up and pick up these young girls. I did recognize some of those girls because they had been in the same class at school as my daughter, so I found that a bit upsetting. I can't remember seeing things like that when I was a child.' The Truman Brewery was fully functioning then and Sally remembers 'the men in their boots and aprons rolling barrels of beer up the street and those old-fashioned carts with the writing on the side, pulled by horses, going into the brewery, and the sound that they made, with their hoofs on the cobblestones'. She described Brick Lane in the 1960s as: 'A place that you would walk through or a place that you would work in, there was no other reason to go there. Nothing was clean, it looked like everything was covered in a layer of dust. The strong and proud community that had been there before had left and all of those front steps that had been religiously scrubbed every morning became covered in grime. It took a while for the next group of immigrants to properly settle, and in those in-between years, I'm talking about the 1950s and 1960s, the place just seemed to be abandoned. Drifter types came for a while and then left again. These weren't the type of people who really took care of property. Many former homes and houses became workshops and factories. This is the way it is before a community gets on its feet. It was the same for the Jews, in fact it was much worse for the Jews, if they did not work they starved.'

I asked Sally how she felt about Brick Lane today and she told me: 'It has become a bit like Covent Garden, and Covent Garden is OK in Covent Garden, but not in the East End. When I go down there I feel like I'm losing my history, but I'll always be especially attached to Brick Lane. My father settled there from Russia after seeking asylum and I've never lost sight of that. If they hadn't let him stay I would not be here and I feel it is important to remember your background and where you come from.'

The Brick Lane I See

Brick lane is a mixture
of aromatic spices
curries, onions and bad drains,
Pakistani restaurants
Jewish trimming shops
and betting shops,
Down at heel workers
and hopeful prostitutes,
cars and vans add to the pollution
with heavy exhaust fumes.
Pavements and gutters
are littered with overspill
from dustbins and workshops.

This is where the immigrant
looks for fulfilment!
This is the breeding ground
for discontent,
Where the Meths drinker mixes
with the down and out,
where Workers are exploited
and small time drug peddlers
sell their dreams!
This is where the thug
dons the crown of King
and bullies thrive,
Where do-gooders
salve their consciences,
This is Brick lane.

Sally Flood, from
A Window on Brick Lane, 1979

10

The Old Truman Brewery

Brick Lane was a run-down East End side street, the brewery
was the main thing there along with lots of second-hand clothes
shops, furniture shops, ethnic food shops, tailors, furriers,
things like that. It was shabby and dirty. That's how I remember
it after the war.

John Williams

I bumped into one of Brick Lane's newer residents recently, an artist
friend of mine called Svar, near the railway bridge in the middle
of the street. He was walking head down against the wind, eating
a bagel out of a paper bag. I hadn't seen him for six months, since
meeting him at a private view in Clerkenwell, where he had been
drunk and morose, having just split from his long-term partner. I
had found him slumped against a pillar in the centre of the gallery
with a bottle of Becks in each hand. He'd grabbed violently at
my arms as I walked past. 'Why, why did she leave me?' he'd said
over and over, sobbing uncontrollably until his friends came and
led him away.

I didn't recognize the gaunt figure walking towards me on Brick
Lane until he was right in front of me. Svar has always been slim but
that day he looked skeletal. He told me he'd been on a life-support
machine in hospital after complications with a burst appendix. Never
one to be body shy, Svar lifted his top to show a thick pink scar
running from his heart down to his groin. Despite this physical
trauma he seemed in a much better state than the last time we'd
met: he had a new girlfriend and a new flat just off Brick Lane.

'The council finally rehoused me from the place in Clapton,' he

said, 'things with the neighbour downstairs had become intolerable.'
I knew about the problems in Clapton, which had started during
his female-to-male transition. As Svar became more masculine the
people around him found the changes harder to accept. 'My barber
commented on my receding hairline and growing sideburns,' he told
me, 'but I didn't grow a beard because people in the dry-cleaners
and bakers just couldn't have coped.' The occasional sideways look
or comment would have been bearable but his neighbour became
violent and abusive. 'We didn't get on before,' said Svar, 'but as
the changes progressed it got worse and worse. He'd spit at me on
the stairs and was really threatening on a daily basis.'

Moving to Brick Lane was an opportunity for Svar to start afresh.
He invited me to come and see the new flat. We took the short walk
together, turning off at Bacon Street and stopping outside a modern
council block. We walked up to the fourth floor and entered a small
apartment with fantastic views over the rooftops of Spitalfields. His
front room overlooks the St Matthias School playground and on the
other side is the back of Marga's commune – if she were standing
at her attic window I could have waved to her.

I asked Svar what he liked most about living there, and, just as
Marga had done, he said the Beigel Bake. Since his operation he
finds it hard to sleep and often visits the bakery in the middle of
the night after waking restless and in pain. 'I'll wander down there
and maybe have a bit of cheesecake,' he said. 'At three, four in the
morning the other customers are young clubbers and late-night
shift workers picking up something for breakfast as well as the
regular junkies and homeless drifters hanging around outside.' This
sounds like a threatening environment for someone just under five
foot and with the kind of physical ambiguity that often attracts the
wrong attention but Svar told me he's had no problems since he
moved to the area. 'It is one of those places that seems to accept
you whatever or whoever you are,' he said.

I sat in Svar's front room and listened as he told me the early
story of his life. Up to a certain point his biography is similar to
mine. We both grew up in Southend in Essex, both went to the

153

local girls' grammar school, both studied sculpture and both changed our names by deed poll as young teenagers. I reclaimed the Polish Jewish family name of Lichtenstein, which had been anglicized to Laurence just before my birth, and Svar dropped the name he had been born with: Yvette. 'At the time this had nothing to do with my transsexualism,' he said. 'It was because I'm small and I felt Yvette was a diminutive, like "Little Eve", and this name just didn't suit my personality, I never related to it.' Svar, which means 'bright space' in Sanskrit, somehow worked. Even when Svar was still Yvette she had an androgynous look, with a flat chest and slim hips. Riding around on motorbikes and getting into constant trouble, Yvette neither looked nor behaved like a typical Essex girl. In 1978 she left Southend for London and wound up at Chelsea Art School, living just off the King's Road as 'a sophisticated London punk, all orange hair and black plastic clothes, getting up to mischief, amphetamines and late-night parties, all sorts of adventures'. She went on to study at Central St Martin's, which was when she first started to visit Brick Lane, becoming a regular at the Sunday market in the early 1980s. Svar began his transition from woman to man after moving to Clapton in 1995. He was thirty-seven at the time, the most common age for female-to-male transsexuals. The process is ongoing; after years of daily testosterone injections his voice has broken, he has facial and body hair and a slight Adam's apple. He hasn't had surgery yet but is thinking about it, although unsurprisingly his stint on the life-support machine has put him off for a while. Many people confuse Svar for a camp, effeminate man, but if you ask him how he defines himself he says, 'I have a cyborg identity but first and foremost I am an artist.' His artwork centres around his changing physical state, with much of it focusing on transmutancy.

In 1991 Svar was one of the first people to rent studio space in the old brewery site on Brick Lane after it stopped trading in 1988. He was one of a collective of twenty-four artists who had studios and a gallery there (opposite where the Vibe Bar is now), run by a man called Christian Anstice with the help of a part-time administrator, Lulu

Kennedy. 'It was the best studio space I ever had,' said Svar. 'I took a long time choosing the right space, there was so much available then. I explored the empty buildings of the brewery by making friends with an electrician on site who showed me around. I was stunned by the vastness of it. Where the brewing equipment had been were immense cavernous spaces. Only the huge empty vats and massive copper pipes were left in warehouses the size of aircraft hangars.' Svar picked a studio on the ground floor, which once housed the old steam-pressure valve, with windows looking out on to Brick Lane. It was perfect for his needs although freezing cold in the winter. Next to him was an artist called Tina, who had the base of the tall brick chimney from the brewery in her studio, which had the word 'Truman' written in large letters down the side.

Situated next to Svar's studio block was the Brick Lane Music Hall. Vincent Hayes, the impresario and owner of the music hall, was well known among the artistic community of Brick Lane in the early 1990s. He had the same determination as the artists to bring to life the derelict and near-empty brewery building. One of the first things Vince did when he opened up in 1991 was to light the outside of the building, which made local people feel safer at night as they walked past the dark, abandoned brewery site. He soon had coachloads of visitors coming for traditional evenings of 'cockney culture' and his music hall saw the first tourists at that part of Brick Lane.

Svar remembers seeing 'Danny La Rue at the Brick Lane Music Hall and other drag queens belting out old favourites in sparkling evening gowns'. Vince used to do special nights for pensioners with a meal, drinks and a show, and sometimes Svar would help out with the stage sets. I met Vince after taking part in a special Jewish East End evening he organized in July 1992 while I was working at the synagogue in Princelet Street. I gave a talk on the history of Jewish immigration to the area, which was followed by a performance of Victorian comedy and song. The final act was Colin Devreaux appearing in drag as the international vaudeville star Sophie Tucker singing 'My Yiddishe Momma'.

In 1995 new owners took over the brewery and rents increased. Svar's collective and the Brick Lane Music Hall all moved on. Vince went to a disused button factory in Hoxton, where the same thing happened again until he moved further out to Canning Town. Despite moving three times he hasn't changed the name of his venture. 'Lots of work went into the Brick Lane Music Hall and to change the name would wipe out that history,' he said. Vincent's core audience has always been white cockneys. Over the years he has met many people who have come to his shows who used to work at Truman's. 'There was once a workforce there of over two thousand people,' he said, 'most of them being local men, who started at fourteen and left when they were handed their pension book, just like their fathers and grandfathers before them.'

Records of the land of the brewery site date back to 1660, when it was fields owned by Sir William Wheler. He released the land to John Stott in 1661, who then laid out Black Eagle Street, Grey Eagle Street, Monmouth Street and Brick Lane before letting part of this land to Thomas Bucknell, a merchant taylor from a large brewing family, who built houses there and possibly erected the first brewery on Brick Lane, although the date is unknown. Joseph Truman may have worked in this brewery for a while but a letter from Truman's archive states that in 1666 Joseph Truman was running the Black

Eagle Brewery in Brick Lane. Joseph's son, Benjamin, inherited the business, and the site expanded over six acres, with large fields, malt and hop lofts, stables and huge warehouses filled with vast copper vats for storing Porter, a popular black stout that brought the brewery international fame in the eighteenth century.

In 1740 King George II knighted Benjamin Truman for his business achievements, and shortly after Sir Benjamin moved into a grand purpose-built Georgian house, no. 91 Brick Lane, which is still there. He commissioned Gainsborough to paint four portraits of him and his grandchildren, and the painting of Sir Benjamin hung in the wood-panelled boardroom of the house until 1977, when Maxwell Joseph auctioned it to raise funds. The other three were sold much earlier, and Truman's own publication, *Truman's the Brewers, 1666–1966*, claims that since the paintings left the brewery the ghost of Sir Benjamin has haunted the building. The workers started a tradition of leaving a jug of Imperial Stout in the drawing room of the house to soothe the angry ghost, and every morning, the jug was found to be empty. I have heard different versions of this story from numerous ex-brewery workers who talked about mysterious occurrences, such as things going missing all the time, strange figures appearing in corridors, and doors opening and closing by themselves.

The Truman dynasty continued until 1789, when there were no male heirs, and then Sampson Hanbury took over. Hanbury employed his nephew, Thomas Buxton, and although the brewery, now known as Truman, Hanbury, Buxton & Co., became a limited company in 1888, there was a member of the Buxton family on the board until the late 1960s. In 1971 Maxwell Joseph (the first Jew to own a brewery in England) and his company, the Grand Metropolitan Group, bought the brewery and merged with Watney in 1972 to create Watney Mann and Truman Holdings.

By the late 1970s the brewery was in decline, sales were dropping and the workforce was gradually being made redundant until, by the mid 1980s, it had been cut in half. In 1988 brewing stopped at the site for the first time in three hundred and twenty-two years.

Apart from the spaces let out to the artists, Atlantis art suppliers and the music hall, the huge site lay dormant as equipment was removed to make the brewery presentable for a private investor. A buyer eventually came forward in 1995 – an Israeli family called the Zeloofs, whose import/export business was located in the area. One member of the family, Ofer Zeloof, had new ideas on how to transform the now eleven-acre site. He began by employing the former administrator of the artists' collective at the brewery, Lulu Kennedy, to start letting out units.

I met Lulu in 1995 when I rented one of the newly available spaces in the brewery. I remembered her as a slim, beautiful young woman who was constantly running around the building looking harassed and holding giant bunches of keys. As I was one of the first to be renting a studio there I was offered a choice of spaces. Lulu showed me the former offices in the mirror-fronted main building on the second and third floor first. She thought I'd like them because they had floor-to-ceiling glass windows and had been especially dedicated for artists. The first floor I saw looked like a gigantic football pitch. Twenty thousand square feet of open space covered in a bright emerald-green carpet. Although there

The old boardroom on the first floor was the grandest in the building. The Gainsborough portrait was still there then and a huge deep-red mahogany table, highly polished with grand high-backed chairs with red upholstery. The downstairs offices were said to be haunted by the ghost of a Huguenot silk weaver who was killed there. I used to work late at night and heard people tell me about women in white walking up and down but I thought it was probably the cleaners.

John Ewing, 2005

were spectacular panoramic rooftop views of Spitalfields from every angle I couldn't imagine working there. The atmosphere felt wrong, there were plug sockets embedded into the floor to feed the computer terminals that had once sat there, and the place had a similar feel to it as the synagogue in Princelet Street – a lingering presence of previous occupiers and an odd energy. We went up to the next floor, which had been partitioned into smaller units, but it was empty and cold, with only about 10 per cent of the spaces let at the time. Lulu took me across the road to look at the former offices in the clockhouse, above the site of the Brick Lane Music Hall. They were clean and had central heating, a major luxury for an artist, and I took one straighta-way and completed much of my Rodinsky research there. It was a strange environment for an artist to work in. Apart from one other painter on my floor the rest of the spaces were leased to dot.com companies, who soon filled the empty site, and I had a feeling even then that this wouldn't be an environment where artists could afford to work from for long.

Lulu was one of the few people to have ever worked in the brewery when the building was actually empty. I wanted to ask her about her impressions of the site when she had first arrived. She still works in the complex, now running an Old Truman Brewery project called Fashion East, housed in the same block where I once had my studio. I went to see her in her office, a small room lit by large Georgian sash windows overlooking Brick Lane. The walls are covered in sketches by and photographs of the young fashion designers she now helps promote. Lulu was the interface between the brewery owners and those renting spaces on the site for years and as a result knows most people working there. She has become part of the fabric of the street, and is as essential to her community of fashion designers, artists and DJs as the caretaker of the mosque is to the Muslim community further down the road. When she first came here ten years ago she knew no one and found the street itself and particularly the brewery to be 'quite desolate, a bit like a ghost town'. In 1995 she started working part-time running the gallery and studios for Svar and the artists. She remembers some of the equipment that came out of the brewery at that time, such as the big copper fermenting vats that had to be cut out on site. She told me: 'They were in Dray Walk, where the Big Chill Bar is now, and if you look up you can see that building has got huge circular holes in the roof where the vats used to sit.'

Lulu started working for the Zeloofs after they visited the gallery one day and offered her a full-time job. She described to me the first time she went into the block that housed the clockhouse, and wandered up the spiral staircase, finding the attic, which was covered in a thick layer of dust: 'Obviously no one had been up there for years and it was filled with all the old brewery merchandising, Truman beer mats and other half-finished graphic-design projects, and none of it had been touched, so it had this real ghostly feel to it. You could almost sense people there. Most of the equipment had been taken out by the time I got there and you could see the marks they left on the walls and ceilings. I remember finding an old corridor with a beautiful tiled fresco of the working brewery, but that's gone now.'

Opposite the clockhouse is the original Georgian house of Sir Benjamin Truman. Lulu told me that the Zeloofs, unaware of the stories I have since read of the lingering ghost of Sir Benjamin,

In 1946 Dray Walk was where the lorries and
the horse and carts used to load up, what we
called the loading bank. The bottling bank was
on the second and third floor. The cooperage
yard was opposite Dray Walk, next to the empty
bank where you'd unload the empties, which
would be pushed down runners and washed out.
Then they'd go underneath the road, through a
tunnel into the brewery up by the racking room
where they were filled up again. If you came
out of Dray Walk and turned left into the main
brewery building, at the end was the Brewers
House. Past there, up some steps, was the
brewing rooms where the big brewing tanks
were. They used to brew porter there before the
war, and stout. Virtually everything was manual
in the 1940s, the only thing that was mechanical
was the machine that filled the bottles up.

Jim Tyler, 2004

have also decided that the building is haunted. Benjamin Truman's old house is grafted on to the 1970s office block designed by Ove Arup in 1976. I asked Lulu how the design worked internally, and she said, 'One minute you are walking through this modern space with high ceilings and walls of glass everywhere and suddenly it's like stepping back in time, all the lines are a bit wonky and the staircases are wobbly.' During her explorations she came across the old workers' canteen. 'I found the key and unlocked the door,' she said, 'it was on the second floor in the main building, and then I found all these old shower blocks and it started to feel like I was in a set for a horror film.'

Again, on entering the main workers' bar, Lulu said, 'It had that feeling that the last occupants had only just left, with a few bits of stray tinsel hanging up and empty glasses sat out on the bar.' Behind the stables she found the remains of the cooperage in 'a small warehouse with a little chimney where they'd bend the wood to make the barrels'.

After the bigger warehouse spaces had been emptied of brewing equipment, cleaned and whitewashed, Lulu started to let them out. In the beginning they 'didn't have many rules and there were quite a lot of wild events'. KLF screened their video *Watch the K-Foundation Burn a Million Quid* in the brewery in 1995, and Hussein Chalayan, a Turkish Cypriot fashion designer, put on shows there, including one with the models in various states of undress, from full *hijab* to completely naked, posing on the top floor of the Atlantis Gallery in front of a crowd of hundreds. Many other parties, art exhibitions and fashion shows followed until the Zeloofs were forced by Tower Hamlets Council to tone things down after repeated complaints from local residents. The programme at the brewery is now strictly regulated and run by a team of events and production managers with health and safety guidelines and sound restrictions after eleven o'clock. These laws do not, however, stop revellers falling drunkenly out of the bars and clubs in the complex and the restaurants on Brick Lane, shouting in the street and keeping the families who live near by awake.

The early period of the brewery redevelopment seemed very optimistic. There were a lot of fashion and dance labels renting spaces then and the Asian contemporary dance music was really starting to happen and it seemed like there was a correlation there and an exciting scene but now it's more like, look at my vintage clothes and my new outfit, and just defiant boozing in the street.

Alan Gilbey, 2006

The Old Truman Brewery is fully occupied again, with a long waiting list of people wanting to rent space there. Some floors are entirely occupied by dot.com companies and the fourth floor is still mostly artists' studios. The rest of the site has filled up with 'mainly creative types' – fashion and graphic designers, music studios, film production companies and artists. There are over two hundred different companies working there, 'a contemporary community of like-minded thinkers', said Lulu. Over the years people have rented spaces there for all sorts of odd ventures. 'We had a Japanese artist here,' said Lulu. 'I went to her studio once and found myself waist-high in ripped-up shredded paper. The artist was rolling around in it and she had all these broken toys everywhere and said she was making some kind of giant installation, but to me it just looked like a human-sized gerbil cage. We had another artist who made a machine that pulsed liquid mercury everywhere.'

Looking through old newspaper articles about the brewery from 1988 I read about early plans to have a bazaar in the building where local Bangladeshi people could sell handmade crafts. This never happened and when the Zeloofs bought the complex seven years later they had no knowledge of these plans. There has never been a curry house on the site: 'We felt there were so many and we wanted to encourage more diversity to the area,' said Lulu. There are small Bangladeshi businesses dotted around the complex and GreenLine Cash and Carry, selling Asian food, leases a whole building. The Old Truman Brewery has also hosted Asian Dreams events over the last few years and *Asiana Magazine* recently held their anniversary party there. Despite this, walking around the site, it is hard to see a visible Bengali presence.

The only place that a restaurant could have operated from, access-wise, was Dray Walk, which was shuttered off until 2000 when the rest of the site was full. After they had built the shopfronts Dray Walk was let out to businesses such as Café 1001, a coffee shop and DJ bar. Dray Walk is now known locally as the 'strip' and is fully occupied with exhibition spaces, boutiques, designer outlets, delicatessens and bars. In the summer it is hard to find space to

When I worked at Truman's in 1962 Brick Lane looked like something out of *Oliver Twist*, with dark narrow streets, filled with strange-looking characters and Hasidic Jews walking around in long black coats mixing with cockney barrow boys selling their wares. The Dickensian nature of the street was only emphasized when you walked into the brewery where people sat at huge sloping desks and wrote by hand in giant leather-bound ledgers.

Peter Bondi, 2005

move there among the young and fashionable crowds sitting outside around the picnic tables on the pedestrianized walkway. Lulu feels that the right balance has been achieved by the Zeloofs in the way they have approached the regeneration of the site:

'They could have charged a lot more money if they had done the whole place up with landscaped gardens but they prefer to keep it real. It's not too trendy, it's tatty enough to feel homely, and the people here are just here to work, not parade about having a lifestyle and posing.'

Talking with Lulu made me appreciate how instrumental the Zeloof Partnership has been in stopping corporate giants like Tesco and Pret A Manger muscling into Brick Lane from the City. The Zeloofs have refused constant offers from the big chains wanting units in Dray Walk. 'They'd obviously pay a lot more money,' said Lulu, 'but it's not what the Zeloofs are interested in. They'd rather give the opportunity to some enterprising new business, like the guy who makes homemade thai noodles.' They have determinedly kept the site intact after lucrative offers to sell parts off and turn them into multistorey car parks and offices. 'Ofer is passionate

Ethnicity here has become a come-on, an opportunity for real-estate speculators to follow the mullets and make a killing catering to the area's latest flotsam and jetsam: students, designers, new media artists, sojourners from Hoxton and Shoreditch seeking the messiness that existing residents would love to escape ('Arrive Hungry, Leave Edgy' reads a sign in the window of one hipster café). For them it's a place to be seen in as much as to live in. They're looking for 'spaces' rather than homes. They pay for 12p bagels with £20 notes and are nowhere to be found at bank holidays or Christmas.

Sukhdev Sandhu, 'Come Hungry, Leave Edgy', *London Review of Books*, 9 October 2003 about the place,' said Lulu. 'He enjoys seeing young, talented, creative people do well.' There is no doubt the brewery complex encourages and supports this and there have been many success stories, particularly among music people, such as Talvin Singh and Groove Rider, a big drum-and-bass producer and DJ, and fashion designers, such as Giles Deacon. The redevelopment of the brewery is largely responsible for Brick Lane's status as the new Mecca for aspiring fashion designers and internet entrepreneurs, and Lulu has played a huge role in this process.

In 2000 Lulu started up Fashion East, one of the brewery's charitable in-house projects, which supports emerging British designers. Another project is Free Range, which sponsors and promotes exhibitions by art and design colleges and universities at the brewery. With these projects the Zeloofs are carrying on the traditions of the former brewery owners, who carried out much philanthropic work in the local community. In 1666, according to *Truman's the Brewers, 1666–1966*, the brewery supplied the firefighters of the Great Fire with beer. In 1816, when many Spitalfields weavers were starving through lack of work, Thomas Buxton helped raise money for them. He also supported the Spitalfields Soup Society, which fed over six thousand people, and helped his mainly illiterate workers by starting a school at the brewery. In the early nineteenth century the brewery equipped the British army with weapons against Napoleon, and during the Second World War Truman's donated a Spitfire to the RAF. It crashed in 1942, was repaired but then subsequently lost on operations later that year. In the Truman boardroom there was a plaque from the Air Ministry thanking the brewery for the plane.

Over the centuries Truman's has supported projects in local schools and at times paid the salary for a curate at Christ Church. Now the brewery helps emerging fashion designers and aspiring artists, reflecting the new community that has developed in the area, particularly during the last ten years with the Free Range and Fashion East ventures. I spoke with a nineteen-year-old contributor to Free Range last year, Poonam from West London, who was

showing her graduate graphic-design show in part of the brewery. She told me she loves being in Brick Lane because it has become the creative hub of London. The day I met her she had just seen the chef Gordon Ramsay in the car park of the building behind her and various other celebrities coming in and out of the large marquee where they were filming the reality television show *Hell's Kitchen*. Earlier on in the year the building next door had housed the controversial 'Bodyworlds' exhibition of plasticated human bodies, which had nearly eight hundred and fifty thousand visitors.

'Brick Lane is really chilled out and down to earth,' said Poonam, 'although it is becoming touristy and pricey.' Poonam first came to the street years ago to have a curry with her Hindu parents. She said they liked Brick Lane because it reminded them of India, with everyone out on the pavement. Poonam doesn't really visit what she calls 'the ethnic end of the street' nowadays; she comes here instead to 'go to the vintage shops, chill, have drinks with friends, hang out on comfortable sofas at 93 Feet East and see live music'. Later I went with Poonam to have a drink in the courtyard of the Vibe Bar. By six-thirty the place was filled with the new brewery workers, a mainly white crowd carefully dressed down in retro gear, busily texting friends and sipping designer beers shipped in from Germany, Mexico and Holland. The bar is in what used to be the old brewmaster's house, and is decorated inside with a garish graffiti mural and filled with battered leather sofas, PlayStation monitors and computers with internet access.

I noticed an elderly Bangladeshi man with a white beard, skullcap and *shalwar kameez* walk past on the other side of the railing. He didn't look at the crowd beside him but focused straight ahead. It was only when a glass broke that he turned briefly for an instant, wincing and adjusting his cap before walking swiftly past, probably on his way for early-evening prayers at the mosque.

There seems to be minimal contact between these two communities. I began to wonder how the old brewery workers had mixed with the former Jewish community of Brick Lane. The only person I knew who had worked at Truman's when it was a functioning brewery was Iain Sinclair, so I called him up to arrange a meeting to talk specifically about his time at the Brick Lane brewery site.

II

A Land of Beer and Blood

The site of the brewery has more of an appearance of a town
itself than of a manufacturing establishment. There are sixty-
five coopers in the cooperage, a wheelwright's shop, a farrier's
shop, a carpenter's shop, one hundred and thirty horses in the
stables, a painter's shop for all the pub signs and at the heart of
the plant is the gigantic steam engine.
                    Truman's the Brewers, 1666–1966

Iain Sinclair is well known now for his pyschogeographic explorations
around East London. His journeys into this territory began when
he was a child living in South Wales, listening to his father's stories
– tales of Bud Flanagan, Jack the Ripper, Middlesex Street and Brick
Lane Market. His father collected books about the area, which Iain
devoured: 'The stories were exotic and Gothic to me,' he said, 'and
the place seemed to be everything that respectable Wales wasn't.'
In 1951, when Iain was eight, the Sinclairs came to London for the
Festival of Britain and Iain's father took him to Victoria Palace to see
the Crazy Gang. The momentum and the fast patter, the characters and
the dancing girls, it all fascinated him. The following day the family
went to Petticoat Lane Market: 'A place filled with fast-talking *spielers*
and astonishing bargains,' said Iain. 'My mother bought some nylon
stockings, which were still hard to come by just after the war, and my
father bought a watch. When we returned to the hotel we found the
stockings had no feet and the watch didn't work but we didn't care
– the experience of the market had been unforgettable.'

After finishing a degree in Dublin in 1966, Iain returned to
London, where he had previously been a film student. After a number

of temporary perches he settled in Hackney and began exploring the local area on foot. 'The minute I entered Brick Lane and Whitechapel, those places became the centre of my creative exploration,' he said. His first impressions of Brick Lane were 'of going under the railway arch and the smoke coming out of the chimney of the brewery, the little Jewish businesses dotted along the street and the Whitechapel Gallery at the other end'. The Jewish presence in Brick Lane wasn't strong then but still visible. He remembers Katz's string shop and 'all these bundles of twine', and 'Hasidic businessmen in the back of clothes and material shops. There was no direct engagement with them, the only time our paths crossed was in the Sunday morning market.' He recalled seeing a few Indian restaurants, including the Nazrul, who catered almost exclusively for Bangladeshi men at the time. Most white working-class people in the area were not eating curry then. 'There were no tourists,' said Iain, 'and Bangladeshi women were not seen on the street. If a white woman walked into one of those cafés she would be presumed to be a prostitute. There were many in the area then, mostly hanging around vans outside Spitalfields Market.'

Iain sometimes ate in the Nazrul with his friend the artist Brian Catling: 'A certain number of non-Asian men would be tolerated but it was unusual,' said Iain. Catling was living in Heneage Street then, just off Brick Lane, above the old synagogue where Rodinsky was once seen at a Kiddush speaking fluent Arabic. Catling later moved to Oxford and wrote *The Stumbling Block*, which Iain describes as 'his best book, about being in that space in Whitechapel, an intense distillation of visions and dreams'. Territory was a joint obsession for Catling and Sinclair, and Whitechapel was the heartland of their imaginations.

Catling, who worked on and off for the brewery, helped Iain get the job at Truman's, and he started working there in 1972, primarily because it was well paid and he had a young family to support. 'Brian fitted in invisibly,' said Iain. 'He had grown up with all of his uncles being geezers working under arches, so his private part that wrote poetry and did sculpture and was interested in obscure things was much more disguised than mine. His voice and stature were right, he fitted in.' For Iain, with his received English and perfect manners, it took longer. 'In the beginning the workers would play tricks on me,' he said, 'but if you responded well you were accepted. I was just assumed to be a student slumming for a time.'

His interview for the job included a medical during which his arms where checked for track marks. 'It was like being interviewed for some Secret Service job in these wood-panelled rooms that looked like an Oxford College,' said Iain. 'Once I was in, I was able to return several times, for periods of three or four months, starting in September or October, until I'd saved enough money to do some writing.' The core of the workforce in the brewery, the old-timers who'd been there for thirty or forty years, had an incredible knowledge of the geography of the area, which they shared with Sinclair. They took him on to the rooftops of the various buildings and told stories about 'bombs falling and buses being upturned – their vision of the East End was filled with these images'. One of the stories Iain remembers well was about the Jewish burial ground behind Durward Street in Whitechapel. A brewery worker who had been a firewatcher during the Blitz saw a bomb land in the burial ground one misty morning. When he opened the gates he was stunned because it looked as though there was a gathering of prophetic elders sitting on the roof of the building at the end of the grounds. The bomb had blown people out of their graves and their body parts had scattered everywhere. Sinclair heard the story told hundreds of times. It was the workers' set piece.

He described the other main group of men who worked at the brewery as 'younger and pushier and mostly living out in Essex. They had flash motors and boasted of their connections with the Krays.' Iain does not remember ever seeing any Jewish workers in the brewery. There were a few women who worked there but only in the bottling shed. 'They were quite rough and ready and would give you a hard time when you went in there.' Sinclair felt the brewery was split into different zones. 'Some were full of machinery and entirely male, like the ullage cellars, and others were exclusively for women, such as the place where the labels were stuck on bottles. The two for the most part were kept entirely separate although there were sparky relations between them when they met. The women were just as tough as the men, if not more so, and would take the piss out of you outrageously if you strayed into their territory. At the same time, when they went out into Brick Lane on payday, men and women would merge together in the betting shops or in the pubs like the Seven Stars, which had strippers.'

Iain remembered an incident one afternoon when 'some of the guys who worked in the brewery picked up a prostitute and brought her back into the building and gave her a tour, but it turned sour because they were drunk and made advances towards her. She got angry because she wasn't doing that then, she was a human being having a tour of the building, and her head was bashed against the pump and there was blood and horror and screaming. It was terrible when these two worlds tried to cross.'

Sinclair's working day started at seven-thirty in the morning with the gruelling physical task of unloading lorries. 'Then there would be a sponsored breakfast in the canteen,' he said, 'and the rest of the day was pretty much yours apart from a few hours in the early evening spent cleaning the hoppers.' In his free time he'd explore the vast underground labyrinthine network of cellars in the brewery, which he thought of as a magical surreal landscape: 'I'd come across huge secret spaces and often get lost.'

There was a free bar in the brewery and 'the whole place seemed to be drunk the entire time'. When Iain came into work there would be a pewter jug filled with two pints waiting for him. Unable to face it at that time in the morning he gave his away. 'Those old boys would drink their pints straight off,' said Iain, 'and then have another with their breakfast and then fall into the free bar in the afternoon and just carry on drinking all day until they fell asleep in their hammocks, which were slung up in the cold store. The drivers would come back with lorries full of beer and then go into the bar and drink pints and pints of Guinness for two or three hours, before getting back into the lorries and driving off again. It seems unbelievable now.'

When I spoke with Iain he had just finished reading *The Italian*

The frontage of the brewery stretched along
Brick Lane and related to Christ Church
because of the round portal windows, as if it
was its own cathedral of Commerce, with this
heady smell. It spread for miles at the back, and
it certainly was the dominating presence on the
street, which at that time was a working place
rather than a tourist area.

Iain Sinclair, 2005

Boy: Murder and Grave-robbery in 1830s London by Sarah Wise, which describes the area when the Resurrectionists were digging up bodies and selling them to hospitals. 'At that time the whole of London seemed to be drunk,' said Iain, 'and the city became a hallucination. It was normal for twelve-year-old children to be drinking then, and they became victim to gangs who'd slip laudanum into their pint of stout. When they fell asleep the murderers would pick up the sleeping children and drown them, and their bodies were slung into the back of a cart and sold to hospitals. The porters receiving the bodies were invariably drunk, as were the doctors and surgeons on grand wines.' Iain thought these stories started to make sense of the Ripper murders, such criminality being better understood perhaps when viewed taking place against the backdrop of a drunken city. In the brewery in the 1970s, 'Everybody was slightly pissed, imagining places beyond the cellars filled with crocodiles or Egyptian gods, and thinking they might be real because they were too drunk to know the difference.'

What fascinated Sinclair as a writer and an artist was a sense of the brewery as a time warp. 'It had an atmosphere of a bygone age,' he said, 'and was filled with cobbled yards, horses out the back, and elderly men who talked to you as if it was still 1945. It seemed as close to Victorian and Edwardian London as you could get.' This was a view I found echoed by many other ex-employees of Truman's.

I spent several fruitless months trying to track down other people who had worked at the brewery, eventually achieving success after placing a request in two brewery pensioner magazines. The response was overwhelming, with over fifty phone calls from people wanting to share their memories. Most of them spoke with BBC accents and separated themselves distinctly from the manual workers at the brewery, calling themselves the 'staff'. They all described Truman's as an antiquated family business.

The firm operated in 'a period gone by', said Rodger Priddle, now seventy-six, who had joined Truman's in 1961 as a building surveyor. 'The directors were all gentlemen from Harrow or Eton,' he said, 'and many of the senior staff were majors, squadron leaders or

Truman's was one of the finest places you could work for. It was hard work but every day was a laugh-and-joke day. You had a beer cupboard on the loading bank and you could go and pour out a half-pint whenever you wanted it and officially each man in the brewery was allowed two free pints a day but in reality we could help ourselves, and if the barrel run dry, as long as the foreman wasn't watching, another would go up in its place.

Jim Tyler, 2004

commanders.' He described the brewery as a typically British institution. The canteen facilities were segregated, and senior managers had a separate and exclusive Luncheon Club with an expensive joining fee and waitress service. On his first day at work Mr Priddle was told he was 'not properly dressed to be representing the company' and was sent to Dunns Gentleman's Outfitters in Bishopsgate to buy a new raincoat, bowler hat and a rolled umbrella.

Mr Priddle was in charge of properties and pubs belonging to the brewery in the 'western area'. He collected cash for beer sold in a briefcase, which he carried with him. 'Occasionally Mr Jolly, the company's chauffeur, would take me out in the Roller with the number plate XX1666,' he said, 'but most of the time I walked.' The company gave him 'boot money' for the repair of worn-out shoes. 'Truman's had a number of antiquated annual ceremonies,' he said, 'such as Carpet Day, where managerial staff had to appear in the boardroom and the directors would announce their increase in salary for the coming year. Old habits die hard in the brewing industry. Another tradition was when a new vat was erected it would be christened like a ship, with a bottle of champagne followed by a meal for the staff. In 1966 the company put on magnificent celebratory dinners to commemorate three hundred years of business at Brick Lane.'

His contact with the manual workers was minimal. 'The facilities were not large enough for everyone to meet together,' he said. 'Senior staff met in the sample room, and the draymen and other workers had breaks in the blowroom.' The only people he got to know at the brewery who actually lived in East London were two elderly East End wide boys who controlled reception and 'could get you anything you wanted'.

The street itself he remembers as a place 'packed with vehicles. There was a constant jam from the early morning till late at night and Brick Lane stunk to high heaven, a strong yeasty smell from the ancient works at the brewery. There were lots of second-hand clothes and wardrobe shops and quite a few Indians around. The top half was narrow and filled with local barrow boys loading up their produce and selling fruit or shellfish. They constantly blocked the street up for the lorries from the brewery and there was always lots of shouting about this.'

Another of the many ex-employees of Truman's I spoke to was Brian Hanks, who started working there in 1967 as a chartered accountant for Watney. When he was relocated to Brick Lane from Hammersmith some of his staff refused to come with him because the area had such a bad reputation. Brian thought Brick Lane 'was a dirty run-down old junk of a place, unhealthy-looking, rat-infested and smelling of decay'. His office inside the brewery was in the newly designed part of the building and in contrast to the street was 'brand new, resplendent and open plan'. There were over two thousand people working on the site in the late 1960s, 'With all the shift people and draymen, it was like its own small town,' said Brian.

Mr Hanks felt the brewery attracted the most extraordinary characters. 'Like these old boys who used to talk about driving up the Great North Road in solid-tyred steam lorries with a candle alight on the side.' He told me a story about the head brewer who always wore a bowler hat. 'He went on holiday once and left his hat hung on a hook on the wall and the room was decorated. For a joke the painter whitewashed the hat, which was left like that on the wall for years.' Another person he remembered was Harry Jones, a gregarious character who gave brewery tours to various groups and societies, 'which always ended up in the sample room where everyone would get smashed'.

A few weeks after speaking to Mr Hanks I received a letter from a man called John Kelly who had been employed at Truman's his entire working life. I telephoned and spoke at first to his wife, Betty, who told me her own memories of Brick Lane: 'When we got married in 1946 a Jewish shop there called Kominsky's made us a bedroom utility suite,' she said. 'He did it special after the war. Another place I remember was the evening-dress shop Goldstein's – John gardened for him at the weekends. Of course, the main thing about Brick Lane was the brewery. John started there in 1935 and retired in 1978. I remember taking our daughters to Truman's in the school holidays to meet their dad and see the beautiful shire horses. I remember the

massive vats of beer with the foam on top and how the brass shone, and also going to the cooperage to see the barrels being made. The firm was great with the children: there were Christmas parties, cricket matches and sports days, all sorts over the years, with sandwiches, cake, tea and beer all laid on by the brewery.'

Over the next few weeks I telephoned and spoke with Mr Kelly a number of times about his memories of Truman's brewery. We couldn't talk for long periods as he is suffering from lung cancer and finds it hard to speak at length. 'I'm eighty-five now,' he told me, 'and I was fifteen when I started at Truman's. Back then it was such a busy place, everything was delivered by horse and cart, and the smell of horses, and the noise of their hoofs on the cobbles, was constant. Dray Walk was where the barrels were washed. They were all oak barrels then. The sniffers worked there, checking the barrels before they were filled up, smelling them, making sure there was no contamination. The bottling plant was opposite, with the vats in the middle. Inside the gate was an old fig tree in a lead cistern that had been there for hundreds of years, and real artesian wells, natural springs, and in the courtyard they kept a live black eagle before the war.'

John Kelly grew up in East London, like most of the brewery workers. On his first day at work he was offered any manual job he

Walking into the offices at Truman's was like stepping back into the seventeenth century. There was a patina of age around the place, with highly polished banisters, a huge marble staircase and antique-looking furniture. It was like a run-down stately home. Downstairs in the counting room were high wooden Victorian desks that the accountants worked on, with places for old inkwells. Nothing was thrown away and it gradually got shipped out to various pubs to be used for decoration.

John Ewing, 2004

wanted because his father had worked there for twenty-eight years as a drayman. After a few months of trying out different jobs he started driving a horse and cart carrying barrels of beer round to the pubs. 'I'd never worked with horses before,' he said, 'they were huge shire horses called Clydesdales, all muscle, with tremendous power and about six foot tall. There was a whole team of people employed to look after them: stable hands and farriers who made the horseshoes.' He left Brick Lane in 1939 and spent six years in the armed forces, stationed all over the world. In 1945 he returned to work at the brewery. 'Truman's continued to operate throughout the war,' he said, 'and was not badly affected by the Blitz.' Motorized vehicles made most of the deliveries from Truman's after the war. Fortunately for Mr Kelly he had learned to drive in the army so he still had a job. 'I missed the horses though,' he told me, 'but I enjoyed the independence of my job. Once the lorry was loaded and you left the brewery you were your own governor.' He was out on the road most of the time, delivering to pubs and off licences as far out as Southend in Essex. 'It was just an old-fashioned brewery,' he said. 'To keep your job you had to work hard. It was a good local employer but the money wasn't excellent. I worked there for forty-three years.' He was made redundant in 1978 and said he was glad to leave, because 'the firm wasn't the same by then. There was no party or anything, just a handshake. That was it.'

Another of the old-timers I spoke to was Jim Tyler, now eighty-eight years old, who started working at Truman's in 1946. 'I was demobbed after the war and couldn't get work,' he said. 'My dad used to go to a Truman's pub and two of his mates there worked in the brewery. They managed to get me a job by pretending I was their cousin as the policy then was to only take on blood relations.' He started off working down the cellars, which was back-breaking work 'in underground tunnels with long railway lines along the floor leading to the racking room. In the racking room they'd fill the barrels up, put the bung in them and roll them down these lines, and us chaps put them wherever they had to be stowed before going out to trade.' After working there for six weeks Jim asked one of the

older men how long he'd have to wait before going up to transport. 'I don't want to frighten you, boy,' he replied, 'but I have had my name down for transport for twenty-five years.' Jim went to see the foreman and handed in his notice. Not wanting to lose him, the foreman went round the cellars and asked if there were any objections to Jim working on the loading bay. Luckily for him nobody minded, and he started work as an extra hand on the lorries.

'The beer would come up from the cellar in casks,' he said, 'by a big rotating machine with two iron fingers that lifted then rolled the casks on to the loading bank upstairs. In them days we had horse drays and hand lorries and the crews of the various vehicles used to get their delivery note and load up accordingly. There were normally two horses pulling a dray, with a drayman to drive, a trouncer to unload the kegs, and a boy. I was sent out with them for a couple of weeks as the boy, to learn how to strike the beer off the lorry. It was an art. You'd rope the cask up and lower it down into the cellar. We had a couple of coopers up on the loading bank who'd go around tightening the casks to stop them leaking. One day, the foreman, Bill Allcock, called me over and said, "Buddy," to him everyone was "buddy", "go out with old Bill Gibbs there and he'll teach you how to shire up a pair of horses." I told him I knew nothing about horses and the reply was, "You bloody soon will do if you go out with him, won't ya?"'

Jim became so skilled with horses he ended up driving his own team and over the years he got very attached to them. 'When I first went out they were Suffolk punches,' he said, 'beautiful, but swines to drive. They were bullet-headed but bright and knew where the pubs were. Some of those old shires even knew when the traffic lights was all right to go by, but they hated zebra crossings. If they trod on the white bit they'd slide down so we had to steer them round them. Nearly all the old team-drivers were from Norfolk and Suffolk – big old boys they was, the most powerful men you ever seen. There was a few who came down from a hunger march up north but most of the workers were from Bethnal Green and Stepney, like me.'

Like Mr Kelly, much of Jim's time was spent delivering. 'The best pubs were run by the Jews,' he said, 'because they'd give you half a crown, the others only gave a shilling.' When he first arrived in Brick Lane it was 99 per cent Jewish: 'All the street doors had them things they used to rub their fingers with,' he said. During the thirty-seven years Mr Tyler worked in Brick Lane he never once entered a Jewish or Bengali shop or café. Most of the time he would have his sandwiches in the brewery canteen, occasionally venturing out to one of the three Truman-owned pubs on Brick

Lane, the Frying Pan, the Two Brewers or the Jolly Butchers, for a glass of beer. He told me a strange story about what he called the 'invasion of the Bangladeshis'. 'It was 1956,' he said, 'and we were coming back to Brick Lane from the fishing club, the brewery used to provide us with a coach once a month to go fishing. When we arrived at the brewery you could not see any pavement at all. There was all these Asian geezers on their blankets going to sleep.'

Mr Tyler retired in 1983 after Grand Metropolitan took over. 'They were asset-strippers,' he said, 'who kept flogging bits off.' During his working life he went from floor sweeper, to driving his own team of drays, then to senior foreman and eventually to depot supervisor in charge of all the men in transport and the warehouse. Every year he goes to a pensioners' reunion, 'to have a few drinks and hear a few yarns'. Last year one of his friends suggested he visit the brewery. 'I couldn't do that,' he said, 'it would break my heart to see what it has become, because I really loved working there. Such comradeship, free beer, we used to have such a laugh. I couldn't bear to see it changed.'

12

Disappearances

Memory embedded in place involves more than simply any
one personal story. There are the wider and deeper narrative
currents that gather together all those who have ever lived there.
Each person effectively reshapes the place by making his or her
story a thread in the meaning of the place and also has to come
to terms with the many layers of the story that already exist in a
given location.

Philip Sheldrake, *Spaces for the Sacred:*
Place, Memory and Identity

I recently met my friend the photographer Daniele Lamarche at
the 1001 Café in Dray Walk. As I walked towards Brick Lane from
Liverpool Street tube station to meet her, I noticed crowds of City
workers in dark suits heading in the same direction, probably going
for lunch in one of the curry restaurants. It was a hot day and the
pavements of Brick Lane were heaving. Roadworks along the length
of the street had slowed the traffic; drivers were leaning out of car
windows, banging on their horns, shouting impatiently at the vehicles in front. A van filled with frozen carcasses pulled up outside
Taj Stores, men in blood-stained white overalls appeared from the
dark interior, hauling headless animals on to their shoulders and
staggering into the back of the shop. A group of American tourists
gathered on the corner of Hanbury Street and Brick Lane, trying to
listen to the gruesome narration of their Ripper Tour guide, who
was shouting to be heard above the noise of the traffic. The touts
crowded around them, smiling and gesticulating, pointing inside
their restaurants, promising the best curry in Brick Lane.

As I approached Dray Walk the smell of exhaust fumes and rubbish was masked by the strong aroma of burgers and kebabs frying on hot coals outside the 1001 Café. Turning off Brick Lane and into Dray Walk, I was reminded of summer festivals I had been to as a student. The pedestrianized narrow walkway was packed with young people, smoking and drinking, sitting in the shade, laughing and chatting loudly around rows of wooden tables. Bassy music pumped out of the bars and the whole scene was slightly obscured by the thick smoke coming off the outdoor barbecues. I found Daniele sitting inside the café on the ground floor with her young son, Theo.

Daniele and Theo live in a council estate near Brick Lane, and Theo's world is truly a multicultural one. Coffee shops, art galleries and organic markets are not the only local spaces he spends time in, unlike many white kids living in the area. Every weekday Theo attends a crèche in Brick Lane housed in a Bengali women's centre, and in January he will start at Christ Church Primary School on Brick Lane. Theo will be one of two white children in a class of thirty. Daniele has some concerns about the lack of cultural diversity at the school, but Bengali customs and culture are not unfamiliar to her. She has lived in Bengali households and spent years as the only white worker on various youth and racial-harassment teams. She has also taken an interest in the history of Bengali immigration to the area and recently initiated research for a new leaflet (later taken on by the London Borough of Tower Hamlets) to guide tourists around the Bengali East End. I remember her telling me about the history of Café Naz at no. 46 Brick Lane: 'It used to be the site of the old Mayfair Cinema,' she said, 'and in the 1960s it became the Naz Cinema, showing Asian films.' The 1999 nail bomb planted by neo-nazi David Copeland exploded outside the Naz; Daniele had been sitting inside the café just before the explosion. 'It was too hot to stay indoors,' she told me, 'so I walked up Brick Lane to the bagel shop and missed the blast by less than five minutes.' Daniele's stories are littered with such fragments of local history, and her vast archive of images of the area and the people who have lived there document the changing face of the street.

Daniele's father worked as an international banker and her childhood was spent on the move; she lived in San Francisco, Paris, Argentina and Panama before arriving in London in 1980 to study. She moved around the city for a while – a squat in Dalston, a bedsit in South Kensington, a flat in Whitechapel – before ending up in Brick Lane in 1981. 'I never intended to stay in London,' she said, 'but something kept me in Brick Lane. It is everyone's and no one's domain; a place that transcends cultures, which gives me a sense of belonging.'

Daniele hauled her laptop out of her bag at the 1001 Café and turned it on. The desktop filled with hundreds of Jpeg files – a small selection of her extensive photo-documentary archive. All around us people were conducting business meetings around their computers. Theo was the only child in the room. 'This was an interesting group of friends,' she said, pointing at a picture of some Asian men and women singing in a small room. 'When I first moved here I lived with a Kurdish refugee and an Iranian woman. It was the time of the Iran–Iraq War and there were many meetings in the flat, people got upset after hearing dreadful news from home about beheadings, as well as other stories of amazing courage too. Lots of Bengali activists used to stop by. People came to talk about local politics, to gossip, to ask for help with writing speeches and funding applications; this is how I was initiated into life in East London. We'd sit around this long table in a tiny room, eating, singing and arguing for hours.'

She made friends easily with many people from different migrant communities who lived near Brick Lane. 'I grew up in so many different places,' she said, 'it was natural for me to walk into new environments and cultures. Say, for example, the *burka*, I never felt threatened by that so I'd approach women wearing it in ways most white people wouldn't, and this attitude made me quickly accepted.' Her own identity often confuses people – her accent is hard to trace and she is sometimes mistaken for being Jewish or Iranian. 'Some of the Bengali men I met made assumptions about me,' she said. 'My local shop was Taj Stores on Brick Lane and I used to exchange hellos with an old man who worked at the till. Sometimes I went into the shop with different people, some of whom were male. One day this man winked at me and said, "No friend today?" It suddenly dawned on me he thought I was a prostitute, as few white women regularly seen on the street at that time weren't.'

Daniele described Brick Lane in the early 1980s as a place filled with class divides. 'I hadn't seen that in other cities in Europe,' she said. 'It was very marked because of the way people spoke. It was a place filled with racism and sexism in a city I had presumed had a progressive culture.' Whether someone had a cockney or a Bengali accent made no difference to Daniele. She couldn't recognize the subtleties in the language, not having grown up in the area, and treated everyone the same, regardless of race, religion or any other agenda. Others accepted her because she was also a foreigner with an accent.

In Brick Lane she found the inspiration for decades' worth of images: Bengali women, gypsy children, homeless people, market traders, Jewish shopkeepers, eccentrics, artists, bohemians, elderly people – all the characters that have crossed over into Daniele's world while she has been living there. She showed me some of the pictures she took when she worked for Race and Housing at Tower Hamlets Council from 1982 to 1986, researching the housing needs of Bengali, Somalian and Vietnamese people. This was a time when racial harassment and violence still dominated the lives of many people, particularly in the Bengali community.

'I went to estates all over the borough,' she said, 'and witnessed why many needed to be moved. As well as seeing severe overcrowding and terrible living conditions, I met families who'd been bombed in

their homes. Many of the worst housing estates were in the Brick
Lane area, but people still wanted to stay there because families
living further east were more isolated from their community and
they suffered the most. I knew a Bengali family who regularly called
the team I was working with. We'd pick up the phone and hear a
terrified voice saying, "There's twenty of them and the police aren't
coming, please help us," and I remember looking around and saying
what are we supposed to do, two women and two men against a gang
of skinheads, but we always went. Usually by the time we arrived
they'd gone but more than anything the families just needed to know
someone cared, someone was coming.' There were repercussions for
Daniele – cracks on the head, threats and verbal abuse.

For many years she had a neighbour in her block of flats who
beat up his girlfriends. She told me about one particularly horrifying
incident when he dragged a pregnant woman by the hair down three
flights of stairs. 'There were over fourteen people watching this doing
nothing,' said Daniele angrily. 'I was the only person who actively
confronted him.' When in the company of Bengali friends Daniele
experienced harassment first hand and was frequently stopped and
searched by police and threatened with arrest. Her car was smashed
up and she was spat at when walking down Brick Lane. 'It was an
interesting position to be in as a white woman, being able to walk
in and out of this community and to get some sense of what they
were experiencing on a daily basis.' People in Bengali and other
communities began to trust Daniele to take pictures of sensitive
issues, a rat infestation, racist graffiti and the evidence of attacks.

She showed me pictures of elderly people, dilapidated shops,
kosher butchers and wine merchants. A series of her photographs
shows the interior of a derelict synagogue in Cheshire Street that
had been squatted by an old rag-and-bone man she knew who kept
hundreds of cats. 'One of the developers had him in court every
week,' she said. 'He stood his ground but of course eventually they
got in, sanitized the whole place, built luxury flats, and another
piece of history was gone. That has been the constant pervading
factor over the last few years – watching whole streets being pulled

down, watching all these people disappear. What really attracted me to Brick Lane was all those hidden places – the warehouses, the animals in people's yards, the studios – and a lot of that has gone along with many of the characters who made the place unique, like him,' she said, pointing to the screen where an image of a man in a wide-brimmed turquoise hat and matching velvet suit had appeared. 'His name was Bangra Raj,' she told me, 'which translates as the "King of Bengal". He was originally a merchant seaman, with a flair for eccentric clothes. He always managed to get into pictures with dignitaries visiting East London, from Prince Charles to Oona King. He also hung around cafés and community centres in Brick Lane. He used to go about talking with people, distributing information, exchanging gossip or managing his imaginary government in exile composed of real people who he regularly appointed and sacked. He could have been sectioned and shut away but he was tolerated and appreciated locally and he had a role to play as a key promoter of local festivals and events.'

Another collection of photographs records the years she spent

working at Spitalfields City Farm. The farm was a tough environment in the 1980s, with alcoholics, junkies, travellers, homeless people and young Bengali kids regularly visiting. Daniele was threatened repeatedly there for sticking up for the 'pakis', and nasty situations occurred with young, violent kids. 'The first year I was working there they slashed twelve tyres on my car and broke three windscreens,' she said. 'One time a boy actually came and apologized: "Really sorry, miss, I didn't mean to hit your car with the brick, I meant to get the girl." I've been threatened on a number of occasions when all the men around have hidden, but if you don't stand up to it or you cower then it only gets worse.' She showed me a photograph of the former head horseman at Truman's called Pinto, who kept the farm supplied with cartwheels, horse tackle and local Maltese gossip. 'He told me about the horses they used to race early on Sundays on the M11 when the ground was wet elsewhere. The horses were kept to the highway lanes by trucks driving slowly behind them.'

Some of her fondest memories are of the traveller children. 'The farm was one of the few places they were welcome,' she said. 'There were signs up all over then saying "No Travellers", like at the Café@ at the corner of Brick Lane and Buxton Street, which used to be a pub.' Daniele spent time making friends with the children, meeting the traveller women and listening to their fears about the authorities taking their children away if they put them into school.

As we sat talking stories overlapped stories: tales of drunken Glaswegians, prison-hardened people and local bully boys. Some of the images of young people who had died from drug-related issues were hard for her to look at. 'The people I met there were extraordinary,' she said, 'an incredible cross-section of ages, races and characters. Spitalfields Farm was a truly unique environment because it was a culturally neutral place for pensioners, policemen and hooligans alike.'

The farm has been running for over twenty years and is embedded into the memories of many people I have spoken to. Situated minutes away from all the noise and cosmopolitan energy of Brick Lane, it is a rural oasis in the middle of the City, a place that transports you out of London with ducks and chickens roaming around and cobbled streets strewn with straw. The noise of traffic disappears and is replaced with birdsong and the sounds of cows mooing and donkeys braying. The violence of the past has subsided and the farm's website is now filled with positive reviews and smiling faces of visiting local schoolchildren. A few years ago an urgent newsflash was added to the homepage stating that the new East London Line extension will be coming right through the middle of the farm. Transport for London now have possession of the land but thankfully the farm will not be displaced, as originally planned. After much negotiating and local protest the

farm has been allowed to remain on the site, although the boundary has shifted and there has been a loss of some of the farm's land. In the summer the fields beside the farm are used to host the Baishaki Mela, the Bengali New Year Festival. Major acts from Bangladesh play on the main stage and thousands of local people crowd into the only sizeable patch of green space near Brick Lane to see their favourite bands playing live on their doorstep.

These fields and the farm are vital parts of the communal landscape for the residents of Brick Lane. Daniele and I sat and talked about other community spaces that have recently disappeared from the area. 'It's not just the buildings,' she said, 'it's the people who are moving away in droves. It seems a whole community of artists, writers and characters who added another alternative layer to Brick Lane has disappeared in the last few years. The world they came to interact with is changing and disappearing. You just don't see those kinds of characters here any more,' she added, showing me a picture of a wild-looking man with long hair standing in the middle of a street with his palm outstretched. 'He was a Sri Lankan homoeopath who came to Brick Lane in the late 1960s and used to treat local

Bangladeshi men. I got to know him and we'd stop on the street and talk. One day he'd just gone. One of the last things he said to a friend was, "If you look in someone's eyes and the irises touch the bottom of the lids you know they are going to die." She looked at his eyes and this is how it was and it was his way of telling her. When he died his Bengali acquaintances didn't know how to bury him because he was a Buddhist, so it fell to an Australian woman to empty his flat and find his family.'

Another eccentric character Daniele told me about was a man called Benjamin Crème, a Scottish mystic claiming to be in telepathic touch with higher beings, who began lecturing all over the world in the 1980s, saying the Brick Lane Asian community was harbouring the next messiah. He predicted that the new messiah would appear if all the world's media were watching. I found newspaper reports backing up her story. On 22 May 1982 Crème gathered about thirty journalists in a teashop on Brick Lane to witness the Second Coming. First, a Pakistani man entered, declaring himself as the messiah, but Crème dismissed him. The Sri Lankan homoeopath also went to join the debate, wondering if the holy man could indeed be himself. Crème said he was too short. The Bengali community thought the whole thing was hilarious. According to Crème the messiah had not appeared that day because not enough of the networks had got involved. Five years later Crème claimed the messiah had materialized in Kenya dressed as Christ.

He said he'd known for thirty years that he was
the Maitreya. He'd been told by holy men back
in Sri Lanka but, at the time, hadn't understood
what they meant. After he had read one of
Benjamin Crème's press conferences, the
publicity for which he'd stumbled upon merely
by 'chance', Crème's pronouncements had
started him wondering – after all, he did work
in the Brick Lane area! But he had sat quiet for
two years and had become confident enough to
announce himself only when the press and all
the people had descended on the Lane that week
of May 22nd.

Timothy Wyllie, 'Whatever Happened to the Maitreya?', 1986

13

Heba

When the children were born and they learned English, life
was easier because they helped me. Brick Lane today is better,
tourists come and I see many different kinds of people. I would
never meet these kinds of people in Bangladesh.
                    Anonymous, Heba Women's Institute

It was time for Theo to go to crèche. Daniele invited me along with
them and we walked together out of Dray Walk, through the crowd
outside and on to Brick Lane, past the brewery, through a small
purple door near Eastside Bookshop and into the Heba Women's
Institute. I followed Daniele and Theo up a narrow staircase and
out on to a small enclosed roof terrace that had been converted
into a children's play area. Theo ran off to join his friends playing
around a red plastic sandpit. The tall brick chimney of Truman's
brewery cast a long shadow over the rooftop playground. Daniele
went to speak to Theo's nursery worker, a young Bengali woman
dressed in jeans, a white jacket and T-shirt with her long black
hair pulled back into a loose ponytail. She agreed to speak with
me about Brick Lane as long as she remained anonymous and I
didn't photograph her face.

Daniele went off to work and I sat down with N in the shade
and watched as Chinese, Algerian, Bengali, Somalian and English
children played happily together in the sun. 'It's what I love most
now about Brick Lane,' said N. 'The chance to meet all these
different cultures.' She offered me a cold drink and I watched her
walk into the nursery building and through to the small adjoining
kitchenette, and was surprised to see Derek Cox there, waving at

me through the window. When she returned N told me that Derek's office shared the kitchen with hers.

'Do you know him well?' I asked.

'All my life,' she told me. 'Most of the kids from round here know Derek. He's always been there for the Bengali people, writing letters, helping them fill in passport applications, taking the kids camping.'

N went on to tell me she had been born in Bangladesh and had been brought as a baby to London, to a flat in Hanbury Street, just off Brick Lane, by her parents. Her sister and three brothers were all born in London. She's been back to Bangladesh twice since then but feels more at home in Brick Lane. When we met she was very worried about the forthcoming move her parents were making to Ilford. 'Lots of families from round here are doing the same thing,' she said, 'because it's cheaper to live there. But I don't want to leave all my family and friends, and I worry about my mother, who speaks little English and has never had to mix with non-Bengali people before.' Her father was insisting on the move, as he didn't like the recent changes on the street and described Brick Lane as 'a business place, with estate agents everywhere and cafés and bars filled with alcohol'.

Her parents have always worried about her going out in Brick Lane. 'When I was a child they feared fascist attacks,' she said, 'which they had experienced directly. When the nail bomb happened they wouldn't let me out for months. They thought it was all starting again. I was scared because I heard all these awful stories from my father who was here in the 1970s. I came here in 1978, and it was still a scary place to be even then, but the worst thing that ever happened to me was having some stones thrown against a window while I was sitting in a restaurant in Brick Lane with my family.' As she got older her parents worried more about the gangs of Bengali youths who roamed the estates and the stories of muggings and drug abuse that followed them around. She thinks things are better now, 'with CCTV and more police and youth clubs and stuff to do', but thinks Brick Lane still has a bad reputation within other parts of the British Bengali community, in Manchester and Birmingham.

After decades of struggle N feels Brick Lane has finally become a good place to live and she is reluctant to move away. 'We have to go because it's too expensive to stay,' she said. 'We need more social housing so extended family can live near by but we are being forced out to Ilford and Manor Park. It seems so unfair – Brick Lane has even been renamed Banglatown and has become the central place for the community outside of Bangladesh, but the community it serves is moving, as it is too hard to live here with a big family.'

'Your parents must be finding it very hard to leave,' I said.

'In many ways, but in others they are ready,' she replied. 'There is so much of our culture here and we love the Mela, the music, the food, all the stars that come over from Bangladesh and the way the whole community joins in. But in the evening they don't feel safe with all the clubbing and stuff. My dad doesn't go to the Brick Lane mosque any more. He goes to the East London one because he finds it too threatening in Brick Lane at night. The elderly people here find all the drinking around the mosque very disrespectful.'

'Are your parents very observant Muslims?' I asked.

'When it comes to religion they are quite laid back, but again when I was younger everyone was into religion. If someone didn't wear a headscarf people used to talk, but now it's not a big deal any more.'

'Do they want you to have an arranged marriage?'

'No, they would not force it though if I do marry it must be to a Muslim man, but I'm still single at twenty-seven. I was encouraged into further education and completed a degree. I worked in the City for a while but hated it and then became a nursery nurse. I love my job now,' she said, smiling. The children obviously love N too and throughout the time we were talking one or other of them would run up and sit on her lap or play with her long hair.

'What else will you miss about Brick Lane if you move?'

'The mix of people here now,' she said. 'I worry if I go to Ilford I'll be in a Bangladeshi ghetto again. I went to Thomas Buxton School and that was all Bengali kids, and St Anne's next door was all white, we used to pass each other every day and never spoke. Now a lot of my friends are English and Somali, which is great but I do notice a lot of the children now can't write in Bengali. My younger brother can't write or read Bengali and that's happened in just ten years. I was fluent in Bengali and Arabic at his age but now there isn't the focus, and my brother doesn't see the need to learn it. He doesn't have such a strong Bengali identity as me. I communicate with my brothers and sisters in English and with my parents in Bengali.'

I followed N through into a small office on the other side of the playground, which overlooks Brick Lane. While N spoke to one of the office administrators I picked up a promotional leaflet for the Heba Women's Institute. I read that as well as the crèche the building housed a training and enterprise project for local women with courses in English, textile design, computer training, sewing and garment production. N came over to me with the office administrator, a Bengali woman in her early thirties called Shoma. 'I hope you write about Heba in your book,' she said. 'We are currently under threat of closure, all of our funding has been slashed and we don't know how long we can continue.' She told me Heba has been running for over twenty years and is the only place where local Muslim women can come and study, meet friends and learn new skills without the threat of intermingling the sexes, which is against their religion. 'Many of the women who come here were really isolated before,' said Shoma. 'Their husbands wouldn't let them go anywhere where they might meet men, but they let them go to Heba. A lot of ladies are sent here from social services with different problems and they really need this service. There are so few community spaces left, particularly on Brick Lane itself,' she said.

Just before we were about to start a tour of the building a woman wearing a green sari came into the room with a young child balanced on her hip. She stood shyly in the doorway until Shoma went over to her and led her gently by the elbow over to the desk, talking to her softly in Bengali the whole time. The woman kept pulling her headscarf further up on to her head, looking nervously around the room. Shoma sat her down and showed her some leaflets. They

spoke for another few minutes and I saw the woman in the green sari sign a few forms before leaving the room, smiling broadly. 'There's an example for you,' said Shoma, 'of why we must not close. That lady does not speak English and wants to learn and have somewhere for her child to go while she takes classes.'

Shoma took me down a narrow corridor where some women wearing long *burkas* were crowded around a tiny kitchen area, making tea. They nodded and smiled as we passed. At the end of the corridor was a door that opened up into a wide airy workshop filled with women sitting around large tables and sewing machines. Most of them were Bengali and they were nearly all dressed traditionally with their heads covered. Many were busily engaged in embroidering words relating to their everyday lives on to silk umbrellas for an exhibition at the Women's Library near by called 'What Women Want'. Their carefully stitched words mirrored the concerns of most contemporary women: diet, exercise, children, happiness. I spoke to a few of the women about what the centre meant to them, and they were unanimous in their support. 'There is such a strong and friendly community here, it's a very special place,' they said. 'We can't believe it is under threat.' That morning over eighty women who regularly attend the centre had turned up to protest at Heba's threatened closure to a visiting member of the council. 'There is Nowhere Else for Us to Go' read one placard in English and Bengali. 'This is our Second Home' read another.

One of the women, an older lady in a mauve *burka*, her teeth stained red from *paan*, who did not want to be named, said she'd talk with me if Shoma agreed to translate. The younger woman held the hand of the older throughout the interview and, with this support, the older woman managed to converse with me in English for over half an hour. She was extremely proud of this achievement and said she didn't think she had ever had such a long conversation in English since she moved to Brick Lane in 1984. After the interview the lady allowed me to photograph her hands, which, apart from her face, were the only parts of her body that were exposed.

Shoma gave the woman a hug before she returned to the sewing room. 'If her husband was still alive I don't think she would have

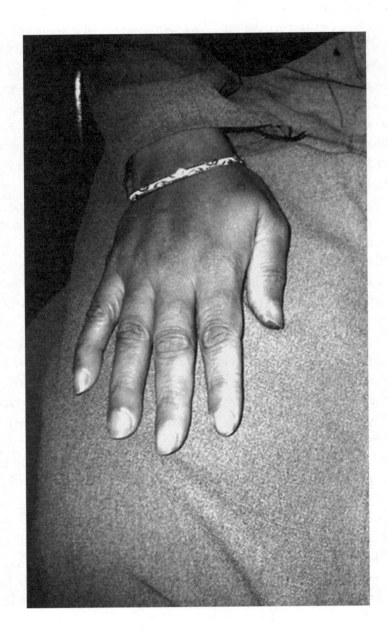

Since I came to this country I have lived in Brick Lane. When I first moved here everything was confusing and I was afraid. I didn't see women on the street, just men. I rarely went out. I was very homesick, very scared. I had an arranged marriage in Bangladesh then my husband moved here to look for work. Many years later he brought me over. It was so cold. Brick Lane was not nice, there was rubbish everywhere, and it was unclean, with people drinking alcohol on the street. I felt miserable because I couldn't speak English, if I went to the shops, the doctor, any place, the whole of life was difficult for me. There was no translator then and I could only go somewhere if I took my husband with me.

I am sad now because I want to go back to Bangladesh to visit my family but it is too expensive. I miss my parents very much. I haven't seen them for twenty years. My husband died two years ago, he used to work in the restaurants.

Anonymous, 2005

spoken with you,' said Shoma. 'She was the first student ever at Heba. She is very upset this place might go, this is were she learned her English.' Shoma related to the older lady's story, having moved to Brick Lane herself from Bangladesh at the age of twelve. 'I understood nothing at all for weeks,' she said, 'but I was not alone. There were always new girls coming from Bangladesh and we all helped each other out.'

Shoma now teaches English to a range of women who come to Heba, from older Bengali ladies to recent immigrants to the area from Somalia and Eastern Europe. 'I understand their problems,' she said, 'and realize how important it is for them to get the language. When I first moved to Brick Lane the only thing that made me feel OK was seeing a majority of Asian faces around.' Shoma loves living in Brick Lane today. 'I know it has a reputation for gangs,' she said, 'but the East End is filled with little mafias so it's not just here. We need to educate the mums because the boys leave school early with no qualifications and can't get a job. They see all this money around them and this is what they want, so they do all this ugly stuff to get it. I still want to live here. I have a boyfriend and we want to get married. I expect we will move out to Ilford or Redbridge. Poor people like me cannot afford to live in Brick Lane any more.'

N came back into the office for her tea break and joined Shoma and me. The two young Bengali women then took turns asking me questions about my life. I showed them the pictures of my children and told them about my own family history and the shop my grandfather had owned on Brick Lane. They wanted to know about my artwork, and I told them about the mosaic I had made with the pupils from Thomas Buxton and St Anne's schools. 'I went to Thomas Buxton School,' said N, smiling. 'There was a wonderful art teacher there called Neela who really encouraged me to go on to further education.'

14
Bengali Lives

Today approximately 300,000 Bengalis live in Britain, most of whom originate from Bangladesh, from the region of Sylhet in the north-east of the country. Now one third of the population of Tower Hamlets is Bengali, the largest Bengali community in the UK.

Dan Jones, 'Exploring Banglatown and the Bengali East End'

Ten years after completing the mosaic at Thomas Buxton I returned to the school to develop another public artwork. The workshops were run jointly by Svar and myself and organized by Freeform Arts Trust. Over many weeks we taught pupils from three local schools, including Thomas Buxton, about the history of Spitalfields. The children made related drawings and wrote poems, and a select few were engraved on to granite slabs and inserted into a floorscape in the recently redeveloped Spitalfields Market. 'Dig Me Up' read one slab; 'Watch Your Back' said another; 'A Drunken Man Laid Here' wrote one boy. Bengali girls decorated their slabs in intricate *mehndi* designs and words like 'Flowing Saris' and 'el Shadoi', which means 'peace'.

The workshops at Thomas Buxton School ran particularly smoothly thanks to Neela, who is still working there as the head of the art department. She is in her early sixties now and has a serious diabetic condition but does not intend to retire any time soon. She is passionate about her role as a teacher and does everything she can to help expand the curriculum and show her Bengali pupils about other cultures and other opportunities. 'Many of the children here have never been outside of Tower Hamlets,' she said. 'Some of them would not even have ventured over to Spitalfields Market. It would be out of their territory, even though the majority of them live in and around Brick Lane.'

Neela has become a spokeswoman for the Bengali community of Brick Lane and recently received an OBE for her work. One of her latest projects is a book of success stories, tales about former pupils of Thomas Buxton School who have gone on to achieve great things, becoming doctors, lawyers and councillors. 'There are so few positive role models in this community and things have been worse since the London bombings and 9/11,' she said. 'I see many young people here with low self-respect and there is such wider fear about the Muslim community in Britain. What goes on in the mosque, what our customs and traditions mean, we need to educate people, we have to learn to be more open.'

Neela grew up in Bangladesh as the eldest daughter of wealthy, liberal parents and was encouraged to achieve. At the age of fourteen she competed in the Asian Games and her O level grades were the highest of any girl in Bangladesh at the time. In 1969, after finishing university, she became a programme producer for Pakistani television. She was one of the very few women in the business. In that same year her parents decided it was time for Neela to get married. The wedding was arranged with a man she had never met, a law student who was studying in England. He returned to Bangladesh to meet his bride and a few months later Neela was on her way to London. After her husband finished his studies they intended to go back to Bangladesh, but political upheaval in the country made it impossible. Their children were born soon after and began to settle in London, and Neela and her husband became like many Bangladeshis who dream of returning to the Desh but never do.

After various part-time jobs, and the tragic death of her younger son, Neela began working with the Bangladeshi community in London, translating Bengali books and legal documents and teaching English to children on Bangla TV. In 1982 she started working at Thomas Buxton. 'The children needed a lot of bilingual support then as many had just arrived from Bangladesh with no English at all,' she said. 'I had posters up everywhere with the English and Bengali words for things – on the doors, the chairs, even on myself.'

In the early 1980s the pupils at Thomas Buxton School were a mixture of Indian, Greek, Bengali and English children. Many of the children's parents worked in leather factories in Brick Lane then, most of which were Jewish-owned. Now the majority of these factories have closed down and nearly all of the pupils at Thomas Buxton are Bengali. Neela is proud of her community's achievements, which are evident from just walking down Brick Lane: 'There are so many Bengali-owned businesses there now and the Brick Lane area has the largest Bengali population outside of Bangladesh,' she said. 'The *melas* are the best time to see Brick Lane, because the smells of good food cooking are everywhere and the street is filled with women in yellow-and-red saris, the colours of spring. The Baishaki Mela is the primary Bengali celebration outside of Bangladesh, and thousands of people from all over the world celebrate with us. It is a great way to show others about our culture and this is something I am really keen to do.'

Neela has watched generations of Bengali families grow up in the area and although she feels most of the changes are positive she is aware of the many problems her community still faces: 'There is a lot of conflict between generations and communication is bad. Mum might not be able to speak English and so stays at home, and Dad often works late, sometimes all night, and rarely sees the children. The parents have no idea what their children are getting up to sometimes until it's too late. Parents need to give more time to the children. They feel they're doing their best earning the money but they need to do a lot more if things are to change. The children are confused. It's one world at home and another outside. They are being influenced by a culture beyond their parents' consciousness and this is why there are so many drug problems. If the parents watched the news it would be better, but at home they just watch Hindi films on Sky and Bangla TV. They need to broaden their knowledge.'

These Bangladeshi teenagers aren't afraid
to show out. Pencil-thin, their hair whippet-
cropped or drenched in product – facial hair
immaculately coiffeured too – they cut a swathe
through the area, chatting into mobiles,
sporting the loudest, proudest labels (Moschino,
Ted Baker, Versace) and munching fries from
the *halal* chip shop. The tightness of their
tapered trousers and their designer rollnecks
make them look like 1960s mods, and
distinguish them not only from the flapping
flares their fathers wore twenty years earlier,
but from the baggy slackness of those Asian
media professionals who are gradually moving
into the area with their white partners.

Sukhdev Sandhu, 'Come Hungry, Leave Edgy', *London
Review of Books*, 9 October 2003

Another of the schools involved in the Spitalfields Floorscape Project was Swanlea Secondary School in Whitechapel. Housed in a new, architect-designed building in Brady Street, the school is one of the largest in the borough. The pupils there are ethnically mixed, although the Bengali students are in the majority.

The first time Svar and I went to the school the covered atrium of the building was teeming with teenage pupils who eyed us suspiciously as we walked by. I started to feel a little nervous about the workshop. It was always hard to predict how people were going to react to Svar. When the class began Svar managed the kids brilliantly, ignoring the jibes from the boys at the back – 'Miss, I mean, sir' and the accompanying sniggers.

There was one girl in the group who had real artistic talent. Her name was Repha. She sat near the front, head down, drawing intricate pictures of the local architecture, which particularly interested her. She was dressed in a *burka* and wearing a *hijab*. I found it hard to communicate with her at first until we began to talk about her artwork. She showed me a file of her paintings and told me she wanted to study art at university. This was unlikely to happen because her parents expected her to have an arranged marriage as soon as she left school. Repha had been born in Brick Lane and still lived there on the Wheeler House Estate. She went to Thomas Buxton School and knew Neela well. She was keen to take part in this book and with the permission of her teachers we sat down privately and talked.

Derek Cox had played a huge part in Repha's childhood, as he had for many local Bengali children. 'He was always organizing stuff for us,' she said. 'Face painting and music in the park, he took us ice-skating, swimming, camping – places my parents would never have taken me.' Repha told me that Derek had got married in Bangladesh. This fact and his conversion to Islam meant her parents trusted him. 'I have known him all my life,' she said.

Repha shares a small council flat with three sisters, one brother and her parents. 'I'm doing my GCSEs now and there's no private space to revise in,' she said. 'I try to study in the bedroom but one sister is listening to music, another's on the computer, the other one's fighting and it's impossible. I just try and work over the noise.' Her parents have lived there since they came to London from Bangladesh eighteen years ago. 'But they would still say they are Bangladeshi not English.' Repha is glad they live near Brick Lane because of the Bangladeshi culture that surrounds them there. 'Brick Lane is like a part of Bangladesh,' she said. 'I feel connected there.'

Her parents are religious and the imam comes to her house every week to teach Repha Arabic. Since 9/11 she has noticed people staring at her more, particularly if she wears the *hijab*, but says, 'it doesn't bother me, I just get on with life'. If she does get married she wants to stay living around Brick Lane. Partly because of the accessibility of *halal* food and everything she needs to live a religious Muslim life but also because she enjoys the more contemporary aspects of Brick Lane. 'I like all the art exhibitions and cafés there,' she said. 'The vintage thing is a new thing and I think it's really cool. I haven't been in one of those shops, even though there is one at the top of my street, but I would like to go. Last week there was a concert and I could hear the music in my room, it was really loud but my parents wouldn't let me go.'

She feels safe in Brick Lane because she knows everyone. 'I'm not bothered by the problems like the gangs and stuff because you get that wherever you go,' she said. 'The gang boys want the space to themselves and they don't want others to come into their place changing things. Even other Bengalis from Brady Street or Bethnal Green will get challenged if they come on to our estate.'

Another student in Repha's class I met who had been born in Brick Lane was Azizul. His parents had lived in a three-bedroom house near Hanbury Street since arriving from Sylhet thirty years ago. In 2003 the family moved to Plaistow, and Azizul was finding the change hard. 'My new area, it's a bit weird 'cause I don't know no one there. The special thing about Brick Lane is the environment, you got all the Bengalis in one community and over there it's a different culture and I find it difficult to mix.' The family

I like Sundays, there's so many people around
and you see all the English people walking past
from Columbia Road with big flowerpots full of
plants. I feel sorry for the English people
walking down Brick Lane who get dragged into
the restaurants and hassled by the people outside
but they don't bother with me. Another thing I
don't like about Brick Lane is it's just full of men
and I feel awkward sometimes because of my
religion. There's always drunk people near our
building screaming and shouting and there's a
whole community asleep right next to them and
they are screaming as if they are the only people
there. Every Saturday and Sunday there is a lot
of noise. I live in a very noisy place.

Repha, 2004

had to move because of financial problems. 'My father is becoming more and more religious,' said Azizul. 'He decided we had to go to pilgrimage, to Haj to Mecca, so he sold the car, everything.' There were other reasons too. Their house was right near the mosque and all the restaurants and the street was sometimes so busy the family were unable to open their own front door. 'Day by day the Bengali community is getting bigger,' he said, 'and Brick Lane is just packed out. The housing is not enough for all the people there and too expensive and that's why we moved to this new area but I miss my friends.'

Azizul described his childhood in Brick Lane: meeting friends to play football in Altab Ali Park; going to the Whitechapel Library to hang out; socializing at the Whitechapel Mosque; using the PlayStations and the gym. 'There were even teachers there who would help you with your homework on a Sunday,' he said. Every time he went out on to Brick Lane he saw people he knew. 'It was a special bond,' he said. Like all the other young Bengali people I have spoken with Azizul enjoyed the multicultural aspect of the street and loved the festivals, parades and the singers coming from Bangladesh. 'I loved the way people talked about Brick Lane and it got so popular with celebrities going there and stuff, that was cool.'

He claimed his involvement with the mosque stopped him getting involved in drugs, unlike many of his friends, sadly. 'The boys around Brick Lane are getting bad,' he told me. 'I used to smoke a bit of spliff and stuff when I lived there but now I am more by myself in this new area, not hanging around in a group. I study more and I can see the advantage of not living in that area. Because the council flats are so small the parents have to let the children out and they do not know what they get up to. I do: smoking, taking drugs, hanging around. There's pressure, they influence you and come and call for you and get you to go out. Those boys used to respect me like an older brother. I was always telling them not to smoke and stuff but now they got no one to tell them what to do and they will struggle when they grow up. Now I am working really hard with my studies, I want to do something with my life. So, yeah, in some ways I'm glad I moved. There is too many temptations in Brick Lane.'

15

On Brick Lane

**When you are on the street in Brick Lane the interior spaces
are external to you. There aren't many reasons to go inside the
buildings and get into these private spaces that hold their time
in a different way to street time, which is always contemporary.**
Iain Sinclair

The day we completed the last workshop at Swanlea School, Svar
and I returned to Brick Lane for a coffee at the internet café on
the corner of Buxton Street. The café was slowly filling up with
people coming out of the old brewery complex. Loitering by a
lamp-post just outside the window were four or five Asian teenage
boys wearing jeans and hooded tops. One of them pointed inside
the café, and for a moment I thought they might come in, but
they turned together and walked slowly up Quaker Street, kicking
a can noisily along the road.

It was hard to talk above the noise of the techno music blasting
out of speakers beside us, and we were hungry too, so we decided
to go and have lunch at Sweet and Spicy, a small restaurant further
down the street that serves traditional Asian sweets and has a limited
menu of hot *halal* food. The business has been there since 1969 and
is run by the son of the original owner. Until recently its clientele
were almost all Bengali men but over the last few years the café has
become popular with other local people, City workers and gallery
owners who have discovered the food there is better than at many
of the more expensive restaurants on the street. My father-in-law,
who is from Pakistan and an excellent cook, will not eat anywhere
else on Brick Lane.

The decor inside Sweet and Spicy is functional and slightly shabby, with Formica tables and red plastic chairs screwed to the scuffed lino floor. The walls are decorated with paintings of famous Bengali wrestlers. On each table is a large aluminium jug of water and some plastic glasses. No alcohol is served, out of respect for their Muslim customers. Sweet and Spicy is one of the few places on Brick Lane where you will see religious, often elderly, Bengali men in the same room as the newer arrivals to the area.

Svar and I ordered a chicken biryani and a few chapatis between us and carried our meal on a brown plastic tray to the only spare table, at the back of the restaurant. The front of the restaurant was filling up with people queuing for takeaways, mainly Bengali men, who brought their own dishes to be filled and taken back to their place of work. After finishing our food we decided to go for a quick pint at the nearby Pride of Spitalfields in Heneage Street.

When Svar and I both had studios in the brewery we'd often go to the Pride after work. In the middle of winter it was a treat for Svar to escape his cold studio and sit by the warm pub stove. The Pride was the kind of pub where you'd see the same old men sitting around the fire every time you went in, although later it became popular with artists and City workers too. Unlike most places on Brick Lane it has yet to be updated and the swirly carpets, dark wooden furniture and velvet seating make it very homely. The walls are covered in flock paper and hundreds of framed sepia prints – porters at the old fruit and vegetable market, photographs of hop pickers and workers from the brewery. Svar told me about a wild night he had there after the former landlord, Kerry, had died. 'I went to pay my respects to him,' he said, 'he was in the saloon bar in an open coffin. His wife was there serving free drinks.'

That day, when Svar and I went in, the bar was nearly empty apart from a few regulars smoking and talking at a table near the back. A buffet was laid out against the far wall for a party of policemen coming in later. I went to get us some drinks and got talking to the barmaid. She told me about the alleged racist attack that had taken place there on 17 June 2003. 'Some Asian

kids threw a petrol bomb in here as one of the barmaids and her
boyfriend was leaving the pub,' she said. 'They were both hurt,
but not fatally, and the doorway was scorched and burned. It
was terrible.'

After a couple of drinks Svar left the pub and I sat and waited
for Iain Sinclair, who had offered to walk around the area with
me again, showing me the holy geometry of Spitalfields and
Whitechapel. He arrived shortly after and we started our tour
directly outside the front of the pub, talking about the building
opposite, a former synagogue, which has been converted into luxury
flats. 'That building became such a focus for my exploration of
Brick Lane and the Whitechapel area,' said Iain. 'Above the synagogue is a room where the artists Boyd Webb and Alison Wilding
lived. They sublet it to Brian Catling and I remember wonderful
meals cooked there by candlelight. The power of the room itself
was extraordinary, like a pool of memory and darkness. Later,
when writing *Downriver*, I discovered this was the room where
David Rodinsky had been seen speaking Arabic after a Kiddush,
and this image turned the room into something spectacular for
me. There used to be an Indian supermarket next door packed
with piles of rice and if you looked up you could see the balcony
of the old synagogue.'

Iain marched up on to Brick Lane and stopped briefly outside the ancient drinking fountain in front of Christ Church School, which he has always thought of as some kind of holy well 'fitting into the mystic geography of this area with the Seven Stars next door, which now lies derelict'. The Seven Stars pub was one of the first places I met Iain in when he was making a film with Chris Petit that included some footage shot in Rodinsky's room. After filming we had gone together to the saloon bar at the back of the Seven Stars – a large barren room, lit by neon strip lighting with vast stretches of red carpet and a pool table in the centre. While we were having our drinks a woman had walked languidly out on to the bar wearing high-heeled shoes and performed a striptease. Iain told me, 'The pub used to be run by a Sikh in a turban, and there was an interesting mix of people in there, and although the place looked rough it was never threatening.' He was in the pub in 1997 when the General Election results came in. 'The Conservatives were finally beaten and suddenly this disparate bunch of lowlife began celebrating,' said Iain.

Iain resumed his fast walking pace before stopping again outside the window of Mr Katz's string and paper bag shop. I had first met Iain back in 1994 after he had seen the artwork I made about my grandfather's watchmaking and jewellery shop in Katz's window. 'It's become a strange parody of its former self,' said Iain, looking at the latest latex and string installation in the window.

We walked on, past the brewery, which Iain described as 'a strange underground university and a paternalist employer who could look after you for the rest of your life'. During the time he was working there he walked around the area obsessively and discovered certain energy paths that he considered were almost like ley lines. 'There was one that went through Cheshire Street and over the little bridge and into the tenter grounds behind and then into the back of the brewery.' Years later he met the writer Emanuel Litvinoff, who talked about his early childhood and how that bridge had become for him a place of sexual fantasies, evoking thoughts of girls under the railway arches, as well as a place of threat when he was beaten up by boys in his class. All the dramas that took place in Litvinoff's childhood seemed to centre around that bridge. For Iain the bridge divides Brick Lane like the wall that once divided East and West Berlin. The place plays a pivotal role in people's memories of the street and has appeared in fictional works, such as Alexander Baron's *King Dido*, a novel whose plot hinges on violent tribalism in the East End in the early 1900s. King Dido has a fight with a local villain on the cobblestones in front of the bridge.

I walked the perimeter of the brewery with Iain before turning off Brick Lane into Woodseer Street, 'a place with mystical associations', said Iain, 'as if it had been occupied by a magician who used woods and forests to see'. Before long we reached the fields beside the farm. 'There were stables and horses there in the 1970s,' he said. 'I would walk out of the back gate of the brewery into this area of fields, which felt like the original Whitechapel which used to be a piece of countryside next to the City – a place where you could smell hops, where animals roamed, a mysterious mixture of country and town. It wasn't built up as it is now but was a wild meadowy space often with horses on it and Georgian buildings, which would have looked more at home in Oxford or Winchester, but were connected to the Church and seemed monastic or secret in some way.'

As we crossed the field and were about to walk up on to the footbridge that goes over the old railway line we saw an abandoned boat on a grass verge. 'I told you it's a river,' said Iain laughing, 'we're just waiting for the rains to come.' The bridge itself, with its high walls of graffiti-covered corrugated iron obscuring all views of the City, has an abandoned and dangerous feel to it. We stopped again on the other side of the bridge in Cheshire Street. 'It's like we've dropped into another world,' said Iain. 'Movements in time and space in this part of London are what give it its singularity.'

We walked down the street, past many abandoned warehouses, which Iain remembers as being filled with rag pickers, junk and old clothes on Sunday mornings. 'There is all this energy and activity here on a Sunday,' he said, 'and the rest of the week, nothing, it becomes a ghost street.' We passed the last pub owned by the Kray Twins, the Carpenters Arms, and Iain pointed out the Masonic symbols that cover its façade. 'This building is an exact reflection of the violence going on in Alexander Baron's novel,' he said. 'The Krays came here on the mythic night of the murder of Jack the Hat, and the church behind is the place where the funerals of the Krays took place. It leads on to Bethnal Green Road and they grew up on Vallance Road, a couple of streets away.' We continued to walk along Cheshire Street, past the old Jewish baths that Sally Flood used to visit as a child, before turning right into Vallance Road, which runs parallel to Brick Lane: 'And if you carry on,' said Iain, 'you just drift naturally down past the London Hospital to Cannon Street Road and then to the river.'

We passed still-derelict bombsites before coming into Whitechapel High Street, which is dominated by the Royal London Hospital. 'I've always thought of it as the memory depository for the zone,' said Iain, pointing to the vast Victorian building: 'They had this archive of photographs and records at the back, library medical

records and histories of anyone who had anything to do with the hospital, and I am fascinated by the idea of the Elephant Man in a little room above.' To our right was the skyline of the City but before long we had dived off again down another small side street into Durward Street, formerly Buck's Row, behind Whitechapel Station, the site of the first of the Ripper murders. Just behind the old school building the nearly decapitated body of Polly Nichols was found in 1888. Behind it I could see the glass-and-steel structure of Swanlea School where I had been earlier that morning.

16
Street Life

HI, Rachel, I just received a card from
Iain Sinclair regarding your Brick Lane
book. I will get back to you after I have
spoken to Dad. He has a fantastic memory.
I just read *Children of the Ghetto* by
Israel Zangwill. It is a masterpiece. Have
you read it?

All the best, Gerry Goldstein

'Archaeologists, revenants and historians' is how Michael Moorcock
described the bookdealers Gerry and Pat Goldstein in his story
'London Bone'. After lengthy email communication I arranged to
meet them at Stanmore tube one afternoon. They were going to take
me to see Pip, Gerry's father, who Iain Sinclair had told me was 'a
friend of Jack Spot with great stories of battles with Blackshirts in
Cable Street, gambling clubs, adventures in the rag trade, forgotten celebrities and market tales'. When I arrived it was nearly dark
and the station was deserted. The time for the meeting came and
went, and after a further twenty minutes of standing in the cold
I was about to turn back when a battered Cortina pulled up in
front of the station. A tall man in his mid fifties tumbled out of the
car, talking continuously and apologizing profusely. He introduced
himself as Gerry and ushered me into the back seat. His wife, Pat,
was driving and the two of them talked at great speed. 'Loved that
book you wrote!' he said loudly. 'Fucking fantastic!'

After driving for about five minutes, Pat pulled into a cul-de-sac
and parked outside a low-rise block of flats. We all piled out of the

car with Gerry enthusing about his father and his stories. I followed
Gerry up two flights of stairs into a small flat on the second floor.
Inside the scene was familiar to me: deep striped sofas, lace curtains,
a large mahogany sideboard filled with sepia family photographs,
a *menorah* and a collection of porcelain plates. A television set was
blaring in the corner, and in front of it was a table laid with tea
and biscuits. Sara and Pip welcomed me into their home like a lost
relative, making me feel instantly welcome. Gerry and Pat sat on
the sofa, Sara sat herself down in one armchair and Pip took the
other. I positioned myself close to Pip and set up the recording
equipment. This was obviously going to be a family interview.

'Go on Dad, talk to her,' said Gerry encouragingly, 'tell her
about Brick Lane.'

Pip settled himself into his chair and began his story. 'I was born at
53 Brunswick Buildings in Goulston Street, in a tenement, opposite
the Brooke Bond Tea factory, on the 14th of August 1918.'

'Incredible, Rachel, isn't it?' said Gerry pointing at his father.
'Look at him, all of his hair, barely a line on his face, eighty-eight
years old this year. Can you believe it?'

I nodded in agreement, and Pip smiled and pointed across the
room to Sara. 'How about her, then,' he said to me. 'Have you ever
seen such a beauty? But of course she's much younger than me.'

Pip's real name is Maurice Charles, and his Hebrew name is
Moshe. 'When I was about three there was a little ditty going
around,' he said, '"Moshe Pippick went to the races and lost his
braces," and that's where my nickname came from.' From the age
of three everyone called him Pip. He lived in a basement flat with
two rooms – a lounge-cum-kitchen and one bedroom. There were
five children. His parents had come to East London as children
from Russia. 'My mother was a wonderful woman,' said Pip, looking fondly at a photograph of her on the sideboard, and then the
words stopped as tears streamed down his face. 'Sorry, darling,' he
said, 'it's making me very emotional to remember.'

When Pip felt ready to continue he started to talk again, but now
everyone else was talking loudly too, so I moved closer, trying to

pick up his memories on my machine over the noise in the room, and politely requested that we turn the television off. Pip transported himself back in time. 'Once a week we visited the public baths in Goulston Street for a penny,' he said smiling, 'the posher bit was sixpence. "Hot water, no. 22!" you'd hear.'

'Oh, yes,' said Sara, joining in, 'I remember that well.'

'Did you grow up there too?' I asked.

'Of course,' came a chorus from around the room, with hands raised in the air.

Looking lovingly at Sara, Pip tapped me gently on the back of the arm and said in his deep gravelly voice, 'She was born in the same block of flats as me. The first time I met her she was six years old and playing with her brother Jacky. I couldn't take my eyes off her. She fascinated me.' He winked at Sara.

'He said he loved me then, didn't you, doll?' said Sara, laughing.

'I never spoke to her until at least twenty years later,' said Pip. 'I was married by then, and when we met up by chance I remembered her and approached her.'

'The rest is history,' said Sara.

'It's a love story,' said Gerry.

'It was a happy life,' continued Pip. 'But we had nothing. My father was a machinist in the rag trade, he worked very hard and times were often tough but we were well looked after. One of the first things I can recall,' said Pip smiling, 'is being three years old and running around doing favours for the stallholders at Petticoat Lane Market, which fascinated me. As a kid I loved the art of salesmanship and I used to watch my Zayde, who was a knicker manufacturer with a stall in the lane outside where we lived in Goulston Street.'

Pip went on to describe a typical Jewish childhood in East London in the early 1920s: playing football on the street, visiting relatives for Shabbos, attending the Jewish Free School in Bell Lane, where Israel Zangwill taught, and visiting the Whitechapel Library.

'My twin brother practically lived there,' he said, 'but I was the little *lobos*, more extrovert and into sports. I left school at fourteen. My mother tried with me but I was such a little bounder, God rest her soul.'

Pip's parents wanted him to become a rabbi and sent him to the Brick Lane Talmud Torah but he was only there for a few weeks. 'We had this teacher,' he said, 'a rabbi, and he was such an animal. He used to knock us around and he hit me once so hard I went for him. I was only a kid. My twin brother went and told my mother what was happening and she never made me go again.'

'All the boys went to *cheder* then,' said Sara. 'It was a totally Jewish world we lived in. It was a revelation to discover there were people in the world who were not Jewish. We didn't have any non-Jewish neighbours.'

Pip visited the Machzike Hadath Synagogue only once and didn't like it there, finding it too vast and imposing. Sara remembered Shevshik's, the Russian Vapour Baths, opposite. 'They'd sit there all day,' she said, 'the Orthodox, they'd take sandwiches in and it was nicknamed the "Shvitz". They would thrash leaves over your back to increase the circulation of your blood and then after the steam you took a cold dip.' An argument started about whether the baths had been bombed during the Blitz or not. 'I'm telling you, Gerald,' said Pip firmly, 'I know it wasn't, I can remember Brick Lane, everything about it, exactly how it looked,' and with that Pip closed his eyes and began to describe the Brick Lane of his childhood.

'Starting at Osborn Street at the Whitechapel end, there was a big stationers called Straikers. Upstairs there was Moss and Roberts, my dentists, and they charged a shilling for extracting a tooth. There'd be a queue like at the supermarket outside his door. Near by was that place called the Warsaw Hotel or Snelvar's Restaurant, where all the Jewish gangsters used to hang out and a lot of communists went there. If you wanted a loan you went to the Achie Betech Loan Society in Osborn Street. At the beginning of Osborn Street was a barber's run by Jack Spot's brother, Pizar, a real gentleman who used to cut my hair. Madame Barr's hat shop was next door, a rather upmarket place it was. On the corner of Old Montague Street was Bloom's. You could have a three-course meal with waitress service there for half a crown. The tailors used to meet there looking for work.'

'Do you remember that little ditty everyone used to sing?' said Sara, breaking into song. '"Maybe it's the rain, that fills Brick Lane, with all such lovely perfume; no, it isn't the rain, it's salt beef from Bloom's."'

'Old Montague Street itself was fascinating,' continued Pip. 'It was the first turning off Brick Lane coming from Osborn Street, and it was a busy Jewish market during the week. There was a kosher butchers shop called Strongwater Mark, a Hebrew bookshop and a high-class deli by the name of Green. I remember a dairy there, a sweet shop where you could get a sarsaparilla drink, and a barber's shop. Just past Bloom's was a little court way called Frostic Walk, with a few dwellings there, and a shop run by two old spinsters who sold pickled herrings and cucumbers and they was always arguing.'

'Don't forget Black Lion Yard, doll,' said Sara, 'it was the famous place for jewellery and could be entered through Old Montague Street or via Whitechapel, opposite the Bell Foundry. Before Hatton Garden everyone went there. You could haggle and get a good deal. And I remember Madame Yanovski, who sold handmade corsets, she was right before you went into the yard. She'd fit you herself. Outside there used to be a *schlepper*. All the shops had them before

the war, particularly the dress shops, they'd pull you in, yank you into the shops.'

'Just before Old Montague Street there was a café that belonged to Curly,' said Pip. 'He was in the fighting business, boxing, and he sang in a band. Gangsters, racing boys, all them type of characters used to meet in there. Coming back on to Brick Lane, further along was the Old Electric Company where you paid your bills. Then there was Collins, the menswear shop. He had handsome boys, older than me – Sam, Albert and Benny. At the top of Flower and Dean Walk was the Rothschild Tenements, which were full of Jewish kids. There was a home for fallen women there too, they were all old *nufke*, prostitutes.'

'Brick Lane was bustling except on Saturdays when it was like a morgue,' said Sara. 'Everything was completely closed up, because it was a religious community.'

'Opposite Flower and Dean Walk was a big factory called Ellis and Goldstein,' said Pip, 'who were in the rag trade. Further along was a famous shop that sold men's cloth called Julius Isaacs. All the club boys, the gamblers and the villains, used to go there to have their suits made because he had the best stuff.'

'Brick Lane was so full of life,' said Sara, 'the streets were filled with people walking about. How about the cinema? Tell her about the cinema, Pip.'

'There was a cinema in Chicksand Street, just past Bloom's, called the Brick Lane Cinema,' said Pip. 'We all used to go.'

'It was entirely Jewish kids in that audience,' said Sara.

'The place comprised of one big hangar, on one level, like a warehouse,' said Pip. 'There used to be a little guy there, like a midget, and he had a *hoicka*, a hump, a *nebbech* he was. He used to sell peanuts. I saw silent films at that cinema before you was born,' he said, pointing to Sara. 'And I saw one of the earliest Technicolor films there, *Broadway Melody* with Eddie Kearns, I'm talking about 1929.'

'When that cinema closed down the Mayfair opened on Brick Lane,' said Sara.

The last turning in Brick Lane before Whitechapel High Street was Old Montague Street and the biggest concentration of Jews were there. It began with a large pub on the corner and continued with small shops up to Black Lion Yard where the diamond shops were, some of them acted as fences. There was a market there, mostly composed of barrows, where the smell was raw fish and poultry both live and dead. The shops were small and the street was so narrow that when a cart came through there was often a row and the language was very forceful. Moishe the Gonoff, the most famous Jewish pickpocket of the time, lived in Old Montague Street. He used to come up Brick Lane and when he appeared all the stallholders would say, 'Watch out, here comes Moishe the Gonoff.'

Raphael Samuel, *East End Underworld: Chapters in the Life of Arthur Harding*, 1981

'Let's not forget Alfe's fish and chip shop,' said Pip. 'It was on the corner by the cinema. The guy who ran it was a thick-set middle-aged guy, it was a penny for chips wrapped in newspapers.'

'It didn't matter where you went,' said Sara, 'the cinema, a walk, a show, you made your way to Alfe's for fish and chips afterwards – it was the meeting place for the youngsters.'

'Further along,' continued Pip, 'were a few wholesale shops, a lingerie place, a knitting shop and a couple of Jewish cafés. It was a working place, the people were poor but it wasn't rough. The kids were well behaved, it was a close-knit community.'

'Predominantly Brick Lane was all shops,' said Sara. 'There were tailor-trimmings places, quite a few material shops on the rolls, silks and things like that. If you wanted to buy cloth that's where you went.'

'Past the Machzike Hadath and the Turkish Baths was a gown shop, which my late father worked for,' said Pip. 'He had a workroom upstairs, and downstairs a retail outlet selling women's wear, coats, dresses and such. It was called Statman Max. Further along was a little Jewish place that sold Jewish books, *menorahs*, silverware. There was Katz's opposite the *shul* selling the string and paper bags, run by a *frummer*. He had a typical fiddler-on-the-roof face, always wore a big homburg. Towards Hanbury Street was a bakers, called Bernstein's.'

'It was the most wonderful pastry shop,' said Sara, 'they used to sell a boat-shaped pastry called a "stuffed monkey", filled with almonds and spices. The top half was chocolate icing and the other half was vanilla.'

'In Princelet Street, there was a *shul* where my brother was *bar mitzvahed*,' said Pip.

'My grandparents were married there too,' I said, 'and they had a shop there on the corner of Princelet Street and Brick Lane, a jewellery and watchmaking shop.'

'Hang on a minute,' said Pip. 'Did they go under the name of Lichtenstein as jewellers?'

I nodded encouragingly, excited about the possibility of Pip remembering the shop, as no photographic record exists.

'Of course, I remember that name,' said Pip. 'Lichtenstein's

The 'brides' were mostly down the other end
of Brick Lane, where the lodging houses were
in Flower and Dean Walk. The 'Seven Stars'
next to Christ Church School was mostly used
by the ladies of the town, and the 'Frying Pan'
on the corner of Thrawl Street and Brick Lane
was famous for being the centre of the red-light
district.

Raphael Samuel, *East End Underworld: Chapters in the Life
of Arthur Harding*, 1981

Watchmakers and Jewellers – I can picture it now from when I was a kid. It looked like a shop from a Victorian era. The façade was very old-fashioned. There were glass shelves in the window with *menorahs* and candlesticks on, but mainly jewellery and watches, particularly pocketwatches. It was painted in black with wood panelling. A Dickensian-looking shop, with gold lettering on the window.'

Overwhelmed to finally have my grandparents' shop described it was my turn to be emotional, and we stopped again for a while to talk about them, although Pip was too young to have known them personally. After more tea we continued our walk up Brick Lane.

'Further along on the left-hand side was a salt-beef shop and then a wine merchants called Rosenbloom,' said Pip. 'Right next door to the Machzike Hadath was a hairdressers I used to go to called Shriebman. They did perms, all sorts. Walking up the street there was a grocers and a chemist called Lasfid. I can picture it all. Of course, one of the most important places in the whole street was the brewery, Truman, Hanbury, Buxton & Co. They took over acres of land either side of the street. It was like going to a new world in there. You couldn't get into the site but you could smell the hops coming out the chimney. You'd see the draymen coming down with the horse and carts piled up with barrels of beer. We used to jump a ride on the back of the carts.'

'Some people slept on the floor of the cooperage in Truman's Brewery during the air raids,' said Sara, 'because the roof provided good cover.'

'Coming towards Bacon Street there was Shoreditch Station and that was as far as I went really,' he continued. 'Maybe to Cheshire Street to the shops, but generally we didn't go past the railway bridge. There was only one bagel shop then but there were two bagel sellers, a mother and daughter. The mother was called Esther, and she was a right old cow. They used to sit on the floor with a sack in the lane, and the bagels was in there – a dozen for sixpence. The daughter would be on the opposite side and they'd curse each other in Yiddish. If you didn't buy from them they'd curse you too. There was a lot of characters then. There was an act called

"Solomon and Levy", two guys who'd do a little dance in Brick Lane, then pass round their hat.'

'Don't forget Izzy Bonn,' said Sara. 'You can't talk about Brick Lane and not mention him. He was a musical-hall character from Brick Lane, on loads of variety programmes, and I think his parents had a salt-beef place in Brick Lane.'

'I loved all the market-stall traders, the auctioneers particularly,' said Pip. 'In Brick Lane people sold fruit and vegetables along the road in barrows, but that was up towards the Bethnal Green end by the railway arch.'

Pip stopped for a while and closed his eyes. 'I nearly forgot to tell you about the gambling club on Brick Lane called Ginger Harry's,' he said. 'I went when I was about eighteen or nineteen to play billiards and cards. It was an illegal place, full of Jewish men. One night in 1937, I came out of there and someone told us some of Mosley's Blackshirts were in Brick Lane. We found them, and chased them with our billiard cues and beat them up. I had no problem in doing this. I was a tough street kid. The next night walking up Whitechapel a couple of girls I didn't know came up and kissed me.

'I was a cobblefighter, a streetfighter,' Pip continued. 'It probably started because someone tried to bully me and I learned to defend myself with my fists. Many of my friends were professional boxers, Jewish boxers like Harry Lazer. His father was known as Ikky Nark,

My father was a cabinetmaker like me and his father before him and all my brothers. That was our trade. I worked in a workshop in Brick Lane from the time I left school until 1939. There was a little narrow turning before you get to the arch coming from Bethnal Green and that's where I worked, in the basement of a little house that had been taken over for our workshop. The whole street was packed full of cabinetmakers then. We worked from eight in the morning till when, by that I mean till when you finished. Being a youngster I never wanted to work that late but the old'uns probably did. Brick Lane, Hackney, Virginia Road, Shoreditch, Gibraltar Walk, it was a cabinetmakers' area. Fournier Street was full of the fur trade and Brick Lane was mainly tailoring.

Jack Kaye, 2004

a *nark* is a grass. He was one of the faces of Brick Lane, a local villain. I wasn't the biggest kid but I was the best fighter, and because of that somehow the leader of the gang. I was utterly fearless and very streetwise. We were a different breed of Jews – tougher – we had to be.' Pip boxed for the Jewish Lads Brigade and wanted to turn professional but his mother wouldn't let him. 'Everyone I knew boxed,' he said. 'The Krays were both semi-professional boxers. It was a part of East End culture when I was growing up.'

I asked Pip about his underworld connections and gangster reputation. 'I knew them all,' he said, 'The Krays and Jack Spot. I'm not proud of it but that was my world. I was standing next to Jack Spot in the Battle of Cable Street. We got out razors and slashed up the police horses because the police were going at everyone with batons and we had to stop them. The first time I met the Krays I was working a stall in Petticoat Lane, auctioneering, pitching curtains. They came and asked for money, they were in the protection racket. I wouldn't like to repeat what I said to them. I was a tough lad and I wasn't scared of them, and who was behind them, Jack Spot, who had his own mob. He'd been charging the Jewish stallholders for years to protect them from the Blackshirts. He called it his Market Traders Association. He had a go at the Krays for harassing me and they apologized and shook my hand. That's how it was then. In 1968 I went to prison over maintenance for him,' he said, pointing at Gerry, 'the judge put me down for two months when the Krays' trial was coming up. I was over fifty then and I was in the exercise yard and someone was calling out from the top "Pip!" and it was one of the Krays. They threw me down a packet of cigarettes and we spoke from time to time. Jack Spot was the villain of my day, along with the Aldgate boys, Bobby Knark and Lazer Knark.'

We sat chatting for another hour or so before they all dropped me back at the station, showering me with kisses and pinching my cheeks. They promised to come and visit me in Essex, which they did shortly after – a memorable day eating fish and chips by the sea and sharing memories of Jewish East London with the legend – Pip Goldstein.

17

Sites of Emptiness

Brick Lane is both the place I was looking for before I even knew about it, and it has become the fulcrum through which I see the rest of the world. It is not a neutral place, it is a place of encounters that repays curiosity. I have lived in other parts of London and they just don't do it to the same extent. I find some of what is missing in the rest of the country in Brick Lane.

Sukhdev Sandhu

Shortly after my visit to the Goldsteins I took a very different walk along Brick Lane with another resident of the street, the film critic, writer and cultural commentator Sukhdev Sandhu. We first met at an evening event in August 2005 at the Whitechapel Library organized by the Jewish East End Celebration Society to commemorate the closing of the building. Well-known Jewish figures, such as the Yiddish actress Anna Tzelniker and Bill Fishman, spoke, and the playwright Bernard Kops read his poem 'Being so hungry I fell on the feast, Whitechapel Library, Aldgate East', which summed up the nostalgic sentiments of many in the audience including Sukhdev. 'It was my local library and meant something to me personally,' he told me, 'its familiarity, its warmth. It welcomed all the people that you never see anywhere else in East London, the tramps, the vulnerable and elderly people, and it is not culturally specific like most other community spaces.'

Sukhdev describes himself as a rambler who looks in the corners of places. He had spent the night before our walk wandering through the sewers of Soho. 'I came across solid lumps of fat and human hair weighing over a ton,' he said, 'blocking the tunnels, choking up the arteries of the city.' The previous night he'd been patrolling the skies in a police helicopter, and later in the week he would witness an exorcism in the early hours – all research for his nocturnal journal, *Night Haunts*, a project for the contemporary art commissioners Artangel.

We started our walk from outside the closed doors of the Whitechapel Library. Sukhdev was yawning and rubbing his eyes with his fists as I approached but was soon talking passionately about the building. 'It is on this sort of crossroads,' he said, pointing at the busy junction in front of us, 'for so many different places, and whether you liked it or not you had to share this space with others.' Sukhdev is an avid reader and used the library a lot; he feels his time spent there allowed him a brief portal into the interior life of people in the area. 'Right up until it closed it was teeming,' he said, 'with people on the internet, talking into their mobiles when they shouldn't be, there was just this kind of chatter going on. It had a vibrant community life and now it's been taken out of action and it feels so wrong. It's surrounded with a certain type of emptiness now.'

As we wandered around the area we passed other places with similar resonances for Sukhdev – Aldgate tube, one of the sites of the 7 July London bombings, the Naz on Brick Lane, where the nail bomb exploded, and A. Elfes Stone Masons in Osborn Street, with its associations of death and burial. Sukhdev seems to be tuned into the weird reverberations of these sites and the residues and resonances of past lives in old buildings. The crumbling nineteenth-century architecture of East London was one of the things that attracted him to the area originally; buildings such as Toynbee Hall, the Whitechapel Library and old Victorian doss-houses. 'The physical texture of steel and glass does not weather or bear the traces of its age or history in the same way that brick does,' he said. Whitechapel was a romantic place of literature, poetry and successive layers of history for Sukhdev, but when he spent some time living in Brick Lane he discovered something else, something unexpected – the beginnings of a personal sense of belonging. We made our way to

Once a remote, tubercular outpost, Brick Lane is one of the few notionally central places in the capital still home to a sizeable non-white population. Maybe that's why it has become a heritage-trail stop-off for inquisitive tourists whose outsize coaches jam the narrow road, to the dismay of local restaurateurs who shout abuse at the people coming to peer at them. At street corners young architects lecture their students about new urbanisms. Curry festivals and street parties abound, patronized by Mayor Livingstone and progressive politicians, who have their photos taken beneath bunting sponsored by Kingfisher, an 'Indian' lager brewed under licence by Shepherd Neame at Faversham. In April 2002 the ward was officially designated Spitalfields/Banglatown; lamp-posts have been painted red and green for the national flag; street names are also written in Bengali, though that's of no use to those locals who speak only Sylheti. Brick Lane has even given its name to a restaurant in the 'Little India' stretch of Manhattan's East Village, as well as a road in Dhaka.

Sukhdev Sandhu, 'Come Hungry, Leave Edgy',
London Review of Books, 9 October 2003

the corner of Fournier Street and pointing at the mosque, Sukhdev said, 'That's one of the main reasons I'm here.'

'I thought you were a practising Sikh,' I said, surprised.

'I am,' he replied, 'I'm talking about the energy of this place. Brick Lane is charged and it's got religion, and I don't want to live in a place that doesn't have a very thick sediment of belief or spirituality. I grew up in Gloucester, a few streets away from where Fred West did his murders, and that place has no strong sense of community, Sikh or otherwise. I didn't grow up with the connective tissue of religion I see around me here.'

Sukhdev feels Brick Lane is both a spiritual and a tolerant place. In other areas he has lived, including West London, he has been attacked, both verbally and physically, because of his appearance. 'I used to have a massive Afro, so big it would catch fire and I wouldn't even notice it until someone came and threw water over me,' he told me. 'I was constantly getting beaten up for it but for some reason me and my hair are accepted in Whitechapel.'

We moved on, past the Nazrul and towards Dray Walk, where a fashion shoot was taking place in front of a metal shutter covered in graffiti. A few people gathered round to see what was going on, but for the most part the locals just walked past.

'Does it annoy you to constantly have the place where you live photographed and documented?' I asked him.

'It is not necessarily a bad thing,' he replied. 'Many local people, including those in the Bangladeshi community, take pride in this and are really happy that people are interested in them and their area. In some ways you could say it makes the community less authentic somehow, or more like performers, because they are used to living within a tourist zone and responding to that, but I feel it is one of the most unique and interesting things about this area, and it is not typical of other Islamic communities around the country. There are parts of Bradford where if you walk down the street with a camera you are putting yourself in physical danger. When the media rush down here to get a soundbite for the news relating to, say, the London bombings, the responses from here are different to everywhere else.'

We passed the main brewery site where a promotional exhibition had recently taken place about Ken Livingstone's plans for Crossrail, a project to build a new railway connection under Central London, which, in addition to the East London Line extension, will impact enormously on the area. Sukhdev, like many local residents, is against the proposed scheme, which would see a huge hole bored into the centre of Hanbury Street. The works could take up to six years, disrupting local businesses with tons of earth and rubble being removed. 'Brick Lane to me is a place of tunnels, secrets and ancient burial grounds,' said Sukhdev, 'sacred places that should not be disturbed.' We carried on walking up towards Bacon Street where Sukhdev lives in a block of flats that houses Brazilians, Scandinavians, Lithuanians and Turks. In the last year or two he has noticed many French people squatting near by in empty warehouses around Brick Lane.

'I think of Brick Lane as a model for the rest of the country or even the rest of the world,' said Sukhdev suddenly. 'I have learned to live with otherness here in so many different ways. People try

to shield themselves away in most places – look at new gated communities, double glazing – but here you hear the ethnic samples, the laughter, the tears, you are forced to interact with what's happening and there is still variety, it's a place of echoes of the past but not in a sentimental way. It is really rich and compacted and could be seen as a model although it has not been set up or designed like this. It is suggestive and haunting in terms of what you can learn from a place.'

Sukhdev was tired and needed to rest before his next nocturnal adventure. We walked together up the street towards his flat, past Shoreditch Station and the iron hoardings covered in posters. As we neared the Bethnal Green end of the street I was aware that something felt different, the street had opened up somehow, it was changed. Then I realized why: the railway bridge had gone. The site of so many encounters over the centuries, the place of conflict and passion, the almost physical divide between communities, had disappeared. Sukhdev thought its removal probably had something to do with the Crossrail redevelopment. A negative impression of the bridge hung across the street. I felt myself instinctively hunch as we walked through the former dark shadows underneath.

After waving Sukhdev off near Cheshire Street, I ambled back down Brick Lane, heading towards the site where my grandparents once had their watchmaking and jewellery shop, which is now a curry restaurant called Eastern Eye. I was curious to speak with the current owners. The Eastern Eye was one of the first restaurants in Brick Lane to try to attract City workers, with a modern interior, chrome chairs and white linen tablecloths. When I reached the building it was about one-thirty in the afternoon and, from a distance, I could see through the full-length glass windows that there were no customers inside. As soon as I stepped through the door I was approached by a waiter, who tried to give me a menu and show me to a table. I explained my reasons for being there and asked to speak with the manager.

'I'm sure he'll see you,' said the waiter, 'as you can see we are not

busy.' He sat me down at a side table and disappeared into the back, emerging a few minutes later with a Bengali man in a dark suit who introduced himself to me as Raju, the manager. He was reluctant to speak with me at first, but warmed to me after hearing about my grandfather's connection to the site. He told me the building had been demolished and re-erected in 1934. 'There is a little plaque just above the doorway,' he said. As he spoke a piece of my own family history fell into place. I had always wondered how my grandparents could have afforded to rent such a large premises; their shop here had been small and modest according to family stories. Then I realized their original shop had probably been demolished to make way for this newer building in 1934, which must have been why they moved to another shop in New Road in Whitechapel.

The waiter who had greeted me at the door brought a pot of coffee over for us and sat down at the table to join in the discussion.

'This is Nur,' said Raju. 'He has lived on Brick Lane his whole life and can tell you some interesting stories.'

'This place, it used to be a vegetarian restaurant before Eastern Eye,' said Nur smiling, 'and before that a launderette and a sari shop.' Nur told me his family had lived on Brick Lane since his father arrived there in 1962 with working vouchers given to him by the British government. He had worked as a presser doing piece-work in the leather industry in a workshop on Brick Lane until his death a few years ago.

'When I started this business there were many leather factories,' said Raju. 'Upstairs on the first floor was one and in the basement was another. Now most of them have gone. Slowly by slowly Brick Lane converted into the restaurant trade, and nowadays it's a tourist place, it's the curry capital. The restaurant trade is now the main employer for Bengali people in Brick Lane. Some are cabbing, a few still work in what is left of the garment trade, but most work in the restaurants.'

'The Nazrul and the Clifton are the oldest restaurants in the street,' said Nur, 'many of the places are doing refurbishment now, trying to appeal to English taste.'

'Like we did,' said Raju. 'English people like it here because of the simple decor and we don't stand outside and pull people in.'

'And we have an excellent chef here,' added Nur.

'Our Bangladeshi chefs are very good but they have no qualifications or the language,' said Raju. 'Some of them have been here since the 1960s, and although their cooking is superb they cannot go to other places because they don't speak English.'

'They can't market themselves, you see,' said Nur. 'They could never become a celebrity chef like Jamie Oliver.'

'Is it usual for the restaurant to be so quiet?' I asked, looking around the empty room.

'Trade has gone down since the bombings,' said Raju. 'Particularly the lunchtime trade, which has drastically reduced, many people died in Aldgate, people are afraid to come because it's an Islamic area and the bombs happened near here.'

'People outside are looking at us differently,' said Nur.

'We are dependent on City people coming here for lunch,' said Raju. 'At this time of day the place used to be packed with customers from the offices. It's the same in the evening, well below average.'

'We want the tourists to come back,' said Nur. 'Not just for the restaurants, the residents like it also. Banglatown is now globally famous and we love the fact that people come here from all places.'

'I hope things pick up after the curry festival,' said Raju. 'Thousands of people come then and we have a stall out on the street, it is a very good event.'

'Do you have many Bengali customers?' I asked.

'Some,' he said, 'but many of them are like tourists now. They have moved out of the area but they always come back and visit. Brick Lane is still the main stop for everyone in the Bangladeshi community in this country, to come and get their shopping, to book a ticket to go to Bangladesh, to send money back home, to visit relatives, organize a wedding.'

'When I was a child it used to be mainly Bangladeshi people walking around here,' said Nur, 'and now it's so mixed it feels like you are in Soho or something.' Looking out of the windows at the busy street outside I could see why Nur felt the analogy was appropriate. I only wished for their sake that some of those people would make their way in. I shook their hands, thanked them for their time and stood to leave. Raju welcomed me back with typical Bengali hospitality, 'Call me if you come with friends,' he said smiling, 'I will make a special meal for you.'

Nur accompanied me to the door, stopping for a while and pointing through the window to the building opposite. 'The Bengal Cuisine – it used to be a launderette,' he said. 'The Shiraz Restaurant used to be a pub, Café Naz was a cinema, and a lot of political meetings used to happen outside.' I nodded, encouraging him to continue with his memory map.

'Taj Stores has always been there, and I remember Harry Fishman's sweet shop, it was small and congested and I used to buy sweets by the weight there with a one-pound note. Bombay Spice was a Jewish man's shop, the Curry Bazaar restaurant was a bicycle-repair shop, and they sold gas there for heaters. Like most Bengali people in the 1980s, we didn't have central heating. I was sent there to get gas. We didn't have a telephone either, no one could afford it, we'd receive telegrams from back home or letters. A real treat was if my father hired a video recorder for the weekend, we would rent Indian films and loads of people would come over to the house to see them. There were many video shops round here then, particularly in Hanbury Street, selling Bollywood films, they were so in demand, now everyone watches them on satellite.'

Nur stepped outside the door with me and stood looking up and down the street; the touts from the other restaurants were all doing the same thing. Nur respected his boss's wishes and restrained himself from directly approaching the passing tourists, but it didn't stop him standing there and politely smiling at people walking past in the hope of enticing them inside.

I left Nur and walked up Princelet Street, past the old synagogue, before crossing Wilkes Street and cutting through Puma Court on to Commercial Street. The traffic outside Spitalfields Market wasn't moving, Brushfield Street was closed off and a large crane took up most of the road, manoeuvring gigantic slabs of concrete for the redevelopment of the back half of the market. I walked on towards Aldgate tube, passing the Ten Bells pub on the corner of Fournier Street. In comparison to the curry restaurants on Brick Lane, the pub was busy. Through the gilded windows I could see groups of young people gathered around low wooden tables lit by candles. Until recently the pub used to be a strip joint, a rough-looking place where local working girls picked up customers. Ripper enthusiasts were the only outsiders who'd visit the place then, entering the murky interior in awe, hungry to breathe in the atmosphere of the building where Jack the Ripper met two of his victims, Catherine Eddowes and Elizabeth Stride. For decades the grisly history of the murders was celebrated inside the pub on a wall of fame exhibiting newspaper cuttings and photographs of victims and sites where bodies were found. Inside you could buy Ripper merchandise – keyrings, coasters and postcards. The pub was called the Jack the Ripper until the late 1980s, when a local committee forced the owners to change the name. The Victorian tiling is now all that remains of the old decor. The newspaper cuttings have gone along with the weighty Rottweiler who once

sat behind the bar, and the Ripper tourists are now sneered at by the *Guardian*-reading crowd inside.

The pub sits opposite Hawksmoor's Christ Church, whose enormous tower looms above the cityscape of Spitalfields, a landmark, a witness. After decades of campaigning and fundraising, the building has now been completely refurbished and is visited by architecture students and hordes of tourists, some of whom are fascinated by its associations with the occult, as mythologized by Peter Ackroyd in his novel *Hawksmoor*. Ackroyd founded the book on research conducted by Iain Sinclair a decade earlier, gleaned during his time spent working as a gardener for the Hawksmoor churches of Tower Hamlets. 'I went a lot deeper into the area when I began cutting the grass at the churches,' said Iain. 'I became invisible, mowing the lawn or walking around with a spike picking up old condoms, beer cans and bits of broken glass. People didn't notice me and I was able to look at the buildings and think about them in a new way.' Iain spoke to everyone, the vagrants sleeping on the benches, the parson and the occasional visitor to the then derelict Christ Church; these interviews gave him a secret insight into the area, which later came out in *Lud Heat*, a poetical work filled with suggestions that the six churches and two obelisks designed by Hawksmoor formed a power matrix over the London landscape that attracted dark happenings.

When I first moved into the area in 1991 Christ Church was closed. Alcoholics and homeless people sat in the gardens or on the stone steps by the basement, waiting for the crypt to open underneath the church, where there was a drop-in shelter and soup kitchen. Back in the 1970s meths drinkers filled the unkempt gardens, huddling around open fires, boiling up soup made from vegetables scavenged from the markets or occasionally having hot food from a stand outside, Fred's Snack Bar, which accepted meal tickets handed out by the rector. A few years ago I noticed the doors to the crypt were permanently closed. The gardens became well tended, gated off and respectable again. The crypt has not been open to general public access for centuries, fuelling urban myths about the place.

The shadow of Christ Church falls across
Spitalfields Gardens and in the shadow of Christ
Church I see a sight I never wish to see again.
There are no flowers in this garden, which is
smaller than my own rose garden at home.
Grass only grows here, and it is surrounded by
a sharp spiked iron fencing, as are all the parks
of London town, so that the homeless men and
women may not come in at night to sleep upon
it. We went up the narrow gravelled walk. On
the benches on either side arrayed a mass of
miserable and distorted humanity, the sight
of which would have impelled Doré to more
diabolical flights of fancy than he ever succeeded
in achieving. A chill, raw wind was blowing, and
these creatures, huddled in their rags, sleeping
for the most part, or trying to sleep. Here were
a dozen women, ranging in age from twenty to
seventy. Next a babe, possibly of nine months,
lying asleep, flat on the hard bench, with neither
pillow or covering, nor anyone looking after it.

Jack London, *The People of the Abyss*, 1903

The most fantastical story I've heard is that during renovations in 1990, the perfectly preserved body of a young girl was discovered inside one of the catacombs in a lead-lined coffin. She was dressed in funeral clothes: a white dress, bonnet and gloves. As the body was exposed to the air it rapidly began to deteriorate and within twenty-four hours she had turned to black dust.

Walking past Christ Church after my walk with Sukhdev and meeting Raju and Nur, I was surprised to see the doors to the crypt open. Curious to get my first look inside the place I went down the worn stone steps, descended beneath the church, and found myself in a dark narrow corridor with a vaulted brick ceiling. The thick stone walls seemed to suck up sound. The constant noise of the traffic above on Commercial Street was absent. I couldn't see anyone, so I wandered around until I found an open vault to my right. It was pitch black inside but as I turned a corner I saw a strange projected light flickering over a rippled surface that seemed to be suspended above the ground. I walked towards the mass of material and realized on closer inspection that it was carpet, which had been draped around one of the central columns in the room. It was clear to me I had stumbled upon an artistic intervention of some sort, and as I looked closer at the shafts of light I could just make out the distorted shapes of wild animals. I heard some footsteps behind me and turned around quickly.

A young white woman with long hair stood in front of me. 'Sorry, I didn't hear you come in,' she said smiling, 'the acoustics are so weird in here, and I was just making tea.' She told me she was the recently appointed curator to the crypt, which had just reopened as an art venue. The work I had seen was the first of four commissioned installations that responded to the crypt. The curator was called Lisa-Raine and she told me she was an active member of Christ Church and worked there as the administrator. I asked what had happened to the homeless hostel and she told me it had been moved to purpose-built premises five years ago. 'I still get many people coming down here wondering where it has gone,' she said. 'The artwork you saw is the first public event in

Ignoring the ancient injunction on the wall bidding them to 'Commit no Nuisance,' these time-honoured figures stage a vile performance of their own. They hurl insults at the concert-goers, begging money from them obscenely and urinating over their smart cars. My sleeve was taken by a man who dragged me through the hellish narrative of twenty-two years spent in gaol. Shuddering with horror at the deteriorated company into which he had been released, this fellow declared his own outlaw ethic in words that should be cut into the stone of the Hawksmoor building: 'I've never raped. I've never mugged. I've never robbed a working-class home.' As he sank away towards the underworld of the crypt, we ascended the hierarchical steps to hear music by Messiaen and Hans Werner Henze. The frisson was undeniable.

Patrick Wright, *A Journey through Ruins: The Last Days of London*, 1991 this crypt for many years. Despite over a thousand people a week using the nave above for worship, concerts, public performances and private functions, this part of the crypt has never been open for public access before.'

Home of the dead for centuries, an air-raid shelter during the Second World War, a homeless hostel and now a venue for contemporary art – the crypt is part of the long history of the area. Standing in the dark subterranean vault I imagined all the people I have spoken to for the purposes of this book converging together there; filling the empty space with their voices, their different stories echoing around the vaults, becoming a part of the fabric of that place.

18

Fournier Street

Fournier Street is unique and has always attracted interesting people to it. There's the City and a Grade I listed church at one end, and at the other end a mosque and Banglatown, which makes it a very dynamic place to live.

Tracey Emin

The following week I returned to the crypt. Lisa-Raine was standing in the corridor, deep in conversation with a bearded man carrying a black bin bag. She drew a map on the back of one of her art leaflets and handed it to him with a smile before waving me towards some chairs. 'He needed directing to the new shelter,' she said. We sat and talked as visitors to the exhibition walked in and out. A man went past, telling a story to his friend about when the crypt was first opened: 'They found spores of the plague virus in the lead coffins and the archaeologists had to be inoculated.'

When Lisa-Raine moved to East London in 2001 she began searching for a church to worship in. She looked at many places but was drawn to Christ Church because of its proactive work in the local community. 'I was also intrigued by the building itself and the three parallel lines of Bishopsgate, Commercial Street and Brick Lane,' she said. 'The City meets the artistic community meets the immigrant community.'

We talked about the long history of the church and she told me that in the 1950s it had nearly been demolished – it was in such a bad state of repair. For decades Christ Church remained derelict, squatted by vagrants and pigeons. 'The congregation couldn't use it,' she said, 'they met in Hanbury Hall or the crypt.' In 1976 a group

I remember breaking into Hawksmoor's Christ Church in the 1970s and going up rickety staircases and it just being open to the elements almost. It was filled with tramps living there and that reflected the state of the whole area. I do have a certain resentment for the art world moving in here. There are still many people living in awful conditions in the area alongside celebrities living in houses worth millions. There's this cheek-by-jowl contradiction going on that doesn't sit well with me.

Eddie, 2004

called the Friends of Christ Church got together to save the building. Over the years they raised millions and with the help of the Heritage Lottery Fund Christ Church was eventually restored back to its original state, with a perfectly refurbished Baroque interior, a hand-cut stone floor, wood-panelled galleries and eighteenth-century chandeliers. The building reopened to the public in 2004 and is now used throughout the year by an active congregation as well as being hired out for events.

I followed Lisa-Raine through to another vaulted space in the crypt arranged with simple wooden pews in front of a small altar decorated with a hand-embroidered cloth. She told me this was where the congregation used to meet before the church was restored. 'Of course, it is nicer to be upstairs,' she said, 'but our church is so much more than the famous Hawksmoor building. It is a living community, a unique mix of people. We have Bengali Christians in our church, many visitors from the Far East, some African and Afro-Caribbean people as well as many Europeans, but the majority are English and live locally.'

Some Bengali Muslims are connected to the church via their Adopt a Family Scheme, which Lisa-Raine is involved in: 'I visit a group of boys to help them with their homework, and in exchange they

Christ Church with its towering spire stands at the borders of the City and the East End, quietly watching over the community it serves; with its fantastic architectural dimensions, the light and space of its interior transforms it into one of our capital's most breathtaking sacred spaces. It stands too as a constant reminder that God is present here in the midst of the hustle and bustle. Visitors and tourists may stand in awe of this building whose size reminds us of His eternal and cosmic sovereignty.

Revd Andy Rider, MA, Rector of Christ Church Spitalfields, 2006 teach me Sylheti, cook for me and invite me to family gatherings and likewise. I've met my next-door neighbours, which can be difficult. There is a great mix here, but the cultures rarely merge in this way but more typically live in parallel.'

Christ Church run many other outreach programmes: visiting elderly people in their homes; a boys' football club at Allen Gardens; homework and language support to local families; Sylheti classes for English speakers; and other activities that bring the Bengali and Christian communities together. The church owns and governs Christ Church School on Brick Lane. They support the school with link charities, run English classes from there, and voluntary workers from the church help Bengali pupils with reading and English language. The school is a Church of England school, and the primarily Bangladeshi children are taught about both Christian and Muslim cultures. Bill Fishman told me that in the 1880s the English teachers at that school had to learn Yiddish to teach the mainly Jewish pupils there.

Christ Church has strong connections with the mosque at the other end of Fournier Street. The interaction the church has had with the local Bengali Muslim community has proved invaluable in recent times: 'After the 7/7 bombings, when it was very difficult here for some of my Muslim friends, I was able to support them,' said Lisa-Raine.

The community work that is undertaken at Christ Church is invisible to most people coming to visit the building, but the church has been helping local people in the area for centuries. When Huguenot weavers were starving in the eighteenth century it established a soup kitchen; and the crypt was used as a homeless shelter from 1965 to 2000. The use of the church hall has always reflected the community living in and around Brick Lane. In 1888 the activist Annie Besant hired the hall to persuade the Bryant and May matchgirls to strike over their terrible pay and working conditions, which caused their jawbones to disintegrate after being exposed to phosphorus used in the factory. In the early part of the twentieth century it was used by Jewish anarchists and Zionists as a meeting

place; and in the 1970s the first English classes for Bengali women were run from there. In 2002 I was fortunate enough to meet the remarkable woman, Juliet Shelbourne, who initiated them.

Juliet is Lisa-Raine's predecessor, the former administrator of Christ Church. We met at the Hawksmoor-designed rectory in Fournier Street. My initial impression of Juliet, a petite, genteel woman in a tweed skirt, was of a rather shy, middle-class lady who seemed a little out of place in Whitechapel. It turned out, however, that her Christian faith has led her to make some unorthodox and brave decisions. In the 1970s a strange dream persuaded her to uproot herself and her four children from a beautiful fifteenth-century house in the country and move to a dilapidated former women's hostel in Cable Street in the East End. Juliet and her husband, Hugh, a bible teacher, renovated and shared their new home with their children and various other people who had nowhere else to go, including a violent and unpredictable homeless woman who often smashed up the furniture.

The Shelbournes started to work with the Bengali community soon after moving to the area, and Juliet set up English classes at the church hall and ran various support groups (alongside establishing eight nursery schools in Uganda and various other remarkable feats). In the last few years she acted as a mentor to a number of young women with high-powered jobs in the City who attended Christ Church, some of whom had lost their jobs and were struggling with personal issues. During this time she became friendly with one of Fournier Street's most famous residents, the artist Tracey Emin. 'Tracey often came to the church,' Juliet said. 'She sometimes seemed quite shy and we talked a lot. She is very involved in the area.'

Tracey Emin is just one in a long line of artists who have chosen to make the streets off Brick Lane their home. Gilbert & George came in the 1960s, along with bohemians such as Raphael Samuel and Mike Farren, when the area was still filled with tailors' workshops and furriers, and was a run-down working place. In the early 1980s the Spitalfields Historic Buildings Trust – a charity set up to purchase and meticulously refurbish buildings of historical interest in the area and sell them on to vetted buyers – began to move in and restore the long-decaying former weavers' homes.

These houses, built by wealthy Huguenots in the eighteenth century, were originally intended for single occupancy. As the weaving industry declined so did the houses, which were split up and converted into smaller dwellings that were rented out to lodgers and workshops for the rag trade, housing up to ten families at any one time. When the Jewish community started to arrive in the 1880s they moved into these rooms and continued in the textile industry, working in dreadful conditions. The fabric of the buildings and their usage remained the same when the Bengali community took over. The original fireplaces were boarded up to keep out draughts, and the original leaking ceilings were covered over to stop the plaster falling. Cornices and banisters survived not through conservation but neglect.

In the late 1980s Spitalfields remained one of the poorest boroughs in London. Prince Charles made a visit in 1987 and was appalled by the poverty and inner-city decay he witnessed. In 1989 Grand Metropolitan sold the brewery site and British Rail sold the Bishopsgate Goods Yard (an area of over twenty-seven acres). A few years later the fruit and vegetable market was gone and the developers moved in. At the same time the Spitalfields Trust arrived, buying up buildings and restoring them for people who wanted to live in one of London's most historic quarters.

The small rag-trade units were pushed out as landlords realized the new real-estate potential of their properties. Local community activists condemned the actions of the Spitalfields Historic Buildings Trust as ignoring the needs of local people, but there is no doubt that the trust's forced occupancy of many of these buildings saved them from demolition. Kay Jordan of Heba predicted in an interview for the *Guardian* in 1989 that 'in five years' time this area will become a part of the City with maybe tiny enclaves of local people that were once the majority'. Spitalfields has shrunk, half of the market has gone, the boundary of Bishopsgate that marked the edge of the City and the beginning of East London for centuries has been blurred, and the immaculately restored properties in Fournier Street are now highly desirable and worth millions. Crowds of tourists wander there daily, admiring the architecture of Spitalfields' most distinctive street, trying to get a peek into Tracey Emin's window, making bad jokes about her 'unmade bed' or listening to the tour guides' tales of master weavers standing outside their grand porticoes, dressed in the finest silks and damasks. The later histories, the poverty, the Dickensian conditions of the buildings, the long hours spent at tailoring benches, are often left out of these stories.

Tracey Emin makes no secret of the fact that she lives in Fournier Street. She bought one of the refurbished Georgian houses a few years ago and has talked about her passion for Spitalfields repeatedly in the press. She is regularly seen walking down the street on her way to her studio, having breakfast in St John's Bread and Wine on Commercial Street or drinking in the nearby Golden Heart. Everyone I meet locally has an opinion about her. I was curious to speak to Tracey myself, not about her work as an artist but about the place she has chosen to make her home.

Tracey told me she first got to know East London in the early 1980s, when she went to college at Sir John Cass, and she described the whole area as 'a giant bombsite then'. From 1992 to 1993 she ran a shop with fellow artist Sarah Lucas in Redchurch Street, just off Bethnal Green Road near the top of Brick Lane. She said she has always felt 'at ease in the area'. She had a studio in Wentworth Street with her then boyfriend Matt Collishaw and started living there before buying a small house in Wilkes Street. 'When I could afford it, it was a natural move around the corner to Fournier Street,' she said.

Tracey's nan used to work in Whitechapel back in 1915, so she feels a real connection to the area, having grown up with stories about the Jews, visits to Bloom's, and the Victorian prostitutes. Her nan wasn't there that long after the Ripper murders and it was still a very rough place. She worked in a furriers making hats somewhere between Whitechapel and Aldgate East stations.

The psychogeography of the area interests Emin. 'Behind my

Conservation here is typically pastiche, as in a costume drama, items are treasured for their period effect. Houses are restored by stripping them of their historicity – the barnacles that have accreted over time.

Raphael Samuel, *Guardian*, 17 October 1987

house in Fournier Street is a runic circle,' she said, 'a bit like a Stonehenge thing buried underground that just touches the boundary of my garden and I think this gives a really good karma to the area. The other thing is Spitalfields used to be a hospital in Roman times. Maybe they placed it there because of some healing energy of the place. I can't exactly explain why but the whole area just makes me feel good. Maybe it's because Brick Lane has always been the place where migrants have gone to, so throughout history it has been filled with people who never quite fitted in and that's the reason why I feel comfortable there.'

Another reason Tracey chooses to live in Fournier Street is because most of the people don't conform to the normal nuclear-family set-up. 'I don't feel like an oddball,' she said, 'like the spinster in the street, which is a good feeling.' She describes the area as village-like and friendly. She feels an accepted part of the community most of the time though she has been verbally attacked for her supposed wealth. One night in her local pub someone said to her, 'You come in and whack your eight hundred grand down and think you've bought a bit of the area.' Tracey was deeply offended by the comment. 'It's not like I'm gentrified, I've always felt connected there. If I'd had a co-op flat I would have been happy too,' she said.

Tracey knows the name of every single person who lives on her street: 'When I go home late at night on my own and get a bit frightened I go through their names in my head, like a mantra, and it makes me feel safe.' The week before I spoke to Tracey she'd been to the house of one of her neighbours to celebrate their newly awarded OBE. 'I meet some great people here,' she said.

She has only one Bangladeshi friend, which she finds incredible but thinks is a generational thing: 'I'm not going to be friends with the older types and the young ones who might be willing to be my friend are probably too young, and the generation in between seems quite private. I think in the next fifteen years there'll be a lot more mixing, and the Bangladeshi community will open up more.'

Tracey occasionally attends Christ Church, and always pays attention to what is going on there. 'The church is part of community

life here,' she said. 'A lot of my neighbours meet on Sunday at St John's Bread and Wine on Commercial Street for breakfast and then go to services at the church. It's a traditional Sunday morning but with an edge.'

For the most part she feels an accepted part of the community. When her cat, Docket, went missing, though, the posters she put up were ripped down and sold as pieces of artwork. 'That upset me and so do the constant comments about my unmade bed,' she said. 'No one in my community would have taken the posters. I thought they could at least have waited until I had found him.'

Tracey celebrates the recent redevelopment of the area and describes herself as pro-commerce, pro-regeneration: 'When you see the reflection of the church in the great sheets of glass on the new Spitalfields Market building it's beautiful. I like the urban nature of where I live, and even if it becomes completely gentrified it will remain a unique place filled with amazing people.'

One of her best friends is Sandra, the landlady at the Golden Heart, whom Tracey described as 'a generous, warm, devout Catholic, with an incredibly good heart. She's a real East Ender and very family orientated and takes care of people like me. When I was terribly ill, and couldn't get out of bed, she came every day with food for me – fish, hot tea and soup, she's got that real old East End spirit.'

Soon after talking with Tracey I attended an event at the Golden Heart to celebrate the first screening of a short film made about the pub's landlady by my friend, the photographer, filmmaker and local councillor Phil Maxwell, and his partner, Hazuan Hashim, entitled *Sandra*. The film celebrates the life of the iconic landlady, capturing a slice of her life at the pub she has run continuously for over twenty-five years.

Phil tried to get Sandra to speak to me for this book but it was impossible to pin her down. Every time I went to meet her she'd be busy working in the bar, chucking out drunken City boys, or talking in corners with the few traders who still come to see her from the old fruit and vegetable market opposite. They used to

form her customer base, but now you are more likely to bump into Gilbert & George, Dan Cruickshank or Tracey Emin there, and the reason they all love her so much is she treats everyone the same. I asked Phil why he wanted to make the film, and he said, 'She encapsulates East End matriarchy and has extraordinary survival skills underpinned by great humour.' Lulu from the brewery complex described her as a 'touchstone person who I always go to see when I celebrate and if things go wrong. She has so much contact with people every day and has gathered huge amounts of wisdom, from the market traders to the new City lot, and they all know they have got to behave if they go in the Golden Heart.'

The film was shown in a gallery opposite the pub. Everyone cheered when Sandra arrived, wearing a vintage dress, pearls and sparkling slippers. 'Chill out, chill out,' she said laughing. The film, with a musical score by Michael Nyman, showed Sandra jiving with punters in the pub, trying to raffle a fairy made by Tracey Emin to raise money for charity, and hula hooping in the saloon bar. After the screening most of the people in the gallery went back into the heaving pub opposite, and the party continued until late. Sandra disappeared for a while, then re-emerged from the basement with her hoop and stood in the centre of Commercial Street hula hooping and waving at the passing cars. A crowd gathered on the street to watch. Eventually she stopped and came over to where I was standing with Phil, red-cheeked and happy, and threw her arms around him. 'He's wonderful, you know, this one,' she said to me, squeezing him tightly. 'I love him, such a fabulous artist, you should speak to him for your book, not me, he's been documenting the area for ever.'

19

Whitechapel Memory

**The new interlopers are marching into this territory and
stripping it bare, taking over the land. Liverpool Street was
distant ten years ago and now the market has half gone, a
boundary has been crossed. History is being effaced, there's
been a physical shift and things are being lost at an unnatural
rate. It's a bring-in-the-bulldozers mentality.**

Jagtar Semplay

I went to visit Phil Maxwell in the high-rise council flat he has
lived in for over twenty-five years, on the east side of Brick Lane,
a very different place from Fournier Street though only a short
walk away. The walls of his block are covered in graffiti and gangs
of hooded teenagers roam around the patch of grass at the front.
I met him on the landing of the twelfth floor, where he lives, and
we stood for a while outside his flat, looking at the views out on to
Brick Lane and the City beyond. 'I find it incredible that this area
boasts the highest and lowest wages in London,' said Phil, pointing
at the council estates below. 'The newcomers, the Trustafarians I
call them, and the middle-class white kids are all buying houses
around Brick Lane, buying into an idea of urban chic, but few of
them cross over to this side of the street.'

Phil was offered his flat in 1980 because as a council employee he
qualified as a key worker. 'It was hard to let at the time, probably
still is,' he said, laughing. He'd moved there from a tough neighbourhood in inner-city Liverpool where he had been working as
a teacher. He left that job because of the homophobic attitude of
parents and staff. His sexuality hasn't been an issue since he moved

to Brick Lane, but he is acutely aware of the racist attitudes around him. 'I experienced it the first time I got off the train at Euston and took a cab here,' he said. 'The driver said to me, "I don't normally take people round here, mate, 'cause it's full of Pakis."' Phil enjoyed the diverse and cosmopolitan nature of Brick Lane, and felt physically safe in the area even though it was economically depressed, but the living conditions of his Bengali neighbours horrified him. 'I saw people living in real squalor,' he said, 'like in Brune House around the corner where a family of ten were in a one-bedroom flat with the kitchen doubling as a bathroom. They had to pull a wooden top, which was quite rotten, over the bath, and that is where they prepared food.'

Phil became a councillor for Tower Hamlets and a passionate campaigner for better housing in the area. 'Spitalfields Housing Association grew out of this struggle,' he said. 'The Bengali community stood up and fought, with the help of people like Terry Fitzpatrick, a white builder, who organized numerous marches and demonstrations.' Phil got to know his Bangladeshi neighbours by protesting with them. Many of them had been involved in the Bangladesh Liberation War, and had remarkable energy. Some of

the successful businessmen with restaurants now in Brick Lane were part of the campaign to change things. 'They were once living in that squalor,' said Phil. 'They remember the skinheads running down Brick Lane, fighting people on the streets. Now they are respectable and well-off, it is a remarkable achievement and has happened relatively quickly. There is jealousy now about the success of some of the Bangladeshi community, just like there was with the Jews. What people don't realize is they had no choice but to set up new ventures within their communities. They couldn't get into mainstream business because there was a colour bar. They went into their industries, which they were skilled in, and worked very long hours, which provided them with the economic base for what they have now.'

Phil still works for Tower Hamlets Council and remains actively involved in local politics. His other great passion is photography. He describes himself as a 'street photographer' who has been obsessively taking pictures in Brick Lane since he moved there. He now has an archive of over ten thousand images of the area. 'I can't go out without a camera, it's my notebook, I take pictures on a daily basis,' he said. Thousands of negatives have yet to be processed. One day he hopes to print them all, but he would need a much

larger storage space than his small flat. His interest has always been people, their faces and how they react with the environment. 'When I go out in the street I see theatre,' he said. 'I love to walk in the area; it is just a complete pleasure. Hearing the different languages being spoken, people interacting, putting their stalls out in the morning, all of life takes place here. Brick Lane is a particularly interesting place to photograph – the juxtaposition of the wealth of the City right next to what was for centuries the poorest part of London.'

He took me through to a small bedroom that doubles up as his office and dark room, and we spent some time sitting on the floor looking through his vast collection of images. His style of social-documentary photography has many similarities to the work of Marketa Luskacova, Ron McComarck and Paul Trevor, who all spent time living and working in East London in the 1970s, getting to know people in the markets and on the streets. They have moved on to other projects but Phil is still living in the area. He has taken photographs all over the world, particularly in Bangladesh, but not a month has gone by in the last twenty-five years when he has not been out on the streets in and around Brick Lane with his camera.

His photo-documentary archive must now be the most extensive record of the area in existence. To celebrate this achievement the Spitalfields Housing Association sponsored an exhibition of his work, entitled 'Spitalfields 25', as part of its Silver Jubilee celebrations. Before I left his flat that day Phil gave me an invitation to the opening night.

The exhibition took place in the Brick House Gallery, the part of the Old Truman Brewery where Svar and the artists' collective once had their studios and gallery space. When I arrived a crowd of people had congregated on the pavement outside, smoking, talking, holding plastic glasses filled with wine. Inside, the large white warehouse was packed. I caught sight of Phil's partner, Huzuan, who came up to me excitedly and said, 'He's already sold three works,' before being whisked away by a journalist looking for Phil. I have been to many openings in and around Brick Lane over the years, but what made Phil's exhibition so different was that the majority of the people there were Bangladeshi. I stood against the wall and watched for a while as local characters wandered around with their families, pointing themselves out in the pictures, which were hung high on the walls. I spotted Phil surrounded by a large huddle of friends and waved before slowly making my way around the show looking at his work.

His remarkable collection of images documented the clearance of slum dwellings and the deprivation of the early 1980s, and featured many of the people he has got to know over the years. His earlier work had a certain resonance to it – many of the places depicted no longer exist, and the kind of characters he photographed are rarely seen around Brick Lane any more: lone figures sitting on upturned crates, elderly women in headscarves pushing empty prams, Hasidic Jews standing in shop doorways, looking as if they had been directly transported from seventeenth-century Krakow. Other images recorded the political activity Phil has been involved in: anti-Nazi demonstrations in Brick Lane; a protest outside the police station in 1984 against the deportation of Afia Begum. One wall was dedicated to photographs taken in the last five years: large

One of the great things about East London is the feeling of cultural inheritance. I was in a Bengali restaurant and these two men were standing outside the door and I took a photograph. It's timeless in that some people might assume it to be an image from sixty or seventy years ago and there remain people from the Jewish community who haven't changed their attire or demeanour for generations.

Phil Maxwell, 'Street Photography: A Century of Change in Pictures', *Rising East*, Vol. 3, no. 3 (1999)

colour images of the Brick Lane Festival; people sitting in coffee bars in the newly regenerated brewery site, the bright neon signs outside the restaurants in Brick Lane and a dozen or so pictures of cranes, bulldozers and building works around Spitalfields Market.

Out of all of these there was one that particularly intrigued me. The photograph had been blown up to about five foot across and showed a section of Brick Lane near to the Old Truman Brewery. Walking down the centre of the street was a lone Bengali woman, so still and beautiful that I wondered at first if she was a shop mannequin. She was dressed in a contemporary way – high-heeled boots, short skirt – and the photograph was sepia-coloured apart from her clothes, which had been hand-coloured in red, reminding me of the child in a red coat at the beginning of *Schindler's List.*

'Stunning, isn't she?' I spun round and there was Phil. I congratulated him on the show and asked about the photograph. 'She didn't even know I was taking that picture,' he said. 'I showed it to her later and she couldn't remember the moment.'

'You know her?' I asked.

'Oh, yes,' he replied, 'her studio is next to mine in the old synagogue in Greatorex Street. She nearly won Miss World once representing Bangladesh, but she is a writer and artist now and lives just off Brick Lane. Her name is Sanchita Islam.'

I had known of Sanchita's work for some time after having purchased her limited-edition book *From Briarwood to Barishal to Brick Lane* at Eastside Bookshop in 2001. The book documents her personal quest to explore her Bengali identity through film, writing, poetry and painting. She invited other Bengali artists to contribute to the publication, but the majority of the illustrations in the book are hers – strange, abstract watercolour landscapes, drawings of rooftops in Calcutta, jungles in Bangladesh, cityscapes in East London. Sanchita's own prose in the book includes a contemporary description of Brick Lane as she sees it. I was keen to meet her. Phil promised to pass on her details.

The following day Phil emailed me Sanchita's address and I got in touch with the Bengali artist. We met up soon after at her flat

When I walk down Brick Lane I see red brick
council flats, hanging saris blowing in the wind.
A chicken bone lying on the street, crisp packets washed up with leaves and bloated jackfruit
spilling on the street. An Asian girl with a thick
black plait wearing jeans that go up her crack
and a top that clings to her flat chest crosses the
road. Another girl, could be a woman, a granny,
don't know because she's hidden behind a cave of
black. Sees her world through a slit of light and
her toes are naked. Three boys with gelled hair
loiter by a car that is half white and brown with
rust. It has no tyres, no doors, no windows, it's
just a shell. 'Hello, nice pussy,' they heckle, 'give
us your number, darling.' Keep my head down,
don't look up in case I grin. Speed past the cash
and carry filled with nine thousand packets of
pink bog roll and sacks of Basmati rice. Hear a
fluttering of a flute, a tink tink, followed by a
high-pitched voice and a tabla beat floating
from a shop. The windows are plastered
with pictures of Bollywood stars. Men with
moustaches wearing tight pants. There's a stink
of onions and rubbish in the air. Eastenders
is filled with locals chewing on kebab rolls
drenched in chilli and minty yoghurt.

Sanchita Islam, *From Briarwood to Barishal to
Brick Lane*, 2001

in Cheshire Street, in the newly converted former Jewish bath-house. Arriving outside the entrance to the building, I pushed the intercom to her flat and waited for the electronic gates to open. Sanchita appeared a few minutes later, running down the central stairway, barefoot, as light as air, heavily made up, with her long dark hair flowing down the back of a bright emerald-green dress. She led me through an open courtyard surrounded by studio flats and up the stairs to her apartment, which consisted of one white room with long French windows at one end and a tiny modern kitchen at the other. All around the walls hung Sanchita's brightly coloured artworks, and soft classical music drifted down from a mezzanine-level bedroom. I took off my shoes and perched on a high red Perspex stool while Sanchita made some green tea. We sat and talked, drinking out of gold porcelain teacups.

Sanchita grew up in Manchester and came to Brick Lane for the first time as a teenager for the Miss World Competition. 'I remember arriving in this long dress and tiara outside Taj Stores,' she said, 'and being jostled around and all these people shouting. It was mad and seemed very foreign and I never imagined then I'd come back and live here.' A decade after the beauty pageant Sanchita did make Brick Lane her home, however. By then she had given up modelling and was working full time as an artist, and Brick Lane had become the perfect environment for her to explore the themes that interested her. She is now deeply involved in the music and performance scene happening at the brewery. She runs a company specializing in live art, called pigmentexplosion, and often performs in the Vibe Bar. She also works intensively with the local Bengali community and she showed me her latest book, *Hidden*, which documents the stories of Bengali women suffering from domestic violence in East London: 'I wanted to tell their stories because I think these women are incredibly brave. Although they have suffered terrible abuse the important thing is that they left, they got out, and they are trying to carve out new lives for themselves and their children.' The common thread running through all of Sanchita's creative work is that it reflects some aspect of Bangladeshi life. 'The typical stereotypes attached to being Bangladeshi,' she told me, 'are either you work in a restaurant or you're repressed and you wear a *burka*, so part of what I try to do is to show a different side.'

Sanchita involves local people in her projects, particularly if they don't have access to the arts themselves. She is currently working on a documentary film based at Avenues Unlimited in Brick Lane, exploring the relationship between Somalian and Bengali youths. The response to her project so far has been mixed. Sanchita goes out on to the street and tries to interview members of local gangs. If she approaches them in a group they jeer and shout abuse. If she manages to get one on their own they will sometimes talk to her. 'This project is the hardest so far,' she told me. 'The women suffering domestic violence just poured everything out, they were desperate to talk, but these kids are keeping things close to their chest, probably because many of their activities are illegal.' Derek Cox is helping Sanchita with the project.

Sanchita showed me another of her publications, *Old Meets Young*, which is based on the relationships she formed with Bengali elders at St Hilda's Community Centre, near the Bethnal Green end of Brick Lane. She spent months getting to know the residents there, many of whom are among the first generation of Bangladeshis to come to Brick Lane in the 1950s and 1960s. Most of the women who feature in the book were brought over by their husbands in the 1970s, 1980s and 1990s. 'It wasn't their dream to live here,' said Sanchita. 'Many never learned to speak English, some are now alone without family, most are wheelchair-bound.' Sanchita showed me a painting she had recently finished of one of the ladies at the centre. 'She'd had a stroke and couldn't speak,' said Sanchita. 'One day I returned to St Hilda's and a care worker told me she had died. They thought she was one hundred and two years old.'

Sanchita feels indebted to these frail elderly people. 'They are the first generation who laid down the foundations for the next,' she said, 'and now there is a third, fourth and even fifth generation living in the Brick Lane area. Their achievements are obvious, particularly in Brick Lane, where Bangladeshi culture is so strong. Brick Lane

to me looks like a street that could have been plucked out of Bangladesh.'

I left soon after looking at that painting as Sanchita had another meeting to go to. Derek Cox was taking her to see a Somalian boy called Golad who speaks fluent Bangla because he hangs out in a Bangla gang. Sanchita was hoping that Golad might take part in her film. She walked me back down to the entrance of the old bathhouse. Cheshire Street was empty of pedestrians and traffic. It is only during Brick Lane Market, which takes place every Sunday from about four or five in the morning until two in the afternoon, that the street really comes to life. This part of Cheshire Street has always been the poorest section of Brick Lane Market. The people trading there try to sell anything to make a bit of extra money: an old coat, cassettes with no cases, a single shoe, out-of-date magazines. Laying out their wares on tatty blankets or bits of wet cardboard, whatever the weather. These pavement sellers reminded Sanchita of the people in the street markets in Bangladesh. 'The way they organized their belongings so carefully,' she said, 'they'll trade with anything they have in Bangladesh, but I didn't expect to see that kind of poverty here.'

20

Brick Lane Market

It is the mother of all the London markets and there is no other
thoroughfare so rich in metaphors of history and memories
of struggle, bravery and desperation as Brick Lane. It is the
original lorry that something fell off: anarchic, disinhibited,
stoic and clamorous.

David Widgery, 'Ripe Bananas and Stolen Bicycles',
Marketa Luskacova: Photographs of Spitalfields

For centuries Brick Lane Market has provided a means for the poor
of East London to make a living. Spreading from Bethnal Green
down to Shoreditch Station, the market has been the focus of local
activity, legal and otherwise, since it originated in Club Row, a
street off the north side of Brick Lane, in the eighteenth century.

299

It began as a place where farmers could sell livestock outside the City walls. Over time it expanded directly into Brick Lane and the surrounding streets, with the animal market continuing alongside all sorts of traders, selling hot food, groceries, anything and everything imaginable.

When thousands of Jewish refugees came into the area in the 1880s the market changed. Stalls selling shellfish, hot eels, pea soup, pickled whelks and boiled meat puddings sat next to new vendors, speaking in rapid Yiddish, dealing in kosher goods, *schmaltz* herring and bagels. The market opened on Sundays instead of Saturdays, because of restrictions on working on the Sabbath. It must have resembled a scene from an Eastern European ghetto then, with squawking chickens, bewigged women in long heavy skirts and bearded men dressed in silk breeches, black coats and wide-brimmed fur hats.

Sally Flood remembers the market in the 1920s as being a very Jewish space that was as much a meeting place as a place to shop, and was frequented entirely by local people. She said it took hours to walk through the market because her mother was always stopping to gossip with neighbours and friends. A weekly trip there was part of the cultural life of the community, buying the basic necessities for the week, exchanging stories, listening to the speakers outside Bloom's. Every week Sally was given a ha'penny pocket money, which she sometimes spent on a chunk of pineapple. If her father wasn't looking she'd give her penny to an ex-serviceman with no arms or legs who used to sit near to the railway arch: 'He had a sign round his neck and sold matches in a little tray. The memory of him still haunts me. I knew he'd fought in the First World War and he looked so desperately lost.'

The Sunday market was part of Majer Bogdanski's life for decades, opening up right outside his front door in Cheshire Street. In the late 1940s he said the customers were a mixture but the stallholders were mainly Jewish: 'Everyone down the Lane on a Sunday morning was speaking Yiddish and all the stalls were Jewish stalls, you could buy Jewish sheet music, records, food, everything.' Many of

the traders were people like him, who had come out of the army or returned from war. Majer ran a stall at Brick Lane for a few years with a former Japanese prisoner-of-war, selling *shmatter*, bits of old cloth and remnants. 'There was a lot of clothing then,' he said, 'mainly second-hand clothing. There was still rationing and people didn't have much, but in the market you could buy anything if you had the money: pots, pans, stockings, books, meat. A huge black market trade took place in Brick Lane after the war.'

In the 1950s John Gardiner remembers 'loads of dodgy characters with hot gear', such as a shifty-looking Jewish man who ran a stall selling stamps and medals: 'He'd look about and then open up his coat and the watches was all up his arms. He'd whip out stuff from his pockets, looking over his shoulder the whole time.' Post-war, money was tight, and the Jewish community still living in the area were poor. The ones who could afford to had moved out after being evacuated, there was nothing to come back to, the houses had all been bombed. The market was a place where people on low wages could buy goods cheaply – much of it was stolen, or 'knocked-off', or second-hand; furniture, clothes, household goods and jewellery were all recycled.

'I remember a little man who done glasses on a stall there,' said John. 'He'd take your frames, find the right lenses and put them in with his Bunsen burner and he weren't half quick. He earned a lot

It is not till we come to Wentworth Street that the strangeness of the Sunday scene reveals itself. Here all the shops are open and the narrow thoroughfare is packed with the stalls of Jewish hawkers. We hear a little English at the top of Wentworth Street, but as we push our way through the seething crowd and get nearer to Brick Lane the English words become rarer and rarer, and presently only the German Hebrew jargon known as 'Yiddish' reaches our ears.

George R. Sims, *Off the Track in London*, 1911

of money, people always wanted second-hand glasses in those days 'cause new ones was real expensive. There was no eye-test, you just tried them on till you found the right pair. Next to him was the sarsaparilla man, who sold cordial drinks. Hot ones in the winter, cold ones in the summer, cost about a penny a glass and tasted wonderful. There were lots of dead-fish stalls with people crowded round, blimey it didn't half smell. They would pick live eels out the barrel and chop them up in front of you, then wrap them in paper. Cheshire Street, or Hare Street as we used to call it, was filled with old bikes. There was an oil shop on the corner of Brick Lane and Hare Street, an ironmongery place, and on the other side was Bacon Street. It was all bombed and there were hundreds of stalls there on a Sunday, lots of second-hand ladies'-clothes stalls in not very vivid colours, everything seemed to be grey in those days.'

John grew up near the Bethnal Green end of Brick Lane in a white working-class community. 'The people at the market were familiar to me,' he said, 'they were like my mum and dad, big women and little men with hats on, and they all seemed to shuffle about rather than walk.' His uncle had a stall there selling second-hand shoes: 'He'd go round knocking on doors collecting old shoes, then mend them at home and flog them at Brick Lane on a Sunday.'

Every week John went with his parents to the market to do the grocery shopping before a trip to one of the local pubs. 'My mum was a stout woman, and always had a fag hanging out of her mouth and swore every other word,' he said. 'She loved a pint. When she finished in the pub we'd walk back up Brick Lane with the bags filled with shopping and visit the bakers. Mum would get a chocolate éclair and we'd have a doughnut for Sunday tea. That was the treat of the week.'

Alan Gilbey felt at least two thirds of Brick Lane was an illegal economy market in the 1960s. He remembers crowds gathered round 'geezers' with suitcases perched on cardboard boxes, filled with fake perfume or jewellery. Goods were stolen to order and exchanged for cash in the early hours. The rest of the market was crammed with grocery stalls, second-hand stuff and junk. The contents of

Like many living in the area in the 1950s I used to buy anything I thought I could sell for a quick shilling. Anything that was easy to carry, to pick up and run with, things like socks, ladies' tights, T-shirts and jewellery. We didn't bother with traders' licences. I remember when a friend of mine called Derek came into the possession of about six hundred empty glass shampoo bottles complete with screw caps, which if I recall correctly said 'Shampooing Tonique' on the labels. A friend who worked in a local Chinese restaurant sold us a large drum of washing-up liquid for ten shillings. We spent all of Saturday night out on Derek's balcony filling those bottles and sold the lot at one shilling and sixpence a bottle in Brick Lane the next morning. Weeks later people were still asking if we had any more of that lovely shampoo, it was a nice little earner but we hadn't any more bottles. The wheeling and dealing that went on was a way of life and good fun most of the time.

Bernard Dray, 2004

whole houses were tipped out on to stalls, which took over the still-empty bombsites in the streets in and around Brick Lane. Alan used to buy stamps and records there while his father went looking for electrical goods and tools. Alan described the market then as 'a monochrome place filled with men in macs moving slowly about in huge crowds'.

Eddie thought Brick Lane Market was an exotic place in the 1960s. He grew up a few streets away from Brick Lane, in a predominantly white area, 'a place of power cuts, poverty, coal smoke and bed bugs'. He was amazed by the diversity of the people he saw every week at Brick Lane Market: 'The first wave of Bengali people had arrived and there were lots of Orthodox Jewish market traders as well as many people from my community, all merging together just for this one morning a week.'

Many people remember the auctioneering that used to be a regular feature of the market. 'It was sheer entertainment,' said Derek Cox. 'People used to go to Brick Lane not even to buy, but just to feel the atmosphere and the laughter. They'd throw the crockery up in the air and catch it. The banter among the traders and public was great fun. It was real street theatre.' Derek's other strong memory of the market from the 1950s to the 1970s is of the dog market in Club Row that used to spread down into Sclater Street. Caged birds, puppies, live rats, goats, snakes, gerbils, kittens, monkeys and even lions were for sale in the pet market, stacked in wire cages and pens piled on top of one another. Iain Sinclair said the animal market was very unregulated and had 'a kind of smell of fear'. It closed down in the 1980s after the RSPCA received thousands of complaints about it. The majority of the animals sold there were either birds or dogs in pens, many of which had been stolen. Fanatical collectors of prize chickens used to congregate on the corner of Sclater Street, looking at the different sorts of roosters, racing pigeons and fluffy-legged chickens for sale. Children crowded round the stalls, petting the dogs and kittens, pressing their faces against the giant tanks filled with tropical fish. Dealers of singing birds and racing dogs came early, looking for a bargain. Among them walked the

I spent a lot of time at the pet market in
Sclater Street in the 1950s where there were
several permanent small-bird traders and a
large branch of Palmer's Bird and Pet Suppliers
as well as the usual Sunday-morning traders.
I have a great love of songbirds. I used to go to
buy a few German roller canaries that were a
little under the weather after the long journey
to the trader's premises. He would let me have
them for half a crown each and with a little TLC
most would make a good recovery in a week.
Then I'd sell them back to the trader for a few
shillings' profit and he'd resell them at the
market. He used to mark his cages with crosses
in chalk, one cross if the bird was in song, two
if he was a good singer and three crosses for an
excellent songster. In those days a lot of
people kept a cock canary or a canary mule for
the beauty of their song. At lunchtime we'd pop
into the Knave of Clubs public house, known
locally as the Bird House, for a sip of ale. Bird
fanciers held singing competitions there, with
the linnets, goldfinches and canary mules. Good
songsters would change hands for considerable
amounts of money. The Knave of Clubs is now a
restaurant called Les Trois Garçons. Dolly the
old landlady must be turning in her grave.

Bernard Dray, 2004

Czech photographer Marketa Luskacova, herself an immigrant to the area from Prague. She moved to London in 1975 and began photographing many of the London markets: Brixton, Portobello Road, Ridley Road and Brick Lane. 'Out of all the markets I photographed, Brick Lane was the only one that caught me and didn't let me go,' she told me. Over a fifteen-year period she visited the market whenever she could.

Marketa felt at home among the mixed-migrant community of Brick Lane Market, where, like her, everyone had an accent. She enjoyed the street life and the vitality of the people who worked and visited the street. There were many travellers and gypsies in the area at that time, who she related to, and she was familiar with Ashkenazi Jewish culture, having come from Eastern Europe. Over many years Marketa got to know some of the stallholders. If she felt it necessary she would ask for someone's permission before photographing them, particularly with religious people, such as the Hasidic traders. She told me about some of the individuals there who made an impression on her, including a man called Ginger, who made his own instruments and was often seen playing a homemade trombone covered in photographs. When he failed to return to his pitch after some weeks Marketa knew it could mean only one thing. Sensing the imminent disappearance of other personalities like Ginger, Marketa continued to photograph the characters of Brick Lane until the early 1990s. Her iconic images of Brick Lane Market now document a lost era. Iain Sinclair feels her images most accurately portray Brick Lane Market in the 1970s.

Throughout the 1970s Iain visited Brick Lane Market every week, arriving at five in the morning to buy boxloads of books, which he would sell on Thursdays in Camden Passage in Islington: 'It was like a kind of religion,' he said. 'I'd be hyped up, dashing around from stall to stall.' He made friends with an old Scotsman, another bookdealer, and helped the older man carry books he bought in Brick Lane back to his car. In return Iain got to pick the cream of the Scotsman's stock at trade prices. 'By the end of the week I expect those books were in Sackville Street and all the posh West

Where Sclater Street crosses Brick Lane, near
the Great Eastern Station, is the market of the
'fancy'. Here the streets are blocked with those
coming to buy or sell pigeons, canaries, rabbits,
fowls, parrots or guinea pigs, and with them or
separately all the appurtenances of bird or pet
keeping. Through this crowd the seller of
shellfish pushes his barrow; on the outskirts of it
are moveable shooting galleries and patent Aunt
Sallies, while some standing up in a dog cart will
dispose of racing tips in sealed envelopes to the
East End sportsman.

Charles Booth, *Life and Labour of the People of London*,
Vol. II, 1892

End shops,' said Iain, 'books from the gutters of Cheshire Street on a Sunday morning. For a time there was this lovely flow of commerce in bookdealing, which began in Brick Lane.'

Alan Dein was a regular visitor to the market in the 1980s. He spent most of his time in Cheshire Street: 'On a Sunday you could really explore, you'd walk down a side road and find half a house, a back wall and one adjoining wall, and inside would be four or five lorries full of tat which had been gathered from house clearances up and down London or Essex and there'd just be stuff pouring out on to tables and the floor. Cheshire Street is not that big but I'd spend hours there, exploring all the nooks and crannies with things spread everywhere. The stuff on the stalls was the detritus of 1950s and 1960s Britain. So in Brick Lane in the early 1980s I found the discarded remnants of the Britain of my childhood.'

I first started visiting Brick Lane Market in 1990. In those days it spanned a wide area from Bethnal Green Road nearly to Bishopsgate right down to the railway bridge at Shoreditch, spreading under railway arches, filling empty bombsites and spilling into adjoining side streets. The most concentrated part of the market was still in Cheshire Street, which became unrecognizable on Sundays. I used to live in Whitechapel and most Sundays I'd make my way up to Brick Lane via Cheshire Street, sifting through the belongings of other people. If I arrived really early, before five or six in the morning, Brick Lane and the surrounding streets would still be congested with vans unloading their goods. Punters and dealers with torches would home in on the vehicles, elbowing each other out of the way in the darkness to inspect the contents inside.

Further up Cheshire Street, past the old Jewish baths, factory buildings that remained shut for the rest of the week would open their padlocked gates and the market would veer off into hidden yards and car parks where you could buy cut-price meat from vans, broken jewellery, picture frames, anything imaginable. Brick Lane was the perfect hunting ground for me as a sculptor. I'd spend my time searching through the lost biographies of thousands,

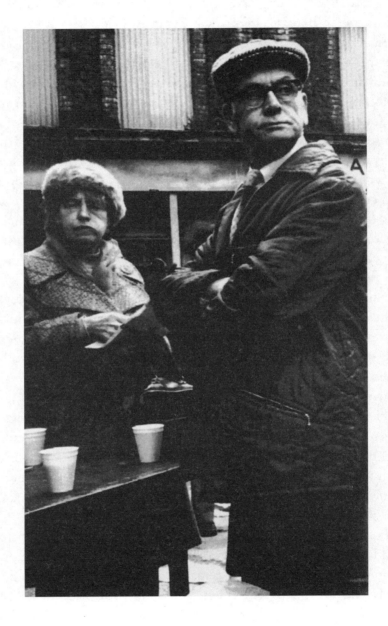

Brick Lane Market in the early 1980s was the place to go to people-watch. It was bedraggled, it smelled, it was gritty, impoverished and virtually in black and white. I always bought a few second-hand records there but mainly I went because I just got a kick out of being in the place, it was unlike anywhere else and it only existed for one morning every week. Come two o'clock it was just washed away like it was never there.

Alan Dein, 2006

seeking objects loaded with personal memory. Among my favourite purchases were: a box of glass negatives from a trip around the Middle East at the turn of the century; a collection of postcards from a granddaughter to her grandfather; a lock of hair still intact inside a dented locket; and a tiny pewter samovar from Russia.

The crowds around Cheshire Street often became so dense I lost my bearings and drifted with the flow of human traffic from one stall to the other, absorbed in the pleasure of examining the things I saw. Most of what was available was junk, grubby old bric-a-brac, job lots of unwanted belongings, but some stalls had real antiques, silver jugs, gold rings, inlaid musical boxes. Moving up to Brick Lane, I'd cross over to Bacon and Sclater streets to explore the lock-ups under the railway arches, which opened only on Sundays – dark cavernous places, stacked to the ceiling with desks, filing cabinets, beds, chairs and dressers. Out on the street, surrounded by sofas, heavy furniture and mountains of loo rolls were the dealers, chain-smoking cigarettes, a bacon roll or a cup of tea in their hands.

Over the next ten years I watched as the market shrank. Redevelopment in Cheshire Street closed down the main artery and the dusty old wonderful stuff disappeared along with the characters who sold it. Rent for stalls went up as the developers tried to squeeze the market out. New refugees in tracksuits flogging counterfeit DVDs and Gucci bags replaced the old-timers with their stalls of Victorian printing presses and copper plates. I stopped visiting.

Svar still wanders around the market every Sunday. Since the Romanians and Albanians came over in the last few years, he feels the market has changed dramatically: 'It has got a lot tougher. It's always been an immigrant market but now it feels more dangerous. There is a lot of drug dealing that takes place there quite openly now.' Svar recently noticed a gang of young Asian and white kids targeting illegal immigrants. A few weeks ago he saw the same gang trying to steal a money bag from a Chinese woman selling DVDs: 'She held on to it so tightly and insistently that they started to beat her with a stick, smashing her in the side of the face. They forced her to run away leaving her goods behind. They keep coming back and harassing her because they know she won't press charges against them. She's an asylum seeker, so she won't go to the police.'

Sukhdev watches the market kick into life every Sunday morning right outside his bedroom window. He describes it as 'a hive of fascination, criminality and characters'. He has been offered cannabis, ecstasy and Bangladeshi porn there: 'Round the corner from Club Row are two guys with a suitcase selling this stuff shot in a flat in Limehouse and by eight in the morning they are gone.'

I recently returned to Brick Lane Market for the first time in years, with Alan Dein and Stephen Watts. We met outside the Whitechapel Art Gallery on a warm Sunday morning in October. Stephen was already there when I arrived, chatting with a *Big Issue* seller, giving away the few pence he had. Alan arrived shortly after, out of breath, hungry and full of stories. The three of us walked together up Brick Lane towards the market, talking and remembering, moving constantly from the pavement into the centre of the road, as the street was being dug up again.

Although it never really gets going till way past Shoreditch Station, the redevelopment of the brewery site has changed the boundary of the market. It now stretches further down the street, but in a diluted version of its former self. Just past Dray Walk we saw a few people peddling without a licence, with pasting tables on the pavement covered in second-hand bits and pieces. Next to them were smart vans selling organic doughnuts and Italian coffee. Near the Bishopsgate Goods Yard were a small group of new hawkers – young fashion students, parodying the old pavement sellers of Cheshire Street, selling directly from blankets spread out on the ground. They looked relaxed, chatting among themselves as they sat in the sun, dressed self-consciously in vintage ensembles. The items they had for sale were last season's unwanted fashion, not the broken belongings of poverty-stricken lives.

We tried to walk up the centre of the road. Range Rovers and Mercedes came up fast behind us, beeping loudly, forcing us back on to the pavement. Stephen was outraged. Every Sunday

for centuries this part of Brick Lane had always been closed to
traffic. 'For a walker this was lovely,' said Stephen. 'I used to
love to walk literally up the middle of Brick Lane on a Sunday.
Now this seems impossible.' As we came past the site of the
old railway bridge the street finally closed down to traffic and
we walked on the road through the once crowded junction of
Brick Lane and Cheshire Street with ease. Apart from the presence of a fruit stall there, it barely felt like a market at all. As
we turned into Cheshire Street Alan looked horrified. 'Where are
all the stalls?' he said, looking anxiously around. 'They've gone,
it's all disappeared.' There were a few vans parked up, a couple
of places selling bedding, some students with rails of clothes, and
a large stall covered in slippers, but whole sections of Cheshire
Street were empty. The once dilapidated rows of shops had been
refurbished and painted in heritage colours. Inside they were
filled with vintage and retro products, sparsely arranged as in
a designer boutique. 'This was the stuff that would have been
out in the street in the stalls for a tenth of the price,' said Alan.
'Now it's been repackaged and is selling at high prices and they

don't even see the irony.' The former bombsites where the market used to spread have all been developed now. The new buildings are gated off, access is now denied to the back yards of Cheshire Street, the market no longer twists and turns as it once did. We noticed the sound in the street had changed: the distinctive voices of the street traders shouting out their wares were another missing element.

We stopped outside Blackman's – a shoe shop selling industrial footwear, boots and trainers. The exterior of the shop is run down, with peeling paint and shutters that are falling apart – a throwback to the old Cheshire Street. I approached the man standing in the doorway, wearing an anorak and a flat cap, and asked him about the shop. He told me it was started by two Jewish brothers in 1935 and is now the longest-running business on the street. The present owner, who did not want to be named, took it over from them some years ago. 'This shop is famous worldwide,' he told me with pride. 'The first Doc Marten shoes you could get in the UK were sold here in the 1960s and 1970s. All the skinheads used to come here to get their boots.' Before running Blackman's the man had worked in Cheshire Street for many years watching the changes taking place there. 'I feel sad being an East End English man,' he said. 'I've lost my roots. I'm a foreigner in my own country now. I have to accept it. My Brick Lane has gone.'

A slight hunched man smoking a roll-up appeared from inside. 'Enough of this chat,' he said, eyeing me suspiciously, 'I've got punters and I need a fiver.' Looking at the microphone he then turned to me. 'Don't you take no pictures,' he said, wagging a finger in my face, 'and if anyone asks, you ain't seen me.' He disappeared into the dark interior.

'Don't mind 'im,' said the owner. 'This market used to be packed out. Until a few years back there was nowhere else to go on a Sunday, nothing else was open apart from the East End markets. Brick Lane was the local market and Petticoat Lane was the posher part. Cheshire Street was the duck-and-dive bit, where people sold anything and everything. If you needed to raise a few quid you went down here and flogged stuff. It was like an early boot fair. The people down here were what we call the "rakers" – they raked stuff over. They wanted something for nothing. When the animal market went it died off a lot.'

Over the years the old traders have died off too. 'They're not replaced,' he said, 'their sons are not interested in carrying it on.' He feels the market is still going only because of the new arrivals to the area, the Eastern Europeans: 'They like a market, and half the people we serve on a Sunday are Eastern Europeans in the building trade, and they've taken over a lot of the stalls.' He suggested we go and speak to his friend Charlie Burns, whose family have had a yard in Bacon Street since the 1860s. Before we left Alan asked him what he imagined would be happening in Cheshire Street in ten years' time. 'It will all be gone,' he said. 'You got a different kind of person who's moved in to the area. It will become like the Old Spitalfields Market, filled with young poshy types. It's a different level of the game and I think the same thing will happen here in Brick Lane. It's already started.'

Leaving Blackman's we walked further down Cheshire Street towards Vallance Road, noticing the street getting quieter and quieter. 'This used to be a real flea market, where people congregated from so many different places,' said Stephen. He has been an observer of the market for decades, a talker and walker, watching people selling and bargaining. 'There is no atmosphere at all now,' he said, 'it feels dead.' The Carpenters Arms was closed down, the old warehouse spaces were all shuttered up, the house-clearance men were gone. There were only two places of intense activity on the street. One was focused around a black people carrier with tinted windows, engine running, parked on the pavement. A multiracial crowd of men gathered around the vehicle four deep. A sign on the side of the car read 'Get your mobile unlocked here'. Cash and phones were passed through the windows to someone inside at great speed. A tall man with a flattened nose paced around the edge of the car with arms folded, looking up and down the street. The only other place that seemed alive was directly in front of the steps to the railway bridge that spans between Cheshire Street and

Spitalfields City Farm, the point where Iain Sinclair feels you drop into another world when you walk down the steps into Cheshire Street. In front of the steps that morning was a tiny pocket of the Brick Lane Market of the past. Men shuffled around stalls, speaking in accents, sifting through old junk that spilled out on to the ground. Russian music was playing from a stereo, a dog sat under a stall chewing on a shoe. Alan jumped happily into the scene, and began rifling through a pile of old records.

Stephen and I left him to browse and walked further down Cheshire Street. I wanted to see what was happening outside the old Jewish bathhouse. Nothing. It had all been cleared away, not a single street seller remained. Stephen imagined they had moved on elsewhere as the market had contracted and they stopped making money. He told me it was a very recent thing. Even a few months before they had been there.

We turned round and walked back up to Brick Lane. Well-dressed people carrying plants from the nearby flower market in Columbia Road were wandering past. They didn't stop. They were just passing through, making their way to Spitalfields Market further

down. Crossing Brick Lane into Sclater Street was like entering a different market. Off Sclater Street are some of the only spaces near Brick Lane that have not yet been developed, which are used as car parks during the week. But on a Sunday they are packed out, mad with life, filled with people of many nationalities, a babble of voices, accents and noise. Hawkers cry out over the top of each other. The stalls are crowded and close together, surrounded by dilapidated buildings and characters reminiscent of the ones Marketa photographed in the 1970s. I passed two women in headscarves pushing an old pram full of tins of food. 'I had a breakdown when I was eighteen,' said one to the other. Sitting on his haunches against the far wall was a man in a parka, the hood zipped right up like a funnel. He wore fingerless gloves and in front of him on a blanket on the floor was one dirty sock. Next to me were some men speaking Polish, rummaging through a pile of old clothes. A gang of black teenagers walked past, talking loudly, elbowing me out of the way. I looked around and realized I had lost Alan and Stephen. It is easily done in that section of the market, which is chaotic and constantly moving. There are no tourists there – it is still an immigrant market for the poor. I found Stephen and Alan sifting through some magazines. Towards Bacon Street we passed the man in the meat van who has been there for decades. He was hacking a side of beef up and auctioning off the pieces to a small crowd gathered in front.

We slowly made our way along Bacon Street towards Charlie Burns' yard, where we found him sitting outside his lock-up on an office chair in the middle of a puddle in the road, holding court. Two elderly ladies sat beside him, laughing at a story he was telling. His hands were clasped over an ample belly, one clutching a walking stick and the other a large wad of cash. It was nearly half past one and the market was starting to wind down. A burly-looking man was shifting the furniture that surrounded Charlie on the street back inside the yard. When asked about his long history in the market Charlie was happy to talk.

'I was born into this work,' he said. 'I've been in this street

One Sunday there was a disaster. We were
playing in Sclater Street, just next to a jellied-eel
stall . . . a fight started. Some of the barrows had
bottles of petrol and when the fighting spread
they got knocked over. 'Bang! Bang! Bang!'
people thought they were guns. The cry went up,
'They're shooting,' and that started a stampede.
It was 1911, the time of Sidney Street, and
everyone thought it was the anarchists and the
police. There was a terrific rush to get away.
Near by in Club Row was the great bird market
and thousands of birds were trampled
underfoot. The stampede broke out like a wheel,
with people running in all directions to get away.
A couple of people were killed.

Raphael Samuel, *East End Underworld: Chapters in the Life of Arthur Harding*, 1981

personally nearly ninety years.' His father and grandfather before
him had been paper merchants, who graduated into general dealing as that business had died out. Anything that came along they
traded in it – office equipment, second-hand clothing, whatever they
could get their hands on. 'Things used to be a little bit harder but
a little bit sweeter,' said Charlie, talking of the market of his youth.
'People were more friendly and helped each other. In the summer
all the people used to bring chairs out of their little houses, which
were all along this street, and sit out and chat. That made conversation, but then those houses were all bombed and the community
changed.'

His memories of the market went back to the early 1900s, when
horses and carts were sold in Sclater Street by girls dressed in riding
clothes. 'It was a very Jewish area then,' he said. 'They were close to
their own but everyone was here to make a living so we did mix in
a business way.' He remembers the market being filled with country
people selling their produce and *lascars* who'd get off the boats at
the docks and come and buy the things they needed. 'We weren't
used to seeing a black face in them days,' he said. 'If one come

along people used to touch 'em for luck.' As he talked tears fell out of his eyes; whether it was the wind or the effect of remembering I do not know. 'This market has always been full of thieves and villains,' he said. 'Loads of pickpockets operate here and fifty years ago it was worse than now. I've seen people lose their watch one end and go up the top and buy it back again.'

'What about all the old characters?' said one of the ladies beside him, touching his arm.

'Oh, yes,' said Charlie, 'the Lunar boys would come down here, men dressed up as women, and dance round an old piano. Prince Monolulu was always here, he was an eccentric racing tipster who dressed up like an African chief in wild outfits with an ostrich-feather headdress and he would dance around, banging drums. He'd lark about with banter like a market trader. There was always a big crowd around him and he'd shout out, "I've gotta horse, I'm gonna make you rich, I've gotta horse that's running today!" and he'd sell the tips, a few pence a time. After they finished telling all their lies they were great people here, a lot of personalities. Like the man with the miniature mangle who'd put in a bit of paper and out came a pound note and people used to buy them. Another used to do a scam with gold watches in closed envelopes but of course when you opened it there was a packet of pins.'

Charlie thinks his business will go within the next few years. He's been offered millions for the properties he owns. I asked what he felt about the market today. 'It's not a market no more,' he said, 'it's just a collection of people.' We left Charlie sitting on his chair and walked back down Brick Lane. Most of the stalls were packing up. 'Hey, professor,' someone called behind us, 'come here.' Stephen automatically turned around. With his long white hair he's commonly called by that name. A group of bearded Islamic students were beckoning him over to their stall. One of them was talking into a loudhailer about the faith of the prophets. Stephen returned a few minutes later with a Koran tucked under his arm. 'They were very friendly,' he said.

The fashion students near the goods yard had packed up and were heading towards the Vibe Bar. The traders in Sclater Street were moving down Brick Lane towards the tube, carrying their purchases in heaving plastic bags. For a few moments the many communities living in and around Brick Lane merged on the street, just like they have always done, as the Sunday market wound down.

The future of Brick Lane Market seems uncertain. I expect the man at Blackman's is right – regeneration of the area will eventually kill the market off. Redevelopment for the 2012 Olympics, the Crossrail project and the East London Line extension will speed the process further as property prices increase with improved transport links. For the communities that are left the temptation to sell up and move further out will probably prove to be too great. Brick Lane is transforming itself for its next phase.

Alan, Stephen and I walked down Brick Lane towards Whitechapel in silence and parted outside Aldgate East tube. I stood for a while in front of the closed doors of the Whitechapel Library and watched as a large group of young people came up out of the station next door and headed towards Brick Lane. In their hands were flyers for a live-music gig at 93 Feet East. I descended into the Underground tunnel, unsure of when I would return to the street. My time on Brick Lane seemed to have reached its natural end.

It is appropriate to think of places as texts, layered with meaning. Every place has an excess of meaning beyond what can be seen or understood at any one time.

Philip Sheldrake, *Spaces for the Sacred: Place, Memory and Identity*, 2001

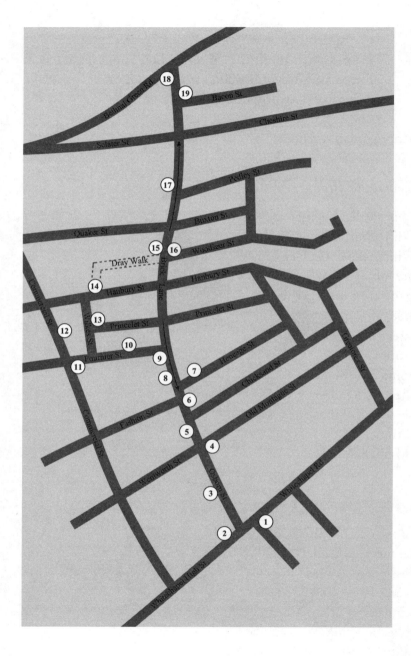

Walking Tour

(Approximately 1 hour)

1. Altab Ali Park

This walk begins at Altab Ali Park, at the junction with Whitechurch Lane and Whitechapel High Street (opposite the Whitechapel Gallery exit for Aldgate East tube). Originally the site of St Mary's Matfelon (the original white chapel, built in 1250, after which the area was named) the park was renamed in 1988 after a Bengali tailor murdered in a racist attack in Adler Street on 4 May 1978. The park has become a starting point for protest marches against racism and the Iraq War and a meeting point for Bengali youths. The church was demolished in 1952 after being damaged in the Blitz and the foundations can still be seen in the grass. The contemporary memorial arch at the entrance to the park sits on the remains of the brick arch to the old chapel.

2. The Whitechapel Library

Cross over Whitechapel High Street to no. 77, the Whitechapel Library and Gallery, founded by the philanthropist liberal MP John Passmore Edwards in 1892, to provide poor local people with free access to art and literature. Jewish migrants named the library the 'University of the Ghetto'. There was a large Yiddish and Hebrew collection there in the 1900s; after the Second World War books in Urdu, Arabic and Bengali were stocked. In 1934 the Whitechapel

Library employed the first specialist ethnic librarian in the UK, a Yiddishist, who was replaced by an expert on Islamic texts in the 1960s. The library closed in 2005 and has relocated to the new Idea Store in Whitechapel. The building has been bought by the Whitechapel Gallery next door.

3. Osborn Street

Turn left into Osborn Street. At no. 17 is A. Elfes Ltd Monumental Stone Masons, est. 1945, the only Jewish business left on the street. At nos 29–33 is the Sonali Bank, the first Bangladeshi bank in the UK. In the 1930s no. 32 Osborn Street was the site of the Warsaw Restaurant (also known as Snevlars), a kosher eatery frequented by anarchists and gangsters.

4. Old Montague Street

Brick Lane begins after the junction with Old Montague and Wentworth streets. Bloom's kosher restaurant was sited on the corner of Old Montague Street and Brick Lane from 1930 to 1952. Garment trade workers would congregate outside looking for work and political meetings took place there on Sundays. Wentworth Street leads directly into Petticoat Lane Market, on the other side of Commercial Street. Old Montague Street was filled with Jewish shops and a busy daily market until the 1950s. The studios and offices on the corner of Old Montague Street and Greatorex Street housed the Great Garden Street Synagogue and Federation of Synagogues Offices from 1894 to 1991, and the Kosher Luncheon Club, which closed in 1994. A small turning, called Black Lion Yard, now demolished, led off Old Montague Street and down to Whitechapel Road; with its fifteen jewellery shops, kosher dairy and bookshops it was known as the 'Hatton Garden of the East End' and was the traditional place for Jewish couples to buy wedding rings and Sabbath candlesticks.

5. Banglatown

Just before the Brick Lane Health Centre at nos 9–11 (built in 1984) is a decorative arch, constructed in 1997, which marks the official entrance to Banglatown. Beside the Shiraz Hotel (formerly the Frying Pan, a Truman pub) is a narrow entrance to Flower and Dean Walk, where one of the first purpose-built council estates for Bangladeshi families in the country was built in the 1980s. In the 1870s this was the site of Thrawl Street and Flower and Dean Walk, notorious slums that were partly cleared in the 1890s with the construction of the Rothschild Buildings – gigantic new tenements built to house working-class families. Funded by the charitable Four Per Cent Industrial Dwellings Company, headed by Baron Meyer de Rothschild, the buildings were occupied almost entirely by Jewish refugees. The entrance arch to the estate in Wentworth Street is all that remains.

6. Café Naz

At nos 46–48 Brick Lane is Café Naz, an Indian restaurant. From the 1960s to the 1980s it was the site of an Asian cinema. Anti-racists met there before political demonstrations in the 1970s. In the 1930s and 1940s the building was called the Mayfair Cinema, and the audience at that time was 99 per cent Jewish. In 1999 a nail bomb set off by the neo-Nazi David Copeland exploded outside the café, but no one was hurt.

7. Christ Church School

In 1874, Christ Church School was erected, in a Gothic revival style, at no. 47a Brick Lane, over the east end of Christ Church's graveyard. The school is still owned and governed by Christ Church although most pupils there are Bengali Muslim now; a century ago the children were nearly all Jewish. After school many of the children there today visit the Brick Lane Mosque for lessons in Arabic and to study the Koran. In the 1900s boys from Christ Church School went to the same building, to learn Hebrew and study Judaism. A Star of David can still be seen at the top of a drainpipe on the front of the building; one of the few symbols left on Brick Lane of its Jewish past.

8. Fashion and Heneage streets

Carry on walking up Brick Lane, passing Bengali-run cafés, wedding shops, travel agents and the last of the textile whole-salers and manufacturers, for which Brick Lane was famous for decades. The oldest remaining is Epra Fabrics at nos 52–56, which has been there since 1950. Fashion Street was occupied from the 1890s until recently by run-down tailors' workshops. The writer Israel Zangwill opens his book *Children of the Ghetto: A Study of a Peculiar People* (1892) with a description of the street, which he names 'rotten row'. The Moorish building to the left was built in 1905 as retail outlets and now houses a private fashion college. Further up Brick Lane, to the right, is a small cobbled turning called Heneage Street. At no. 3 is the Pride of Spitalfields, a traditional East End pub frequented mainly by white locals. It was petrol-bombed in 2003 in an alleged racist attack by a gang of Asian youths. Opposite the pub is the site of the former Eretz Chaim Synagogue, now flats.

9. Brick Lane Mosque

The history of this building reflects the changing population of Brick Lane over the past two hundred and fifty years. It was erected in 1743 as a Protestant church, called La Neuve Eglise, and used mainly by French Huguenots who settled in the area from the 1680s onwards after fleeing religious persecution in France. In 1809 the church was sold to the London Society for Promoting Christianity Among the Jews before becoming a Methodist church in 1819. The ultra-Orthodox Machzike Hadath Jewish community bought the building in 1897, when it became the Spitalfields Great Synagogue.

The Brick Lane Talmud Torah School was attached next door. In 1976 the building was sold to the Bangladeshi community, and is now the Jamme Masjid, or the Brick Lane Mosque (sometimes called the Great London Mosque). High on the wall, above the Fournier Street entrance, is the Latin inscription 'Umbra Sumus', which translates as 'We are Shadows'. Opposite the mosque is a Bangladeshi cash and carry, the site of the former Russian Vapour Baths, which were destroyed during the Blitz.

10. Fournier Street

Turn left into Fournier Street to see some of the best examples of domestic Georgian architecture in London. The houses date from the 1720s and were built as grand residences for Huguenot master weavers. The finest is no. 2, the Minister's House, which was designed by Nicholas Hawksmoor (a student of Christopher Wren) and completed in 1731. Note the wide windows in the attics, allowing the maximum daylight into the rooms for weaving. By the 1880s most had been converted into small furrier and clothing manufacturing workshops and were occupied by Jewish migrant workers, later replaced by Asian migrants who continued in the same trade. In the past thirty years the Spitalfields Historic Buildings Trust have bought many of the houses and restored them before selling them on. The Bangladeshi Welfare Association, at no. 39, is the largest Bengali community organization in the UK. There was a Huguenot charity based there in the eighteenth century to help local weavers in financial difficulty and a Jewish charity at the end of the nineteenth century.

11. Christ Church

Christ Church, at the junction of Fournier and Commercial streets, was designed by Hawksmoor and completed in 1729. Originally built as an Anglican church it was mainly used in the eighteenth century by Protestant Huguenots. By the 1950s the church was

335

derelict and nearly demolished. From 1976 onwards the Friends of Christ Church began fundraising to save the building. Restoration work was completed in 2004 and the church is now used by a multicultural congregation, as well as being hired out for events. The gardens attached were once a much larger cemetery, which spread nearly halfway down Commercial Street and backed on to Brick Lane. The council removed the remaining graves in the 1950s; a few headstones can still be seen, stacked against a far wall. In the 1890s the gardens became a sleeping place for the destitute and were known as 'itchy park'. The crypt below the church has been used over the centuries for burials, as an air-raid shelter during the war, as a hostel for the homeless and, more recently, as an art venue.

12. Spitalfields Market

On the other side of Commercial Street is Spitalfields Market. The original building was erected between 1885 and 1893, and designed as London's main fruit and vegetable market. Part of it can still be seen on Commercial Street. The back half of the market was recently demolished, after much local protest. Archaeological remains, including a roman burial site, were discovered underneath before the site was built on again. The fruit and vegetable market relocated to Leyton in 1991 and since then the site has been re-developed into an indoor antique, craft, fashion and organic food market, as well as housing offices, shops, bars and restaurants.

13. Princelet Street

Past the Ten Bells pub, turn right into Puma Court, which takes you into Wilkes Street, another recently gentrified Georgian street. No. 6 Princelet Street was the site of the first Yiddish theatre in London. A tragedy took place there on 18 January 1887 when someone cried fire during a performance; seventeen people were killed in the panic to escape. No. 19 is the Spitalfields Heritage Centre, which aims to represent all communities in the area. The house was built in 1719 by master carpenter Samuel Worrall, and was the home of Huguenot weavers. In 1889 a synagogue was constructed in the back garden and is now the second oldest still standing in London. The recluse David Rodinsky lived in the attic rooms of the building until his disappearance in 1969.

14. Hanbury Street

Continue along Wilkes Street and turn right at the junction with Hanbury Street. No. 22, was built as a French church in 1719, converted into Christ Church's Parish Hall in 1887, and is still used for community projects. Charles Dickens gave readings there and in the 1880s and 1890s the building was hired out for radical strike meetings. The entertainer Bud Flanagan (Chaim Reuven Weintrop) of the Crazy Gang was born in Hanbury Street in 1896. At no. 20 is the Kobi Nazrul Centre, a Bengali arts centre, which opened in 1982. Cross over Hanbury Street and enter the Old Truman Brewery site, then turn right into Dray Walk, formerly Black Eagle Street, now known as the 'strip'. This was the loading bay and bottling site when the brewery was still functioning.

15. Truman's Brewery

Truman's Brewery was the largest employer of local people in the area, from the time it opened in 1666 until its closure in 1988. Originally named the Black Eagle Brewery, the company was started by Joseph Truman. In the eighteenth century the brewery became internationally famous under the leadership of Joseph's son Benjamin, due to the popularity of the black stout called Porter brewed there. The brewery spread over acres of land around Brick Lane. Benjamin Truman was knighted and built a grand Georgian house at no. 91 Brick Lane. He died in 1780, and his ghost allegedly still haunts the house. The brewery passed to Benjamin's great-grandsons, before being taken over in 1789 by Sampson Hanbury. Thomas Fowell Buxton, Hanbury's nephew, joined in 1808, and the brewery expanded again after converting to steam power. A member of the Buxton family was on the board until the late 1960s. Generations from the same family worked at Truman's as labourers and draymen; most were local white East Enders, who stayed in the job for life. In 1971 Maxwell Joseph's company, the Grand Metropolitan Group, bought Truman's and merged with Watney in 1972, creating Watney Mann and Truman Holdings. In 1988 brewing stopped on Brick Lane for the first time in three hundred and twenty-two years. In 1995 the Zeloof Partnership bought and redeveloped the derelict site into a cultural venue with bars, nightclubs, cafés, galleries, offices and studios. A tall brick chimney with the word 'Truman' on it is still visible from Brick Lane.

16. Brick Lane

Between Woodseer and Fournier streets is the section of Brick Lane known as 'curry mile', which has over fifty Indian restaurants. Originally established as small working-men's cafés in the 1950s to provide *halal* food for migrant workers from Bangladesh and Pakistan, they now mainly cater for tourists. The Nazrul at no. 130 and Sweet and Spicy at no. 40 have been there the longest. In 1797 the Spitalfields' Soup and Ladling Society was based at nos 114–122 Brick Lane, helping starving weavers. At no. 112 is Taj Stores, est. 1930, making it the oldest Asian grocery store in the UK.

17. Bishopsgate Goods Yard

Turn left and walk up Brick Lane, past the brewery complex. At no. 164 Brick Lane is Heba, an education and day-care centre for Bangladeshi women. Past Pedley Street is the site of Shoreditch

Station, which closed in 2006. Opposite is the former Brick Lane entrance to the Bishopsgate Goods Yard; once a vast underground network of brick arched tunnels and large open spaces, which spread over ten acres. It was built in 1840 as the original London passenger terminus of Eastern Counties Railway and converted into a goods station in 1881. Most of the site was demolished in 2004 to make way for the East London Line extension. Between Wheler Street and Brick Lane eight hundred and fifty-nine feet of the Grade-II listed Braithwaite Viaduct remain. In the 1930s the goods yard resembled an underground town, with kitchens, a police office, cross passages, sub-basement storerooms and workshops; over a thousand people worked there. The passenger station closed in 1875 but the goods yard continued until much of it was destroyed by fire in 1964. Giant hydraulic hoists were used to lift goods up to the lines above, which carried trains to and from Bishopsgate Station. The bridge that transported these trains across Brick Lane was thought of by the Jewish community that lived there as the boundary line that separated Jewish and gentile sections of the street. It was recently pulled down.

18. Leather and Bagels

Walking further up, past the Spital Square Mosaic made by children from two local schools in 1995, you can see the last of the leather manufacturers, which used to line the street on both sides of the top half of Brick Lane up until the 1990s. They have recently been replaced by estate agents and vintage-clothing stores. Cabinet makers' workshops were common here before the Second World War, mostly run by Jewish craftsmen. The two bagel bakeries are the last places in the area where you can eat Jewish food, although they are not kosher. The Beigel Bake at no. 157 has been there since 1855.

19. Brick Lane Market

From dawn till two o'clock in the afternoon, every Sunday, the weekly market takes place. It originated in Club Row, north of Brick Lane, in the eighteenth century, as a place for farmers to sell livestock outside the City walls. Over time the market expanded into Brick Lane and the surrounding streets, selling anything and everything imaginable. When Jewish refugees arrived in the area, the market opened on Sundays instead of Saturdays, because of restrictions on working on the Sabbath. The animal market continued in Club Row and Sclater Street until the late 1980s. It was possible to buy snakes, dogs, chickens and even lion cubs there. Today there are traders from Eastern Europe, China and Bangladesh working in Brick Lane Market, reflecting new waves of migration to the area. During the last ten years the market has shrunk dramatically. Former bombsites where the market once spread have now been built upon. In a few years it may not be there at all.

Acknowledgements

This book has taken over five years to research and produce and would not have been possible without the help of countless individuals. I would like to thank Simon Prosser at Hamish Hamilton for his support and patience. A special thanks to Sarah Coward for her careful copyediting. Many thanks to my agent, John Parker, for all his help, and a special thanks to Iain Sinclair, Professor Bill Fishman, David Jacobs and Alain Dein for sharing their memories, contacts, historical knowledge and rare books and for their editorial advice. Their continued support of my work is invaluable to me. A special thanks to the following for their generosity of time and for sharing their stories with me: Atiqul, Azizul, Denise Bangs, Norman Barber, Marga Bell, Bodrul, Majer Bogdanski, Peter Bondi, Charlie Burns, Mohini Chandra, Mr Choudury, Derek Cox, Bernard Dray, Eddie, Charles Ellis, Tracey Emin, Leonard Epstein, Sandra Esqulant, John Ewing, Sally Flood, John Gardiner, Alan Gilbey, Pip, Sara, Gerry and Pat Goldstein, Brian Hanks, Vincent Hayes, Lisa-Raine Hunt, Sanchita Islam, Alana Jelenick, Dan and Denise Jones, Leslie Kay, Jack Kaye, John Kelly, Lulu Kennedy, Daniele Lamarche, Ken Leech, Bernard Levine, Marketa Luskacova, Marion, Phil Maxwell, Neela Momen, Nur, Rodger Priddle, Raju, Repha, Andy Rider, Harold Rosen, Saleck, Sukhdev Sandhu, Chris Searle, Jagtar Semplay, Juliet Shelbourne, Svar Simpson, Jim Tyler, Stephen Watts, John Williams and Zoinul. There were so many others with whom I made contact during the course of the project and for various reasons was unable to interview, in particular all the people who replied to my adverts in the brewery pensioner magazines *Scenario* and *Diagio*. Unfortunately due to time and space constrictions I was able to include only a few

341

of the many wonderful stories about the brewery, but I thank those people for getting in touch, and thanks also to Jeff Sechiari, to Rodger Green of the Brewery Historical Society for his help with Chapter 10, and to Alan Byrne for letting me use his wonderful pictures of life at Truman's. Throughout the course of writing this book I have needed to research at a number of institutions. Many thanks to: Sarah Gilnes and the staff at the Jewish Museum for all their help; special thanks to Chris Lloydd for his help and for sharing his amazing knowledge of the area at the Tower Hamlets Local History Library in Bancroft Road; Helen Carpenter for her help with information on the festival of the Jewish East End in 1987; Nayia Yiakoumaki, archivist at the Whitechapel Library; Rachel Hoffbrand and family for information on Rabbi Avram Werner; and in particular to Ramsey Homa. Thanks also to: Ofer Zeloof for his information on the Old Truman Brewery development; everyone at Avenues Unlimited, especially Derek, who has been an invaluable help throughout the project; the Bishopsgate Institute; the British Library, in particular Bridget McKenzie for allowing me the opportunity to become the first Creative Research Fellow there, where much of the initial research for this book was undertaken; to Kay Jordan of Heba Women's Institute and all the women who gave their time to be interviewed and wished to remain anonymous; the Museum of London; the Moving Here website; the London Metropolitan Archives; Stepney Day Centre; Swanlea Secondary School; Thomas Buxton School; the Whitechapel Library; and to Susannah Rayner, the head archivist at SOAS, for permission to look at the Stencl archives. Special thanks to the Tower Hamlets Local History Library, Daniele Lamarche, Alan Dein, Sanchita Islam, Phil Maxwell and Marketa Luskacova for allowing me to use so many of their wonderful images. A special thanks to everyone at Christ Church for hosting the launch of this book.

Some names and details have been changed to protect the identity of those that requested it. Unless otherwise stated all quotes are from people I have interviewed over the past five years who have willingly agreed to take part in this project. As far as I am aware their stories are as true as memory and time allow.

Text and Illustrations Permissions

Text

While all efforts have been made to trace the copyright owners of all extracts of published works it has not always been possible to do so and the author apologizes for any omissions. Many thanks to the following for their kind permission to reproduce copyright material.

Miriam Becker for the poem 'Whitechapel Britain' by Avram Stencl (translated by Monte Richardson), from *This is Whitechapel* (Whitechapel Gallery, 1971); Alain de Botton for extract from *The Art of Travel* (Hamish Hamilton, 2002); William J. Fishman for extract from *The Streets of East London* (Duckworth & Co., Ltd, 1979); Sally Flood for her poem 'The Brick Lane I See' and extract from 'Brick Lane' from her book of poetry, *A Window on Brick Lane* (Basement Writers, 1979); Alan Gilbey for his poem 'Watney Street' from *Stepney Words* (Centreprise Publications, 1971); Guardian News and Media Ltd for extract of article by Raphael Samuel (17 October 1987); Mark Holborn for extract from his essay 'Marketa Luskacova' in Marketa Luskacova's exhibition catalogue, *Marketa Luskacova: Photographs of Spitalfields* (Whitechapel Art Gallery, 1991); Ramsey Homa for extracts from *A Fortress in Anglo-Jewry* by Bernard Homa (Shapiro Vallentine & Co., 1953); Sanchita Islam for extracts from *From Briarwood to Barishal to Brick Lane* (Arts Council, 2001) and *Old Meets Young* (Arts Council, 2004); the *Jewish Chronicle* for extract from article by A. B. Levy (1948); Dan Jones for extract from leaflet 'Exploring Banglatown and the Bengali East End' (Tower Hamlets Council, 2005); Revd Kenneth

Leech for extract from *Brick Lane, 1978: The Events and Their Significance* (Affor, 1980); Alison Light for extracts from *East End Underworld: Chapters in the Life of Arthur Harding* by Raphael Samuel (History Workshop Series, Routledge & Kegan Paul, 1981); Phil Maxwell and *Rising East* for extract from 'Street Photography: A Century of Change in Pictures', *Rising East*, Vol. 3, no. 3 (1999); Revd Andy Rider, MA, Rector of Christ Church, for extract from www.christchurchspitalfields.org; Harold Rosen for his memories of the Whitechapel Library (from interview with Alan Dein, 1999); Sukhdev Sandhu for extracts from 'Come Hungry, Leave Edgy', *London Review of Books* (9 October 2003); Philip Sheldrake for extracts from *Spaces for the Sacred: Place, Memory and Identity* (SCM Press, 2001); Stephen Watts for 'Brick Lane Mela Poem' (2002); the Whitechapel Art Gallery for extracts from David Widgery's essay 'Ripe Bananas and Stolen Bicycles' in Marketa Luskacova's exhibition catalogue, *Marketa Luskacova: Photographs of Spitalfields* (Whitechapel Art Gallery, 1991); Patrick Wright for extract from *A Journey through Ruins: The Last Days of London* (Paladin, 1991); Shirley Zangwill for extracts from *Children of the Ghetto: A Study of a Peculiar People* by Israel Zangwill (Heinemann, 1892).

Illustrations

All pictures are copyright of Rachel Lichtenstein except where otherwise noted in the List of Illustrations. All effort has been made to contact copyright holders of images. Apologies for any omissions.

Many thanks to the following for their kind permission to reproduce these images:

Marga Bell, p. 65; Alan Byrne, pp. 182, 186, 188; Mohini Chandra, p. 57, Mat Collishaw, p. 161; J. E. Connor, p. 256; Alan Dein, pp. 54, 112, 301; John Gardiner, p. 146; Alan Gilbey and Steve Wells, p. 133; Pip Goldstein, p. 236; Brian Hanks, p. 171; Sanchita Islam, p. 298; David Jacobs, pp. 102, 103, 228; Daniele Lamarche, pp. 193, 194, 196, 197, 198, 199, 202; London Metropolitan Archives, p. 19; Marketa Luskacova, pp. 299, 310, 312; Phil Maxwell, pp. 4,

285, 287, 288, 290 (top and bottom), 292 (top and bottom), 294, 314; Jewish Museum, pp. 99, 110; Tower Hamlets Local History Library, pp. 24, 35, 245, 302, 307; RIBA Library Photographs Collection, p. 31; Johnnie Shand Kydd (Courtesy Jay Jopling/White Cube), p. 280.

The author has tried unsuccessfully to contact the estate of Wilfred M. Fryer whose sketch of the brewery is shown on p. 185.

Glossary

Ashkenazi: Central and Eastern European Jews (Yiddish)

Baruch atah Adonai: Blessed are You, O Lord our God (Hebrew)

bar mitzvah: ceremony for a Jewish boy on his thirteenth birthday (Hebrew)

bemah: raised platform in the synagogue from where services are led (Hebrew)

Buba: grandmother (Yiddish)

burka: an all-enveloping loose garment worn by observant Muslim women. A full *burka* covers the entire body and face with slits for the eyes (Urdu)

chazan: cantor in the synagogue (Hebrew)

cholla: plaited bread used for Jewish celebrations (Hebrew)

cheder: elementary Jewish school (Hebrew)

chollant: traditional Sabbath stew made from meat, potatoes and beans (Hebrew)

daven/ doven: praying (Yiddish)

Desh: home/homeland (Bengali)

Eid: Muslim festival marking the end of Ramadan (Arabic)

el Shadoi: Peace (Arabic)

frum/ frummer: Orthodox Jewish/very religious person (Yiddish)

gonoff: thief (Yiddish)

Gulags: a network of forced-labour camps in the former Soviet Union (Russian)

halal: Muslim religious dietary requirements (Islamic)

hamishe: the old country/traditional/home (Yiddish)

Hasid: Jewish ultra-Orthodox person from the Hasidic sect, which originated in Poland in the eighteenth century (Yiddish)

hijab: literally 'concealing/screening'. Western use of the word
 normally refers to a woman's head and body covering (Arabic)
hoicka: hump (Yiddish)
Imam: religious leader of a Muslim congregation/anyone who leads
 the congregation in prayer
Kaddish: Jewish memorial prayer for the dead (Hebrew)
kashrut: Jewish laws concerning food (Hebrew)
kibbutzing: chatting/talking/hanging out (Yiddish)
Kiddush: Hebrew blessing over a cup of kosher wine
Kol Nidre: solemn prayer on the eve of Yom Kippur that ushers in
 the Day of Atonement (Hebrew)
kufi: knitted cap worn by some Muslim men (Urdu)
landsman: person from same town, village or region (Yiddish)
lascar: Eastern Indian sailor or military servant (Urdu)
lobos: rascal (Yiddish)
maariv: evening prayer in Judaism (Hebrew)
machzor: prayer book used on high holy days in Judaism (Hebrew)
madrasah: mosque school (Arabic)
Magen David: Star/Shield of David. The symbol commonly
 associated with Judaism (Hebrew)
Maitreya: The future world ruler (Sanskrit)
mehndi: temporary henna paintings on hands and feet of women
 for Muslim celebrations (Hindustani)
mela: Asian festival, incorporating music, dance and food (modern
 use of the Sanskrit word in the UK)
melamed: teacher (Hebrew)
menorah: nine-branched candelabrum used during the festival of
 Hanukah (Hebrew)
mezuzah: small container of verses from Deuteronomy fixed to
 Jewish doorposts (Hebrew)
mikvah: ritual bath of pure rain water used for immersion in
 Jewish purification ceremonies (Hebrew)
mincah: daily afternoon prayers in Judaism (Hebrew)
minyan: quorum of ten adult males needed for prayers and services
 in Judaism (Hebrew)

mitzvah: good deed (Hebrew)

meshugge: idiot/fool/crazy (Yiddish)

muezzin: mosque official who summons the faithful to prayer from a minaret (Arabic)

nark: grass/informer (Yiddish)

nebbech: fool/simple person (Yiddish)

nufke: prostitute (Yiddish)

paan: spices, fruits, sugar and tobacco wrapped in betel-nut leaf (Urdu)

parana: feather-stuffed duvet used in Russia and Poland (Yiddish)

rachmones: compassion (Hebrew)

Ramadan: the ninth month of the Islamic calendar, and the holiest time of the Islamic year, when devout Muslims fast from sunrise to sunset during the month of Ramadan (Arabic)

rebbetzin: wife of a rabbi (Hebrew)

Salaam Aleikum: Peace unto You (Arabic)

Shalom Aleichum: Peace unto You (Hebrew)

shalwar kameez: outfit consisting of a long tunic (*kameez*) worn over pants (*shalwar*), which is part of traditional Islamic dress (Arabic)

schleppers: from the term *schlep*, meaning 'to drag'. Roughly translated as someone who brings customers off the street into a shop (Yiddish)

schmaltz: something (like art, music or literature) that is overly sentimental. Also used to describe something sweet like *schmaltz* herring (Yiddish)

seder: meal and ceremony on Passover eve (Hebrew)

sepharim: torah scrolls (Hebrew)

Shabbas/Shabbos: weekly day of rest and celebratory meal in Judaism (Yiddish)

shammas: beadle or caretaker of a synagogue (Hebrew)

sheytl: wig worn by Orthodox Jewish women (Yiddish)

shidduch: matchmaking/Orthodox Jewish arranged marriage (Yiddish)

shlock: inferior or shoddy things/someone who is badly dressed or slovenly (Yiddish) *shmatter*: old rags/rubbish (Yiddish)

shul: synagogue (Yiddish)

shvitz: vapour bath (Yiddish)

Siddur: authorized daily prayer book of the Jews in Hebrew

spieler: a salesperson who will talk extravagantly at great length (Yiddish)

stiebel: Hasidic house of prayer. Literally, a 'small room' (Yiddish)

Sylheti: language of Sylhet proper, the north-east regions of Bangladesh and southern districts of Assam

tallis: Jewish prayer shawl (Hebrew)

Talmud: record of rabbinic discussions, thinking and commentaries over the centuries on Jewish law, ethics, customs and history (Hebrew)

tefillin: leather boxes with straps, used in Jewish prayer, containing biblical verses, also called phylacteries (Hebrew)

tzedoka: giving charity or alms to the poor (Hebrew)

yarmulke: skullcap worn by observant Jewish men (Yiddish)

yeshiva: school for rabbinical and Talmudic studies (Hebrew)

Yom Kippur: Day of Atonement, the most holy day of the Jewish calendar (Hebrew)

zayde: grandfather (Yiddish)

Bibliography

Caroline Adams, *Across Seven Seas* (London: Eastside, 1987)

Chaim Bermant, *London's East End* (New York: Macmillan Publishing, 1975)

Ian Berry, *This is Whitechapel* (London: Whitechapel Art Gallery, 1972)

Lionel Birch, *The Story of Beer*, 2nd edn (London: Truman, Hanbury, Buxton & Co. Ltd, 1965)

Blood on the Streets' (a report on racial attacks in East London) (London: Bethnal Green and Stepney Trades Council, 1978)

Alain de Botton, *The Art of Travel* (London: Hamish Hamilton, 2002)

Curio (accompanying catalogue to exhibition curated by Alana Jelenick) (London: Terra Incognita, 2003)

Kathi Diamant, *Kafka's Last Love: The Mystery of Dora Diamant* (London: Vintage, 2004)

William J. Fishman, *East End 1988* (London: Duckworth & Co. Ltd, 1988)

——, *The Streets of East London* (London: Duckworth & Co. Ltd, 1979)

——, 'Stencl' (article in *Elam*, 1965)

Charlie Forman, *Spitalfields: A Battle for Land* (London: Hilary Shipman Ltd, 1989)

Mark Girouard, Dan Cruickshank, Raphael Samuel, et al., *The Saving of Spitalfields* (London: The Spitalfields Historic Buildings Trust, 1989)

Mr Goldsmith, 'Stencl', *Jewish Chronicle* (31 March 1967)

Bernard Homa, *A Fortress in Anglo-Jewry* (London: Shapiro Vallentine & Co., 1953)

Sanchita Islam, *From Briarwood to Barishal to Brick Lane* (London: Arts Council, 2001)

——, *Old Meets Young* (London: Arts Council, 2004)

Dan Jones, 'Exploring Banglatown and the Bengali East End' (London: Tower Hamlets Council, 2005)

Journal of Brewery History, no. 57 (September, 1989)

Dovid Katz, 'Stencl of Whitechapel', *Mendele Review: Yiddish Literature and Language*, Vol. 07.003 (March 2003)

Revd Kenneth Leech, *Brick Lane, 1978: The Events and Their Significance* (Birmingham: Affor, 1980)

——, *Through our Long Exile* (London: Darton, Longman and Todd, 2001)

A. B. Levy, *East End Story* (London: Constellation Books, 1957)

Rachel Lichtenstein, *Keeping Pace* (London: The Women's Library, 2003)

—— and Iain Sinclair, *Rodinsky's Room* (London: Granta Books, 1999)

Emanuel Litvinoff, *Journey through a Small Planet* (London: Penguin Books, 1972)

Jack London, *The People of the Abyss* (London: Isbister, 1903)

Marketa Luskacova: Photographs of Spitalfields (with essays by Chris Killip, Mark Holborn and David Widgery) (London: Whitechapel Art Gallery, 1991)

Phil Maxwell, *Spitalfields 25* (London: Spitalfields Housing Association Ltd, 2005)

Michael Moorcock, *London Bone* (London: Simon & Schuster, 1997)

Robert Poole, *London E1* (London: Secker & Warburg, 1961)

Leonard Prager, 'A. N. Stencl – Poet of Whitechapel: The First Annual Stencl Lecture' (Oxford: Oxford Centre for Postgraduate Hebrew Studies, 1983)

S. S. Prawer, 'A. N. Stencl – Poet of Whitechapel', *Times Literary Supplement* (Oxford: Oxford Centre for Postgraduate Hebrew Studies, 1984)

Andrew Rose, *Stinie: Murder on the Common* (London: Bodley Head Ltd, 1985)

Raphael Samuel, *East End Underworld: Chapters in the Life of Arthur Harding* (London: Routledge & Kegan Paul, 1981)

Sukhdev Sandhu, 'Come Hungry, Leave Edgy' (London: *London Review of Books* (9 October 2003)

Truman's the Brewers, 1666–1966 (London: Truman, Hanbury, Buxton & Co. Ltd, 1966)

Heather Valencia, 'Czeladz. Berlin and Whitechapel: The World of Abraham Nokhem Stencl', *Edinburgh Star*, Vol. 5 (May 1993)

——, 'Stencl's Berlin Period', *Mendele Review: Yiddish Literature and Language*, Vol. 07.004 [Sequential number 130] (April 2003)

Stephen Watts, *The Blue Bag* (London: Aark Arts, 2004)

Jerry White, *Rothschild Buildings: Life in an East End Tenement Block, 1887–1920* (London: Pimlico, 1980)

Sarah Wise, *The Italian Boy: Murder and Grave-robbery in 1830s London* (London: Jonathan Cape, 2004)

Patrick Wright, *A Journey through Ruins: The Last Days of London* (London: Paladin, 1991)

Michael Young and Peter Willmott, *Family and Kinship in East London* (London: Pelican, 1957)

Israel Zangwill, *Children of the Ghetto: A Study of a Peculiar People* (London: Heinemann, 1892)

www.breweryhistory.com
www.christchurchspitalfields.org
www.eastlondonhistory.com
www.Irb.co.uk
www.mernick.co.uk/thhol (Tower Hamlets history online)
www.movinghere.org.uk
www.philmaxwell.co.uk
www.pigmentexplosion.co.uk
www.subbrit.org.uk

Whitechapel to me was the portal for any form of imaginative life about London. It has always been a place of immigration, criminality and people arriving who could disappear and reinvent themselves, and the two zones, the City and Whitechapel, were side by side, connected by these little labyrinth passageways that you could go through and emerge into this other place. It had everything, the market, the church (which you could never get into at that time as it was always locked) and the hospital, which to me defined a secret city, and the interactions between it in terms of street trade and people who had come from all over the world who survived a new life here.

Iain Sinclair, 2004